The Lesbian and Gay
Christian Movement

The Lesbian and Gay Christian Movement

Campaigning for Justice, Truth and Love

Edited by Sean Gill

CASSELL

London and New York

For all members of LGCM past, present and to come

For a catalogue of related titles in our
Gender Studies list
Please write to us at an address below

Cassell
Wellington House
125 Strand
London
WC2R OBB

370 Lexington Avenue
New York, NY 10017-6550

First published 1998

British Library Cataloguing-in-Publication Data
A catalogue record for this book is available from the British Library

ISBN 0-304-337781 (hardback)
     0-304-33779X (paperback)

Typeset by Ben Cracknell Studios

Printed and bound in Great Britain by Biddles Ltd, Guildford and King's Lynn

Contents

—————◆—————

Preface

To many people both inside and outside the Christian churches, the name of the Lesbian and Gay Christian Movement is an oxymoron of a peculiarly scandalous and threatening kind. To the fundamentalist religious believer it seems to be a negation of his faith, whilst it strikes the secular liberationist as an unintelligible collaboration with the deadliest of enemies. This book recounts the story of an organization which has had the courage to chart such an uncomfortable course and to analyse the reasons why in doing so it has provoked such frenzied opposition. It is not, however, an official history. With characteristic generosity and enthusiasm its General Secretary, Richard Kirker, has encouraged me throughout its writing, and has allowed me unrestricted access to all the records of LGCM deposited in both the London School of Economics, and in the movement's offices in Oxford House in London. He has also saved me from a number of errors of fact and given me some useful leads, but responsibility for the selection and interpretation of the material is entirely mine. Nor is this an account written by an insider. I have been a member of LGCM for most of its life, and the mere fact of its existence has been a tremendous help and inspiration to me at different times, but I have never served on any of its committees and decision-making bodies. In this respect I am very aware of how much I owe to the courage and hard work of others who will, I hope, forgive me if either lack of space – or more likely obtuseness on my part – has led me to ignore or underestimate their part in its history. I have also taken to heart some words of Michael Johnson on the limitations of written sources which he wrote in an editorial foreword to LGCM's magazine *Gay Christian* in November 1984:

> We came together then for strength, for confirmation, for
> healing. What was never recorded in the minutes of AGMs or
> Committee meetings was the effort we put into loving each
> other, into doing our utmost to heal the wounds of those who

had been so desperately hurt, perhaps even damaged by the Church, or by some unthinking or thoughtless representative of it. Sometimes it even appeared that centuries of sorrow were being expressed for the first time.[1]

I have tried to ensure that something of that sense of empowerment, solidarity, pain and joy has been captured here, particularly in the selection of writings which forms the second section of the book. These include both previously published and unpublished letters and articles by members of LGCM and those sympathetic to its aims. The book concludes with essays by two distinguished gay and lesbian theologians, Dr Robert Goss, and Dr Elizabeth Stuart, who have situated LGCM's past and future agenda in the broader context of current debates over the liberating potentialities of queer theory and practice.

Retaining some distance from most of the events described here has some compensating advantages. Thus whilst this is not an 'objective' or 'neutral' account – and quite unapologetically so in these postmodern times – I have tried to draw attention to the weaknesses and unsolved problems as well as to the strengths and successes of the movement in its first 21 years. Moreover, since LGCM has been the largest and most high-profile of the British organizations working for the liberation of lesbian and gay Christians in this period, I hope that its history will be of use to anyone seeking to understand the sexual politics of modern British society. It is for this reason that I have devoted some space to analysing the changing social and political context within which the movement has had to operate.

Most recent historical analyses of the gay and lesbian rights movement have shown little interest in the evolving attitudes of the Christian churches in this area, which is understandable given their appalling track record of prejudice and discrimination.[2] Moreover the increasing secularization and pluralism of British society, which calls into question the long-term survival of any kind of Christian belief, must make the opposing sides in this debate appear to outsiders rather like two alcoholics fighting over the last drink on the *Titanic*. Yet there are grounds for thinking that this neglect is mistaken. Although Steve Bruce's recent sociological survey of religion in modern Britain takes as one of its themes the declining influence of orthodox Christianity in British society, it also draws attention to the fact that the connection between moral values and religion remains a powerful one for many people. This explains why the proportion of the population which thinks it important that religious education should still be taught in schools has remained remarkably constant at around two-thirds of adults in the period since 1951, even though most other indices of church attendance and belief have spiralled downward.[3] The vestigial influence of Christianity in shaping ethical and social norms also explains why religious moralism played a far from neglible part in the assault upon the gay and lesbian community which culminated in the passage of Section 28, and why efforts to fight Christian homophobia from within are of wider significance and interest than those who view British society as essentially secular might suppose. I hope, too, that a history of a campaigning organization which has tried to encompass theological, denominational and gender differences whilst retaining a sense of common purpose born of shared oppression, may make a contribution to the growing literature on collective identity construction within social movements.[4] This kind of interpretative approach, I would argue, raises important questions of political strategy for all gay and lesbian liberation movements in the future.

I would like to thank those who have answered my queries, given me valuable recollections or provided me with material, including Norman Boakes, Malcolm Johnson, Diarmaid McCulloch and Janet Webber. Steve Cook and latterly Roz Hopkins of Cassell, and Robert Goss and Liz Stuart, have been models of faith, hope and charity which eventually shamed me into finishing. My mother has continued to be a great support. My greatest debt is to Richard Hawley, who not only has had to bear with my lengthy absences, both physical and mental, whilst working on this book, but has allowed me to experience in my own life the truth for which LGCM stands.

Notes

1 *Gay Christian*, **34**, November 1984, p. 2.
2 This is true, for example, of J. Weeks (1977) *Coming Out: Homosexual Politics in Britain, from the Nineteenth Century to the Present* (London: Quartet Books), and S. Shepherd and M.Wallis (eds) (1989) *Coming on Strong: Gay Politics and Culture* (London: Unwin Hyman). The impact of religious moralism upon one aspect of the struggle for gay and lesbian rights is briefly discussed by R. Thompson, 'Unholy Alliances: The Recent Politics of Sex Education', in J. Bristow and A. Wilson (1993) *Activating Theory: Lesbian, Gay, Bi-Sexual Politics* (London: Lawrence & Wishart), pp. 219–45.
3 S. Bruce (1995) *Religion in Modern Britain* (Oxford: Oxford University Press), p. 53.
4 For a helpful brief introduction to this field see J. Gamson, 'Must Identity Movements Self-Destruct: A Queer Dilemma', in S. Seidman (ed.) (1996) *Queer Theory/Sociology* (Oxford: Blackwell), pp. 395–420.

PART I

History

ONE

———— ◆ ————

Finding a voice 1976–77

*In the cause of silence each one of us draws the face of her own
fear – fear of contempt, of censure, or some judgement, or
recognition, of challenge, of annihilation. But most of all, I think,
we fear the very visibility without which we cannot truly live.*

Audre Lorde[1]

The beginnings of LGCM

The inaugural meeting of the Gay Christian Movement was held at the
Sir John Cass Primary School in the City of London on Saturday 3 April
1976 and was attended by some 150 people.[2] It began in silence. Yet
the silent prayer and reflection that morning were very different from
the dishonest and intimidating silence with which the Christian
churches had traditionally sought to suppress or distort the truth about
the lives of many of the men and women who came together there.
This hostility was partly a product of the long history of spirit/body
dualism which had been a constituent part of Christian thought and
praxis from its inception.[3] Its enduring legacy – doubtless exacerbated
by English reticence – was an acute sense of shame, embarrassment and
denial when Christians were confronted with issues of human sexuality.
It was also the outcome of centuries of homophobic demonization of
sexual difference by the churches.[4] If all talk about sex was by definition
dirty, then this was the dirtiest discourse of them all.

The new movement was not the first of the gay and lesbian Christian
organizations which set out to combat the injustice of this tradition.
All of them were heirs of the changes brought about in the 1960s, a
decade which had seen the questioning within the churches of

previously accepted teaching about sexuality and morality. Indicative of the new mood was John Robinson's 1963 book *Honest to God* which called for a new Christian ethic grounded on love rather than prescriptive legalism. This outraged traditionalists by suggesting that in some circumstances divorce, and sexual relationships outside marriage, might be acceptable options for Christians. That Robinson was Bishop of Woolwich only made his challenge to complacent and unthinking orthodoxy even more pointed. But more than anything else it was the circumscribed decriminalization of male homosexual acts in 1967 which allowed – even as it attempted to limit – the articulation of an open and affirmative gay identity, making possible the emergence of gay liberation movements within the churches as had occurred in secular society.

The American Metropolitan Community Church's study group had been established in London in 1972 and in the following year it became the first fully incorporated church in Britain of the United Fellowship of Metropolitan Churches. Disillusioned by the negativity of the mainstream denominations, the MCC sought to create its own inclusive churches where gay people would feel at home. In 1973 both the Roman Catholic organization Quest, and the Friends Homosexual Fellowship were founded, and 1975 saw the setting up of the Open Church Group, an interdenominational fellowship for gay Christians mainly in London and the Home Counties. A number of the early members of LGCM had also been involved in the activities of Reach, which began in February 1973, and which sought to bring about change in the Church's attitudes to homosexuality primarily through education. As its Director, the Rev Denis Nadin explained, the organization's name pointed to its efforts to bridge the gap between the Church's general image of the homosexual and the reality, and between isolated homosexual Christians within their respective denominations. Early members of LGCM had also contributed to the activities of the Campaign for Homosexual Equality and its religious study group. Others had worked for the counselling services provided by Friend and the Albany Trust.

It was dissatisfaction with the leadership of Reach, and the desire to create an organization which would act as an umbrella group for all Christian organizations, which led to some 70 people meeting on 17 January 1976 to set up an interim committee and to make preparations for the launch of the new movement.[5] As its first Honorary Secretary, Jim Cotter, who was Chaplain at Gonville and Caius College, Cambridge, later recalled, LGCM began from 'meetings of friends, scattered members of Reach slowly realising that something bigger than they'd thought was going on'.⁶ LGCM did not seek to compete with other organizations already in the field at this time, but it did set out to provide something distinctive and ambitious: it was to be ecumenical; it would provide local support groups as well as a programme of campaigning; it was to be national in its coverage; and it aimed to be inclusive in its membership, seeking the support of all those, whatever their sexual orientation, who could subscribe to its aims and statement of conviction. It also insisted from the outset on including in its leadership those who were willing to openly declare their homosexuality as something to be proud of – a decision which was to place a heavy burden in the early days on a small number of individuals, some of them clergy. Coming out – which had been seen as an essential step in combating homophobia and oppression in the gay liberation movement of the early 1970s – was now to face the test of the most inimical of all environments: the Christian churches.⁷

'The desert of the institutional church'

In a letter to Jim Cotter in July 1976, Laurie Roberts expressed the feelings of many of LGCM's first members when he wrote that 'the launching of this movement has filled many of us with hope and a sense of not being "all alone" in the desert of the institutional church'.⁸ This was an apt enough description of the official pronouncements of the major English denominations on the subject of same-sex relationships, nearly all of which referred exclusively to male homosexuality. The erasure of lesbianism from theological discourse was not an indication of a more welcoming attitude, but rather a reflection of the patriarchalism of Church teaching, which had always regarded any undermining of traditional models of masculinity as a far more serious threat to the traditional ordering of society. In December 1975 the Vatican's Sacred Congregation for the Doctrine of the Faith had reiterated the Roman Catholic Church's teaching concerning homosexuality. On the basis of its reading of biblical texts, and by an appeal to the doctrine of immutable natural law – of which it claimed to be the sole authoritative custodian and interpreter – homosexual acts were declared to be intrinsically disordered. Arguing that theologically there had to be a link between sexual acts and their openness to the possibility of procreation – which involved the condemnation of masturbation and contraception as well – the Declaration denounced homosexual sex as lacking an essential and indispensable finality. Consequently it was in no circumstances to be regarded as acceptable within the Church.[9]

Most Protestant opinion on the subject was less dogmatically expressed, but little more affirmative. The Quaker pamphlet of 1963, *Towards a Quaker View of Sex*, has often rightly been regarded as the earliest and most significant statement of a more positive Christian attitude towards homosexuality. This was the work of a study group of concerned Quakers, including lawyers, teachers and psychiatrists, which first met in 1957. Judging every sexual act by what it called its 'inner worth', the group concluded that 'homosexual affection can be as selfless as heterosexual affection, and therefore we cannot see that it is in some way morally worse'.[10] Yet what is often overlooked is that this document was in no sense an official statement and it caused what John Shackleton later described as a considerable storm within Quakerism.[11] It was also a characteristic product of Quaker theology in which the promptings of the inner light of God's spirit in the present were more important than the pronouncements of received tradition. As the authors were at pains to emphasize, 'For Friends, God's will for man can never be circumscribed by any statement, however inspired; the last word has never yet been spoken on the implications of Christianity'.[12] It was a theology which had often in the past led Quakers to adopt far more radical social and political stances than other Christians. Most Protestants took a much more rigid and less evolutionary view of authority within the Christian tradition. They were certain that the last word had been spoken on homosexuality and that it was one of unequivocal condemnation.

The Methodist Conference in 1958 came out in support of the decriminalization of homosexual acts as recommended by the Wolfenden Committee, and favoured 21 not 18 as the legal age of consent. However, it did so by arguing that a clear distinction could and should be drawn between crime and sin. In 1971 it received, but did not endorse, a report which, although sympathetic to what it described as the plight of those of homosexual orientation, shied away from controversy by concluding – like some prim schoolteacher of delicate sensibilities and advanced years – that with regard to physical sexual acts 'on these delicate and difficult matters we express no final judgement'.[13]

The distinction between crime and sin which characterized the Methodist approach to law reform in the 1960s was also central to the stance adopted by the Church of England. In its evidence to the Wolfenden Committee, its Moral Welfare Council based its support for decriminalization on what it regarded as the generally accepted principle that the British law does not concern itself with the private irregular or immoral sexual relationships of consenting men and women.[14] This made it clear that there had been no paradigm shift in the Anglican Church's view of homosexuality. As the report put it, the homosexual 'is an anomaly whose sexual disorientation bears its own tragic witness to the disordering of humanity by sin'.[15]

The Moral Welfare Council's secretary was Dr Sherwin Bailey, who has been credited with moving the Church of England in a more liberal direction, and with making a significant contribution to the passage of the 1967 Sexual Offences Act. Yet a closer examination of his arguments illustrates just how equivocal so-called liberal opinion within Anglicanism could be. It was Bailey's article in the journal *Theology* in 1952 which sparked off serious postwar debate of the subject, and in his 1955 book *Homosexuality and the Western Christian Tradition*, he spelled out the premises which lay behind his advocacy of legal reform. Here he made several important contributions to the discussion, particularly in his review of the biblical material. He showed that the churches' traditional identification of the sins of Sodom and Gomorrah with homosexuality was erroneous, and argued that since St Paul had no understanding of the modern notion of a fixed and unchosen sexual orientation, his strictures against homosexuality carried less theological weight than many conservatives supposed. The Labouchère Amendment of 1885, which criminalized all forms of male homosexual activity, he regarded as a blackmailer's charter having no deterrent or ameliorative effect. That it was important to achieve such an effect by other means he did not for one moment doubt. Homosexuality – 'this mysterious and unfortunate condition' as he described it – was in his view a consequence of inadequate parenting and the increasing breakdown of family life. Resorting to traditional biblical tropes, he sonorously concluded that it illustrated 'in a remarkable way the visitation of the sins of the fathers upon the children'. What this meant was that:

> Homosexual perversion, therefore, is not itself a fount of corrupting influence, but only, as it were, the ineluctable consequence of a corrosion which has already left its mark upon marriage and family life and, if not checked, may ultimately undermine the whole social order and lead to sexual anarchy.[16]

Legally based persecution of sexual minorities was to give way to a socio-moral analysis in which they were demonized as a symptom of the evils he saw afflicting Western society in a period of rapid social change. Rather like the way in which Christianity had to be eradicated in Stalin's Russia because its presence called into question the achievement of the socialist utopia which should have made its functions redundant, the continued existence of lesbian and gay people in British society seemed to Sherwin Bailey to be a measure of the nation's social and moral decay.

With such confused and largely hostile attitudes prevalent in even the more liberal wing of the Church of England, it is not surprising that there was barely a majority in favour of decriminalization when the matter was debated by the Church Assembly in 1957. The vote was only 155 in favour of change and 138 against with less than half of those eligible to vote doing so. Something of the climate of opinion at the Assembly can be gauged by the contribution of one delegate from Oxford who cited the Epistle to the Romans in support of retaining criminalization, arguing that under Old Testament Law 'This was a crime worthy of death because it was contrary to God's whole order, and undermined the whole order of humanity.'[17] As Canon Peter Coleman has suggested, the Church Assembly's vote did not imply majority support amongst Anglicans for law reform, but rather the acceptance of the fact that the Moral Welfare Council's report to the Wolfenden Committee was in effect a *fait accompli*.[18] But for the same reason, it is also doubtful whether the Church of England was as influential in the deliberations of that Committee as Coleman suggests.[19]

As Archbishop of Canterbury, Michael Ramsey spoke in favour of decriminalization in the House of Lords and took some hard knocks for doing so. Was it really right, Lord Brockett demanded, that the leader of the Church of England should publicly discuss the differences, both physical and moral, between anal and oral sex and thereby turn the august pages of Hansard into a lurid bestseller?[20] Nevertheless, speaking against an amendment by Lord Dilthorne, which would have excluded anal intercourse from decriminalization, Ramsey followed the unanimous tenor of the debate in describing all forms of homosexual behaviour as 'utterly abominable'. The Methodist Peer, Lord Soper, came as close as any Christian speaker in the debate to adopting a more positive view when he refused to make a distinction between different kinds of same-sex activity since in his view any of them could be expressions of love. But even he was prepared to apply the word 'abominable' to them. The very use of the term harked back to the Act of 1553 which transferred jurisdiction in cases of 'the detestable and abominable vice of buggery' from the ecclesiastical to the royal courts and which imposed penalties ranging from hanging to mutilation and deportation. It was also the language of those implacably opposed to law reform. This was expressed most memorably by Viscount Montgomery of Alamein who professed to regard 'the act of homosexuality in any form as the most abominable bestiality that any human being can take part in which reduces him almost to the status of an animal'.[21]

The use of words such as 'abominable' by Church leaders, even as they sought to distance themselves from the vicious diatribes of men like Montgomery, was an early indication of what was to be one of the most serious weaknesses of the liberal Christian advocacy of legal change. The failure to go beyond support of decriminalization to any kind of positive endorsement of lesbian and gay relationships fuelled rather than checked the virulent homophobia which existed in British society and in the churches.[22] Pious talk about loving the sinner but not the sin merely provided a means by which Christians gave themselves permission to give unbridled vent to their fear, ignorance and hatred – a hatred which was only too evident in the early reactions to the formation of LGCM.

Even before the official launch its first President, the Rev Peter Elers, came under attack when his chairmanship of the January preparatory meeting, and his declaration of his own homosexuality, came to public notice. Elers was appropriately enough Vicar of Thaxted in Essex, which had achieved notoriety in the early part of the century as the base from which the Rev Conrad Noel preached his uncompromising and eccentric brand of Anglo-Catholic socialism.[23] It was now once again to be a storm-centre within the Church of England. The Bishops of Chelmsford and Colchester, John Trillo and Roderick Coote, resisted calls for Elers' resignation on the cautiously worded grounds that he merely shared with others 'a certain disposition' and had done nothing wrong.[24] This did not appease Thaxted's churchwardens, who wrote to a local paper seeking to disassociate their church from any form of approval of homosexual practices and criticized the bishops for not doing so in more forthright terms.[25] A major-general and his wife were more vehement:

> The Bishops of Chelmsford and Colchester commenting on the recent controversy surrounding the Vicar of Thaxted and his promotion of the rights of homosexuals within the Church, appear, as reported, to make no condemnation of the most insidious perversion known to man, to which they refer by the astounding euphemism of 'a certain disposition' by inference

excusing it on the grounds that it is shared 'with millions of others'.

It was, they concluded, high time that the clergy paid more attention to the opinions of lay members of the Church of England like themselves and rather less to those of 'way out extrovert vicars'.[26] The publicity surrounding the inaugural meeting of LGCM did nothing to diminish such venomous responses, moving John Trillo to write in a pastoral letter that he had been 'horrified and disgusted by the vindictive and hateful letters I have recently received which have demonstrated a deep loathing of homosexuals as such, whether they practised homosexual acts or not'.[27] Kennedy Thom, the Anglican chaplain at Essex University, was also attacked when his involvement with LGCM became known. One of the former churchwardens of Thaxted, who had resigned when Peter Elers became LGCM's first president, wrote to both the Queen and the Archbishop of Canterbury claiming that no priest could belong to such an organization. He regarded it as appalling that anyone professing Kennedy Thom's views should hold the post of a university chaplain.[28] Thom replied that LGCM was seeking responsibly and carefully to look again at some aspects of the churches' traditional teaching in the light of more recent and fuller understandings of human sexuality. To regard such questioning as wicked, he argued, was to impose a kind of totalitarianism upon the life of the Church.[29]

That was exactly what many inside the churches were seeking to do by avoiding any public debate of the issues. Thus the Bishop of Chester warned in the *Chester Diocesan News* that 'no goodwill can come of activities which sought to parade publicly that which should be essentially private'.[30] The anonymous writer of the preface to *Crockford's Clerical Directory* for 1975–6 agreed. What lay men and women did in private could best be left to their own consciences, but 'Christians should never be so charitable to deviants as to cease to oppose the flaunting of homosexual behaviour.'[31] It was clear from responses such as these, that the churches' support for law reform in 1967 conformed to the intentions of its promoters which had not been the validation of gay and lesbian lifestyles, but rather their legal and cultural containment. A limited degree of toleration was granted, the price for which was to be discretion and silence on the part of its grateful beneficiaries. Any attempt, inside the churches as outside, to put forward a more affirmative self-identity was repeatedly to be dismissed as a provocation and a flaunting of deviancy. As the *Crockford's* preface concluded, 'The recent formation of a Gay Christian Movement in England, imitating similar groups in the United States and supported by some priests, seems to us worse than foolish.'[32] The Bishop of Wakefield, Eric Treacy, took the same line. Homosexuality seemed to puzzle him, and he regarded it as rather like the bizarre goings-on of some newly discovered primitive tribe. He disapproved of discrimination against non-practising gay clergy, confiding to his flock that 'It is a curious thing which I don't pretend to understand, but the male homosexual has a tenderness, an imaginative sympathy that others don't have.' He went on, however, to make it crystal clear that he had no time 'for those who flaunt their sexuality', and 'no time for Gay Liberation Movements'.[33] For the Christian churches, as for society at large, heterosexuality and homosexuality were differently conjugated both ethically and politically: we 'celebrate' our God-given gift of sexuality, but they 'flaunt' their unhappy perversion.

The pressing need for the kind of education and debate which LGCM set out to stimulate within the churches was only too evident from the kind of ignorance, confusion and prejudice exhibited by many of those who sought to prevent honest discussion from taking place. Thus critics of LGCM veered between regarding homosexuality as on the one hand so evil, unnatural and disgusting a practice as to be mercifully rare, and on the other hand as so potentially common or contagious as to threaten the whole fabric of society. It was as infectious as measles, warned the distraught ex-churchwarden of Thaxted. The writer of the *Crockford's* preface agreed, suggesting that one powerful reason for refusing to give the subject a public airing was that it might turn large numbers of people away from wedlock, since 'The category of the marriageable includes large numbers with some homosexual inclination and experience'. E. R. Shackleton, who was honorary legal adviser to the fundamentalist Nationwide Festival of Light, exhibited the same kind of confusion:

> All human society has its roots in the family, and of all the threats to family life today none is so direct and so powerful as militant homosexuality. To condone is the first step towards approval, and to approve will soon lead to participation.[34]

LGCM committee member Anthony Coxon's reply, arguing that sexual orientation was determined at an early age and was to a large extent unalterable, had more logical force but less emotive appeal to the readers of the *Church Times*.[35] The chimera of the family in danger was to be used again and again by LGCM's opponents in the future.

Other early responses to the setting up of LGCM were similarly hysterical. A lieutenant-colonel from Oxford, who had served as a pathologist, came up with the lurid claim that 'In many cases of murder and suicide there was an element of sexual aberration'. There was also, he insinuated, a connection between a homosexual orientation and sexual irresponsibility. A parish priest had to enter into family life in times of birth, death and bereavement, and at such times 'one does not want to wonder, even for one second, whether he is making advances to one's teenage son'. What purported to be less hostile opinions were often no less sickening. Writing to *Reform*, the journal of the United Reformed Church in February 1977, one correspondent argued for what she called a more sympathetic attitude on the part of Christians towards homosexuals. She did so on the grounds that heterosexuals could no more understand their problems than those of 'the mongol or the spastic', though she conceded that they often made up for their deficiencies by being 'very sensitive and gifted people'.[36]

It would be wrong to conclude that there were not those within the Christian churches who took a more knowledgeable and compassionate view, but they were in a minority. Long before the 1967 Act, there were clergy who helped and counselled homosexuals, including their colleagues. Enlightened liberal opinion was most publicly expressed by Dr Norman Pittenger, Honorary Fellow of King's College, Cambridge, who in October 1967 published what he later called a broadsheet entitled *Time for Consent? A Christian's Approach to Homosexuality*. The kernel of the argument was his plea that 'the time has come for the Church to alter its attitude to homosexuals'. Pittenger had originally put forward his case in the somewhat restricted confines of the radical journal *New Christian*, and most of the responses he received were favourable, many of them coming from clergymen. The publication of the argument in book form, and the attendant publicity surrounding it, provoked much wider comment. As Pittenger later recalled, 'I received dozens of letters which were more than vituperative; they were hateful in attitude consigning all homosexuals to hell and myself to utter condemnation for daring to write and publish anything kindly about those whom my correspondents called "filthy creatures", "disgusting perverts", "damnable sinners", and the like.'[37]

Convictions and the problem of identity

Having the very considerable courage to speak out in such a climate was only one part of the challenge facing LGCM: formulating its beliefs and objectives, and creating a public identity was the other. Not surprisingly, many of those who first became involved with the movement were at different stages in the process of coming to terms with their own sexuality, and of seeking to reconfigure traditional Christian teaching. They also differed in their views as to the kind of priorities and tactics which should be adopted. The inaugural meeting in April 1976 agreed on what still remains LGCM's statement of conviction:

> It is the conviction of the members of GCM that human sexuality in all its richness is a gift of God gladly to be accepted, enjoyed and honoured as a way of both expressing and growing in love, in accordance with the life and teaching of Jesus Christ. Therefore it is their conviction that it is entirely compatible with the Christian faith not only to love another person of the same sex, but also to express that love fully in a personal sexual relationship.

An exchange of letters between Jim Cotter and Tony Reed, the convener of the Leeds branch of the Campaign for Homosexual Equality, makes it plain that this statement was not accepted in this form without considerable debate. Reed wanted the final clause to refer to 'relationships' in the plural.[38] Jim Cotter agreed that ideally this should have been the case, but explained that on 3 April 'that particular grammatical battle went ding-dong at the meeting at more than one juncture!' The final outcome was a compromise since 'the concern at the meeting on the 3rd April was to have a minimum statement which would at least put all the members firmly in opposition to the traditional stance of the Church'.[39] What was at stake, he believed, was 'a tension that is bound to be part of the life of GCM. Oversimplifying, I suppose it's gay monogamy vs. a more radical approach to human sexuality as a whole.' Writing in LGCM's magazine *Gay Christian* in 1986, Malcolm Macourt, a founding member of the committee, made the same point more acerbically, describing LGCM in its early days as a compromise between gay liberationists with Christian roots, and more timid Christians who wanted to be Christians and indulge in homosexuality.[40] This issue was a sensitive one since the movement's opponents, and some of its would-be membership, might easily reduce it to a simple ethical judgement on fidelity versus promiscuity. As Kennedy Thom put it in a letter to Jim Cotter two days after the inaugural meeting, 'it was very clear that the main problem in the Statement of Conviction debate revolved round the point at which it was proper to leap into bed with one's friend'. Thom feared that LGCM might be sucked into what he called 'the irresponsibility and promiscuity that seems to mark Gay Lib', and he regarded it as an urgent priority to arrive at some theological and ethical principles for the regulation of sexual expression outside of marriage.[41] This complex question has continued to exercise LGCM members. Were lesbian and gay Christians to seek toleration as permissible exceptions within the traditional framework of heterosexual marriage, or were they to work for a fundamental recasting of the Christian understanding of human sexuality? Were they to accept the status of a benign category mistake within the ordering of human sexuality, or were they to challenge the fundamental hierarchical classifications of sexuality and gender which rendered them deviant in the first place? Macourt's position also had wider implications in which the re-envisioning of sexual relationships was a necessary part of a much larger programme of social and political transformation.

To many of those considering joining or supporting the new movement, such campaigning radicalism was either unwelcome or of secondary importance. One way this was expressed was by suggestions that the organization should be given an innocuous name that did not include the word 'gay' as being too divisive and confrontational. Two rather cosy suggestions were the Aelred Association, and the Fellowship of Homosexual Christians. Jim Cotter replied that the word 'movement' expressed an important element of what the organization should be about, and that 'gay' was 'an assertive word, but I don't think that's a bad thing at this stage'.[42] Tentative heterosexual supporters were particularly uncomfortable with the term. A curate from Oldham, who was involved in the Campaign for Homosexual Equality, was one of a number of correspondents who rejected the idea of what he called 'the gay/straight divide'. In reply Jim Cotter stressed that LGCM wanted both gay and non-gay members, but went on to say that 'there has to be, at the moment at least, a rather exaggerated emphasis on gay identity just because gay sexuality has never before been really explored'.[43]

Unease amongst some of the early membership that too much time and energy was being devoted to campaigning and not enough to mutual support was frequently expressed. One Anglican layman, who resigned after the first year, explained that he did so because he had envisaged the organization as primarily providing care for those isolated in their local churches and communities, whereas what he called the radical view was now paramount in LGCM. Far more changes in public and ecclesiastical opinion could be achieved, he believed, by individuals discreetly and deferentially 'making their own position clear to the right people, in the right way, at the right time'.[44] One of two women from Devon who had joined in December 1976 preferred to concentrate her efforts on running a local group, concluding wryly that 'I cannot but express the conclusion that we should not try, like teenage dreamers to change the face of the established Church of England.'[45] LGCM continued to dream.

In fact, notwithstanding the inevitable differences of emphasis within the movement, and the debates surrounding the implications of its statement of conviction, Peter Elers was correct in drawing attention to its significance when he told the first annual general meeting in March 1977 that 'For many traditionalists within the Church, our Statement of Conviction constitutes a revolution, and we should be proud to be in the vanguard of such a revolution, while recognising how costly this role must be.'[46] The assertion of the inherent moral worth of same-sex relationships ran counter to Church teaching which viewed them as sinful, and in doing so LGCM was typical of the wider gay liberation movement of the time which sought to go beyond limited and grudging legal toleration to the affirmation of the positive value of gay and lesbian lifestyles. At the same time the acceptance of human sexuality in all its richness as a God-given gift presaged the much later celebration of difference in queer theory and practice, even if many of its members at the time had yet to appreciate its full ramifications. Uncompromising, generous and insightful, it has not lost its relevance a generation later.

The question of the identity of the movement had not, however, been entirely resolved as events a few weeks after the AGM were to reveal. On 17 April 1977 the BBC screened a programme titled *The Lord is my Shepherd and He Knows I'm Gay*. This provided the first serious and extended coverage of LGCM and its objectives, and judging by the correspondence it stimulated, it was undoubtedly a great encouragement to many isolated people struggling to reconcile their sexuality with their Christian faith. One man wrote in response to the programme:

> I am in my early thirties, married and a committed Christian. I have known for twenty years that I am gay but I am only just beginning to face the fact and in the present changing climate see the possibility of living how I feel. The pressures one has to live under in order to be faithful to one's marriage vows, one's

Christian faith and all the social pressures are enormous when
pitted against the emotional strains of being gay and scared to
death to risk any one knowing. I know that I cannot bear these
pressures for much longer. You must have heard the story a
hundred times ... I have sought help from straight sources
within the church and found understanding and the will to
change me, but not the willingness to accept me and help me
be what I am.[47]

Despite such heartfelt and grateful reactions to the film, many within
LGCM were dismayed by the image of the movement which they
thought it projected. Giles Hibbert, a Dominican at Blackfriars, Oxford
and LGCM's Vice-President, and Malcolm Macourt, its Treasurer, were
particularly outspoken in their criticism. In a long memorandum to all
committee members, Jim Cotter summed up and reflected upon their
comments. Peter Elers' contribution to the film came in for particular
fire. It seemed to identify LGCM too much with the problems of married
clergy, and with the issue of homosexuality narrowly defined, whereas
Giles Hibbert argued that the movement's real concern should be with
the Church's understanding and acceptance of human sexuality in its
entirety.[48] The President's frank discussion of the psychological
difficulties he faced in touching his wife were felt to be inappropriate
and had been eagerly seized upon and distorted by the *Sun*.[49] More
sensitive still was Giles Hibbert's contention that the President's style
and manner – 'something between the parsonical and camp' – identified
LGCM far too much with a particular section of the Anglo-Catholic
world of which Hibbert took a pretty dim view.[50] Not that he himself
escaped censure for claiming that he had chosen his homosexuality.
This, Jim Cotter reflected, raised thorny questions about the extent to
which sexual orientation was biologically given rather than chosen.
The former, he believed, was the view held by most of the membership.
As for his own contribution to the film, Cotter accepted the criticism
that it portrayed gayness too negatively. One other important issue
concerned the organizational structure of LGCM, and particularly the
very prominent role of its President. As Cotter put it, 'Peter is a person
who cannot be ignored: like it or not, he and Thaxted are bound to get
publicity, however much Peter himself deflects the media and asks the
rest of us to respond with comments instead of him.'[51] Summing up
what he accepted was a serious image problem, Cotter urged that the
movement needed to become less clerical, less Anglican, less narrowly
intellectual, and to involve more women and members of other

denominations, and to make space for a variety of theological per-spectives ranging from radical through liberal to evangelical.[52]

At an extraordinary general meeting in Manchester on 21 May 1977, the posts of President and Vice-President were abolished to be replaced by Chairperson and Vice-Chairperson. Behind this seemingly minor linguistic adjustment lay a desire to make LGCM more democratic and less hierarchical in its structures, and thereby representative of many different shades of opinion. In retrospect, one is struck by the underlying goodwill and sense of cooperation with which this crisis was surmounted. This was nowhere more evident than in the magnan-imity with which Peter Elers accepted criticism and with which he and his wife Gill continued to loyally support the movement's work. Nor were the issues fundamentally about personalities. LGCM was in largely uncharted territory for Christians. Intellectual differences over the significance of human sexuality in general, and of homosexuality in particular, were evident throughout the gay liberation movement at this time and were soon to lead to acrimonious debates over essentialist and social constructionist views of sexual identity.[53]

As part of a Church which had simply ignored or condemned their sexuality, lesbian and gay Christians had even fewer resources to draw upon than their secular counterparts. The decision that the organization should be as inclusive as possible and incorporate widely differing theological, denominational and intellectual perpectives, also made tremendous demands upon people's patience and goodwill, and upon the sensitivity and flexibility of the leadership if such potentially fissile groupings were to be held together. As the demise of the Gay Liberation Front in 1972 had shown, making common cause against heterosexual oppression was not of itself enough to guarantee the degree of unity necessary for survival. Nor would the tensions surrounding a high-profile leadership go away, for as Jim Cotter realized, they were media-driven. The need to provide instant, consistent and headline-catching responses to events was bound to place anyone who undertook this role in an exposed position. *'Le mouvement c'est moi'* was never remotely true, but it could easily look that way.

What stands out from the first year of LGCM's existence is not that there were problems in setting up the organization and in defining its agenda, but that these were so effectively overcome in an ecclesiastical environment that was overwhelmingly hostile. The first conference, led by Sara Coggin and Jim Cotter, was held in Birmingham on 18 September 1976 on the theme of 'Sexual Expression and Moral Chaos' and it led to the publication of LGCM's first two pamphlets. In his paper on 'The Shaping of Gay Relationships' Jim Cotter spoke in the gay liberationist language of the period about the increasing self-confidence of gay Christians:

> But we are beginning to know – and we're beginning to be strong enough to say that we know – that we're moving in the right direction. We see those in authority without the resources and insight to cope: they evade (it's OK being homosexual but don't act on it – and we've seen how that makes a truly moral life impossible); they postpone (wait until a working party reports); they repress (priests are gently persuaded to go quietly). But quite simply we are beginning to give good and positive messages to ourselves, and to 'know that we have passed from death to life because we love one another'.[54]

At the first AGM on 26 March 1977, addressed by Malcolm Macourt and Alison Hennegan, it was reported that in the first year 365 members had joined. Peter Elers referred to the flood of desperate letters which had been received from those deeply hurt and demoralized by the homophobic moralism of the churches, but who now felt encouraged by the foundation of LGCM to see that there were new and creative ways of combining their sexuality with their Christian belief. He went on to remind the meeting that the movement existed to meet these needs and challenges: 'we are not a club but a campaign for truth and love and justice'.[55] LGCM had found its voice.

Notes

1 A. Lorde (1996) *The Audre Lorde Compendium* (London: HarperCollins), p. 14.
2 The Gay Christian Movement changed its title to include the word 'Lesbian' in 1987. Throughout I have referred to the movement by its current title, except when quoting from sources in which the earlier name appears.
3 For helpful discussions of this theme see G. Moore (1992) *The Body in Context* (London: SCM Press); B. Nelson & S. Longfellow (eds) (1994) *Sexuality and the Sacred: Sources for Theological Reflection* (London: Mowbray); A. Thatcher and E. Stuart (eds) (1996) *Christian Perspectives on Sexuality and Gender* (Leominster: Gracewing).
4 For the earlier part of the Christian era this view has been partially modified in J. Boswell (1980) *Christianity, Social Tolerance and Homosexuality* (Chicago: Chicago University Press). For the much more rigorous proscription of same-sex relations in the later medieval period see R. Moore (1987) *The Formation of a Persecuting Society* (Oxford: Blackwell);

and J. Richards (1991) *Sex, Dissidence and Damnation: Minority Groups in the Middle Ages* (London: Routledge).

5 Hall Carpenter Archive, London School of Economics, GCM 4/19/291. Hereafter all references to this archive are given as HCA followed by the GCM classification number.

6 *Gay Christian*, **33**, August 1984, p. 13.

7 The importance of including in its leadership those who were willing to declare their homosexuality openly is evident from a comment by Eric Brown, the convenor of the North Western Gay Christian Fellowship founded in 1972. He admitted that although the organization had done much useful work, it had been hampered by the problem of its non-out membership who were unable to take public responsibility for its activities. HCA GCM/4/2/254.

8 HCA GCM/4/19/297.

9 These views did not go unchallenged within the Catholic Church. For example the Catholic Theological Society of America published a study in 1977 which called into question the Vatican's reading of Scripture; rejected the possibility of our having infallible access to natural law which could transcend the limitations of our own culture and knowledge; and called for the replacement of an act-orientated view of sexual ethics by one in which human growth and love were to be the sole criteria of evaluation. See A. Kosnick *et al.* (1977) *Human Sexuality: New Directions in Catholic Thought.* (London: Search Press). *The Declaration on Certain Questions Concerning Sexual Ethics*, which first appeared in *L'Osservatore Romano* on 22 January 1976, is printed as an appendix in the Kosnick volume.

10 A. Heron (ed.) (1963) *Towards a Quaker View of Sex*, p. 36.

11 *Friends Homosexual Newsletter*, **44**, November 1985, p. 7. Shackleton was writing about his experience of coming out in his monthly meeting in April 1973 and of the acceptance which he found within Quakerism. Nevertheless he spoke of the hurt which some gay and lesbian people were experiencing even in 1985 in what has traditionally been the most theologically and socially radical of English Christian denominations.

12 Heron (1963), p. 8.

13 HCA GCM/4/2/277.

14 D. Sherwin Bailey (ed.) (1956) *Sexual Offenders and Social Punishment* (London: The Church of England Moral Welfare Council), pp. 14–15.

15 *Ibid.*, p. 76.

16 D. Sherwin Bailey (1955) *Homosexuality and the Western Christian Tradition* (London: Longmans Green and Co.), p. 166.

17 P. Coleman (1989) *Gay Christians: A Moral Dilemma* (London: SCM Press), p. 132.

18 *Ibid.*

19 *Ibid.*, p. 128. The contrary view to Coleman's is taken by P. Higgins (1996) *The Heterosexual Dictatorship: Male Homosexuality in Postwar Britain* (London: Fourth Estate), p. 35.

20 *Hansard*, 5th Series, vol. 268, col. 411.

21 *Hansard*, 5th Series, vol. 267, col. 301.

22 I have taken homophobia here and throughout to be an irrational fear and hostility towards gays and lesbians, and have applied it to many

Christian groups and individuals who repudiate the label. I hope that the quotations from their own writings will serve as ample justification for so doing. I am also conscious, however, that both the context and content of homophobic discourse need to be analysed in specific instances if the term is to have any explanatory value.

23 Noel advocated the class war, daily communion, English patriotism, and a united Ireland with equal fervour. On St George's day the red flag, the flag of St George, and that of Sinn Fein could all be seen flying from Thaxted's church. See A. Hastings (1986) *A History of English Christianity 1920–1985* (London: Collins), p. 174.
24 *Church Times*, 13 February 1976.
25 *Essex County Standard*, 19 March 1976.
26 *Essex County Standard*, 5 March 1976.
27 *Church Times*, 7 May 1976.
28 *Colchester Gazette*, 8 February 1977.
29 *Ibid.*
30 *Church Times* , 2 July 1976.
31 *Crockford's Clerical Directory 1975–6* (Oxford: Oxford University Press), p. xx.
32 *Ibid.*
33 *Church Times*, 4 November 1977.
34 *Church Times*, 16 December 1977.
35 *Church Times*, 6 January 1978.
36 *Reform*, February 1977. The letter was answered by Iain MacDonald who was later to play a leading role in LGCM's United Reformed Church caucus.
37 N. Pittenger (1976) *Time for Consent: A Christian's Approach to Homosexuality*, pp. vii–viii. Norman Pittenger was a founding member and lifelong supporter of LGCM who died in June 1997. A memorial service was held on 8 November 1997 in King's College Chapel, Cambridge at which the movement was represented. It also decided to set up a Memorial Fund to honour his contribution to the creation of a more open and tolerant climate of opinion.
38 HCA GCM/4/19/259.
39 HCA GCM/4/19/258.
40 *Gay Christian*, **39**, February 1986, p. 21.
41 Kennedy Thom to Jim Cotter, 5 April 1976. All references to documents other than those deposited in the Hall Carpenter Archive refer to material which has not yet been transferred there but is still in the LGCM office in Oxford House, Derbyshire Street, London. Although this material has not yet been fully catalogued, I have tried to give precise enough details to identify it.
42 HCA GCM/4/2/289.
43 HCA GCM/4/19/287–8.
44 HCA GCM/4/19/440–3.
45 HCA GCM/4/1/77.
46 Minutes of the First Annual General Meeting, 26 March 1977.
47 HCA GCM4/5/151.
48 Giles Hibbert to Peter Elers, 21 April 1977.

49 Malcolm Macourt to Jim Cotter, 20 April 1977.
50 Hibbert to Elers, 21 April 1977.
51 Jim Cotter, Memorandum to All Committee Members, 26 April 1977.
52 *Ibid.*, p. 3.
53 There is a balanced and clear discussion of these issues in C. Vance 'Social Construction Theory: Problems in the History of Sexuality', in D. Altman *et al.* (1989) *Homosexuality, Which Homosexuality?* (London: Gay Men's Press), pp. 13–34.
54 J. Cotter (1976) *Freedom and Framework: The Study of Gay Relationships* (London: GCM), p. 11.
55 Minutes of the First AGM, 26 March 1977.

TWO

———— ◆ ————

Progress 1977–84

*For gay Christians to be able to love, give, and find meaning in
a world that rejects and isolates them, the cruel gash
separating their sexuality from their spirituality must be
healed. Their freedom to love and give in a hostile world
hinges upon their coming to believe in their wholeness and
in their having a rightful place in God's universe.*

John Fortunato[1]

Aims

At its inaugural meeting in April 1976 LGCM drew up an ambitious list
of objectives:

1. To encourage fellowship, friendship, and support among
   individual gay Christians through prayer, study and action,
   wherever possible in local groups, and especially to support
   those gay Christians subjected to discrimination.

2. To help the whole Church re-examine its understanding of
   human sexuality, and to work for a positive acceptance of gay
   relationships within the framework outlined in the Statement
   of Conviction, so that all homosexuals may be able to live
   without fear of rejection or recrimination, and that
   homosexual Christians may be able to contribute fully to the
   life and ministry of the Church.

3. To encourage members to witness to their Christian faith and
   experience within the gay community, and to witness to their
   convictions about human sexuality within the Church.

4. To maintain and strengthen links with other lesbian and gay
Christian groups, both in Britain and elsewhere.

This was a daunting programme, and as the report on the atmosphere
at the September 1976 conference in Birmingham indicated, the plenary
session on policy went less well than the more informal small groups,
partly because 'a realisation dawned of the sheer size of our task in
GCM, and that we can easily be overwhelmed and a bit scared by this'.[2]

Central organization

If the movement was to stand any chance of implementing its agenda
it needed money and some form of central coordination, since it was
simply not possible for a dispersed national committee to act with
sufficient speed and coherence. At the AGM on 26 March 1977 an
appeal was launched to raise money for the appointment of a full-time
secretary, and suffucent funds were rapidly raised to enable the
committee to make a part-time appointment of 20 hours a week. In
November Fiona Morgan accepted the offer of the post to be held in
conjunction with that of part-time secretary to the Rector of St Botolph's
Aldgate, the Rev Malcolm Johnson. By this means LGCM was able to
establish an office of its own at St Botolph's in the City of London.
Malcolm Johnson was himself a founding member of LGCM and played
a vital part in the establishment of its first home. He had already begun
to provide pastoral care for London's burgeoning gay community, and
had offered LGCM the use of the Sir John Cass primary school, of which
he was chairman of the governors, and his adjoining church for its
inaugural meeting. The decision was not welcomed by the formidable
Bishop of London, Gerald Ellison. On the morning of the meeting
Johnson was summoned before the bishop, who berated him for not
consulting him in advance, several times saying, 'Why don't you keep
quiet? I don't tell everyone what Mrs Ellison and I do in bed.'[3] What
insights into episcopal sexual practices were lost by such reticence must
forever remain a matter for conjecture.

Despite the establishment of a base, the committee soon lost
confidence in its administrative secretary's abilities, and on 1 January
1979 the Rev Richard Kirker, who had previously been a member of the
national committee, began work as her replacement. Denied ordination
beyond the diaconate by the then Bishop of St Albans, Robert Runcie,
because of his openly gay lifestyle, Kirker set about restoring order to
the national office. Often, as the committee acknowledged, he worked

many hours a week beyond those for which he was contracted. With the memory of the débâcle caused by LGCM's first television appearance still fresh in its mind, the national committee stipulated that the administrative secretary was to make no statement to the media concerning the affairs of the movement unless specifically instructed to do so by the management sub-committee set up to oversee his work.[4] In practice this proved unrealistic, and in May 1979 the contract was amended such that statements to the press should wherever possible be cleared with a member of the sub-committee which oversaw his work, or at least reported to it after the event. This in reality was a first step towards the evolution of the administrative secretary's post into that of the spokesperson for the movement, though the potential tension between such a necessity if LGCM was to be an effective campaigning organization, and the desire to retain a collective sense of leadership and responsibility had once again surfaced. After a further successful appeal for funds to the membership, Richard Kirker became full-time from October 1979, further reinforcing the pivotal role of the position within the movement. LGCM's ability to pay for such a post was in itself a significant achievement. No other British or European lesbian and gay Christian organization has been willing or able to do so, which goes some way to explaining the high profile which the organization has created for itself in the debates surrounding gay issues in the churches.

The work of local groups

The creation of a national network of local groups was listed first amongst the priorities of the new movement. This was a recognition of the isolation and fear in which many lesbian and gay Christians lived at this time. As already indicated, for many would-be members the opportunity to meet others in a supportive environment was far more important than subscribing to campaigning objectives. The speed and spontaneity with which local groups were set up (by September 1978 there were 45 of them), is an indication of how pressing were the needs which they sought to meet. Running such a group effectively was, however, uncharted territory. In response to a query from someone seeking advice on how to do so, Kennedy Thom could only reply that 'There is not much advice that I can give you on how to start up a group as I am still feeling my way.'[5] Reporting to the national committee in July 1977 on a meeting which he had held with the southern groups, the national convenor, Michael Peet, commented on 'the gulf which existed between the grass-roots and the thinking of the Committee', and on the difficulties faced by local convenors, not all of whom were themselves out as gay.

LGCM's reliance upon the energies and abilities of local convenors was a theme taken up again the following year by Anthony Coxon in a survey of their work carried out for the national committee. The rapid growth of so many groups also meant that there were problems of communication between them and the national office. His other conclusions from the 34 replies to his questionnaire were that about half could be described as active and meeting regularly; that most included elements of prayer and worship as well as social activities in their programmes; that those attending were predominantly male, in their twenties and thirties; and that whilst many individuals were involved in the life of local churches, there was little formal contact with church officials and organizations. On the last point, he noted that a number of groups had circulated all the clergy in their catchment areas, but the response had been far from encouraging – 'typically eliciting everything from outright hostility, through indifference, to an average of two replies in support'.[6] His recommendations, which were taken up by the national committee, were that convenors needed more help and information, and that training and support should be offered through day conferences.

Inevitably the activities of the groups continued to wax and wane according to circumstances and the needs and enthusiasm of their members. A description of the life of the Nottingham and Derby group in 1983 by its secretary Paul Griffiths, indicates the way in which at their best they have created vital systems of support for their members, and also how gay and lesbian campaigning for change in the churches has been rooted in the lived experience of pain, self-help and transformation at grass-roots level:

> At the simplest level, the Group provides a regular opportunity
> for members to meet other gay Christians in an atmosphere
> where they are free to be themselves ... The Group is, however,
> more than just a 'get together' for people who enjoy each
> other's company. It is vital that all newcomers are welcomed,
> particularly those who are not immediately attractive and those
> who bring a heavy burden of problems. I think the wide variety
> of the present membership is a hopeful sign – the Group
> includes women and men, ranges in age from 23 to about 65
> and has a refreshing mixture of occupations and social

backgrounds ... In short I like to think that the Group has helped all its members to understand and accept themselves more deeply and to be more confident as a result. This development (liberation?) of individuals has been the Group's main contribution to the Church and to the gay community. Our members have become better able to live and contribute to both. Several have, for instance, become more involved in the Church since joining the Group and realising that they can be fully Christian and gay. The Group has also begun to approach the churches directly and has started a plan to contact the main local church leaders.[7]

As this passage indicates, local groups have provided the creative matrix out of which LGCM's liberation theology and praxis have grown. The movement's history can all too easily be made to read like a series of abstract theological debates and internecine ecclesiastical disputes. In reality it has sought to be a genuine liberation community, the chief characteristic of which according to Mary Nagel and Susan Thistle-thwaite is that 'Theology done in these communities grows out of solidarity with those suffering and in need and is rooted in particular social justice contexts.'[8]

Counselling

One of the earliest and most difficult challenges which LGCM took up was that of offering help and counselling to the many people who began to contact the organization having suffered emotional and psychological stress as a result of social and ecclesiastical prejudice and ostracism. Not untypical were these experiences, the first from a young woman:

I am seventeen years old and gay. I don't know where to turn as I am a Christian and cannot see that I can still be acceptable before God. Please help as I have very confused feelings about all of this. I have found myself contemplating suicide a number of times. I am really low. I thought of discussing the matter with my vicar but I just could not face him. Please help! Where do I fit in? I feel like a complete outsider to the world.[9]

And the second from an 18-year-old man hoping to go to university:

I have been aware of being gay for about six years, and owing to a much emphasised feeling of guilt, and a continuous bombardment of self-condemnation, I have increasingly sublimated my sexuality. My guilty feelings were greatly exacerbated during the period when I attended my first church. That was about four years ago. It was a Pentecostal church, and there was no tolerance of non-conforming attitudes, and a very anti-gay feeling. Of course, at this time I was rather impressionable, and the hostile attitude of these beautiful loving Christians towards homosexuality made me feel very wicked, and as a consequence I developed some type of nervous disorder. I went to this church on and off for about a year, and then left. My personal problems were so great that I could not get my spirituality off the ground, and could not mature as a Christian.[10]

In order to meet these needs, LGCM sought volunteers who were vetted as to their suitability and experience, and Sara Coggin, who had herself been a counsellor with Friend, reported to the national committee in July 1977 that of 48 volunteers who had offered their services 12 had been recognized as counsellors. By that time there had been 14 referrals to the national office, nine women and five men.[11] The following year Jim Cotter reported to the AGM that there had been two training days, the second of which had been led by members of the British Association for Counselling. LGCM became affiliated to this body in 1979.

The provision of properly supervised and sympathetic counselling services for gay and lesbian Christians was important because of the existence of other so-called counselling agencies run by fundamentalist Christian groups. Their aim was not the holistic integration of the sexual and spiritual needs and aspirations of gay and lesbian Christians so clearly sought in the letters cited above, but rather their rending asunder. Despite the overwhelming evidence to the contrary, organizations such as Pilot, which the Nationwide Festival of Light helped to create, persisted in believing that same-sex orientation could somehow be 'cured' or kept under control by a kind of spiritual aversion therapy. Writing to the *Church Times* in January 1978 to recount the tale of 'a young man lately delivered from homosexual bondage' (the choice of words was perhaps unfortunate), the Festival's Director, O. R. Johnston, saw no real problem in effecting such remarkable transformations. According to him, 'A man is only "created homosexual" in the same sense as others may be created with a predominantly proud, avaricious, lazy or cowardly nature.'[12] This statement was typical of the superficial and damaging attitudes which permeated these groups, and it provoked a strong riposte from Antony Grey, an executive committee member of the British Association for Counselling. As he observed, organizations such as Pilot and the True Freedom Trust were engaged not in counselling but in indoctrination, since it was of the essence of ethically responsible counselling that it sought to help the individuals to arrive at their own resolution of their problems. [13]

Worship, ethics and spirituality

Those who participated in the early years of the movement had a very strong sense of being pioneers. Because the churches had by and large offered their gay and lesbian members nothing but blanket condemnation they were left to wrestle creatively with a whole range of new questions. What kind of ethical values should guide their beliefs and behaviour? Which sorts of relationship were true to the Gospel and which were not? What forms of prayer and worship could be created consonant with the reality of their lives? Were there indeed specifically gay and lesbian forms of spirituality which derived from people's unique experiences of the power of love to overcome oppression and hatred?

At its weekend meeting in July 1977 the national committee discussed the question of developing a liturgy derived specifically from the experience of being gay, and wondered whether it was therefore a mistake simply to take over the existing Eucharistic liturgies of the churches. In October 1981 a day conference was held in Cambridge with the theme 'Worship: An Expression of Ourselves' which explored the use of music, drama and images in liturgy. It also addressed two issues of particular importance to gay and lesbian Christians: the question of power and authority in worship, and that of language as it related to male and female roles in the Church.

One particularly important task in this area which LGCM undertook from its inception, was the provision of services of blessing as a help for those seeking to establish and sustain lasting relationships. In a conference held in Bristol in September 1978, the form which these might take was discussed. The result was published in 1980 as a pamphlet, *Exploring Lifestyles: An Introduction to Services of Blessing for Gay Couples*, which included a sample liturgy. As Malcolm Johnson put it, 'Today gay people are realizing that their love is as deep as heterosexuals, no better, no worse', adding wryly that 'if clergy can bless battleships and budgerigars we can bless two men or two women who are in love and wish to make solemn vows to each other'.[14] Events were to show that many clergy were about as likely to bless a neo-Nazi rally as the endeavours of two human beings to love each other. The creation of suitable liturgies also presented difficulties. There was, Johnson advised, a need 'to avoid language which smacks of bridal veils, buttonholes and mothers weeping in the front pew, but similarities to the wedding service are inevitable, despite the differences which need to be clearly stated'. The justification for solemnizing same-sex relationships was to be sought, he argued, in the theology of God as loving creator rather than in the sacramental theology of marriage.[15] The possible form of the service should include, it was suggested, a blessing, an exchange of vows, gifts or rings, suitable readings from both biblical and other sources, and a celebration of the Eucharist.

Not all clergy were hostile to the idea of such services, and LGCM established a list of those willing to officiate so that it could put the many enquirers who contacted the office in touch with an appropriate person. This was not the usual response from the ecclesiastical hierarchy and the press. In October 1976 Peter Elers conducted a service of blessing for two lesbian couples in his church at Thaxted. In its coverage of the occasion, although the *Daily Express* reported Peter Elers' insistence that the service was not a wedding, the paper's headline shrieked 'Girl "weds" girl', and described the service as a travesty of the marriage service. One of the former churchwardens weighed in with a demand that the church be reconsecrated since it was now unclean.[16] In a letter to the Bishop of Chelmsford, John Trillo, Kennedy Thom reiterated the point that what had taken place was not a parody of the marriage service; what was at issue was whether a loving relationship between men and women of the same sex could be offered to God, consecrated and blessed. He went on to say – prophetically but not perhaps diplomatically – that questions of so-called genital activity were of secondary importance.[17] The bishop was not persuaded, issuing a statement condemning Elers' action and eliciting from him a solemn undertaking not to conduct such services in the future.[18]

Services of blessing nevertheless continued, many of them held in private homes, but an increasing number in churches. In the latter case some kind of public outcry was always a possibility. For example when Brian Holt, the Vicar of Glodwick in Oldham, held a service of blessing for two gay men in January 1983, complaints were made to the Bishop of Manchester, Stanley Booth-Clibborn. Holt justified his actions by referring to his experience of counselling homosexual Christians whose difficulties had led to many tragedies. Booth-Clibborn, the first president of the Movement for the Ordination of Women, and no episcopal dinosaur, replied in measured terms that the service had broken no

Church laws, though he would have preferred to have been asked about it in advance since what was done was 'liable to misunderstanding, and so has caused offence in a number of quarters'. One of these was the Glodwick Mothers' Union whose annual general meeting the following month heard the by now familiar charge that the church had been defiled and desecrated. The argument was not, though, entirely one-sided – the meeting ending as the *Church Times* cryptically reported, 'in some disarray'.[19] As with so many issues surrounding lesbian and gay liberation, those who vociferously opposed church support for men and women seeking help in strengthening and sustaining committed relationships exhibited one of the most pronounced characteristics of those guilty of prejudice and discrimination: blaming the victim of oppression rather than the perpetrator. The first to stereotype gay people as promiscuous and unstable in their relationships, they themselves by their attitudes and actions were doing everything in their power to destabilize them.

Developing a Christian ethic for same-sex relationships was also a major challenge. By dismissing all forms of gay and lesbian sex as sinful, the traditional denominations again provided no help or guidance in this area. Many early members of the movement, such as Kennedy Thom, were unhappy simply to follow what they regarded as the promiscuous free-for-all of the gay scene, but at the same time it was recognized that the inherited Christian model of monogamous marriage was not the best basis for developing a gay and lesbian sexual ethic. Perhaps, it was suggested at the committee meeting in July 1977, there was a parallel between the ethical challenge posed to the churches by lesbian and gay relationships, and that which Christian missionaries faced in evaluating polygamy in the nineteenth century? However ingenious this historical comparison might be, it did not appear to provide sufficient inspiration to resolve the question, the committee noting that 'it needs to be sorted out and discussed carefully and prayerfully'.[20] An outstanding early contribution to this debate was made by Norman Pittenger in his pamphlet *Some Notes on an Ethic for Homosexuals* published by the movement in 1978. After criticizing the inadequacy of naïve appeals to either uncontextualized scriptural texts, or to rigidly prescribed notions of natural law as the basis for a Christian sexual ethic, Pittenger went on to argue for an ethic of love and responsibility in human relationships as the basis for judging particular sexual acts. Such an ethic could be stringent in its demands. 'When I use another,' he warned, 'even with their consent to such use, but have no further or more inclusive awareness of their concrete existence, I am acting inhumanly because I am acting unlovingly.' But he also took a realistic view of many gay people's experience:

> Let me say frankly that I believe that any and all sexual contact, genital or otherwise, is good – provided that it does not violate the intentional understanding of each other human as a person and not simply and solely a *thing*. Some of us would be prepared to say that the 'one-night-stand', for instance, cannot be called evil in itself; there is genuine goodness there, insofar as loneliness is overcome, some slight sense of companionship is given, strong desire is released and to some degree satisfied; and perhaps a kind of concern or care, usually rather small to be sure, is present.

Rather than simply condemning such encounters, he suggested that they could be seen as expressions of the search for a deeper and better form of relationship based upon commitment and permanence.[21]

Pittenger's challenging, humane and sensitive discussion of gay sexuality and ethics was a useful starting point for the movement's developing understanding of gay Christian lifestyles, but this could never be an easy journey to embark on given the novelty of the task and the inherited negativity of traditional teaching. At the AGM in 1983, it was reported that 'there was a nagging anxiety around that we might be better at being gay than at being Christians', and questions were asked about the movement's theology and spirituality and what it actually meant to witness to Christ in the gay community.[22] The same anxieties had also been voiced at the first-ever conference of group convenors held in February, which explored the content of a gay theology and re-emphasized the need for a specifically gay ethic if the movement was not to be guilty of 'throwing out the ethical baby with the bath water'.[23] The editor of *Gay Christian*, Robin Green, articulated some of these doubts and aspirations in an editorial foreword to the May 1983 magazine:

> Christian spirituality at its best is about the direction of our whole life towards God. It is about a person in his or her wholeness 'wholly attending'. To embark therefore on this new pilgrimage may be a dangerous and nasty business. It may challenge some of our comfortable assumptions about being gay. It may also at times make it more difficult to build alliances with the wider gay community. Christian spirituality discovered in a form that makes sense to gay Christians may

challenge many gay norms. There is an inescapable dimension
to all Christian Spirituality: at some point it finds itself at the
foot of a cross.[24]

Such self-questioning was a sign not of weakness but of growing
maturity. Homosexuality had been decriminalized only 15 years before,
and the development of affirmative gay and lesbian identities was
therefore even more recent. For Christians that process was still in its
infancy. Contrary to the derogatory stereotypes of LGCM put about by
its opponents in the churches, the movement was setting about that
task with a deep sense of ethical responsibility and commitment. That
this had to be an ongoing process was made clear at a conference held
in Bristol in January 1984 titled 'Towards a Gay Ethic'.

The challenge of inclusiveness

One of LGCM's stated aims was to create an inclusive Church in which
all Christians, whatever their sexual orientation, could participate fully,
but this also raised questions applicable to the movement itself. Implicit
in its *raison d'être* was the assumption, common to gay liberation
movements at the time, that sexual oppression and injustice created a
unity of identity and purpose amongst all those who suffered from
them. Yet in reality this common purpose did not of itself transcend
differences of gender, as the Gay Liberation Front discovered to its cost
in the early 1970s.[25] In the case of a Christian organization significant
denominational differences also had to be accommodated. One of the
most profound challenges that LGCM faced was how to evolve
structures and foster ways of relating in which difference could flourish
without the movement being torn apart by the centrifugal energies
which this process generated.

As its name, and the original formulation of its aims indicates, the
Gay Christian Movement at its inception was a male orientated
organization. Nor could the very prominent part played by Sara Coggin
on its national committee in its early days disguise the fact that its
membership and leadership were largely made up of men. Concern
about this imbalance was expressed at an early date. It was, for example,
an element in the crisis of identity which led to Peter Elers' resignation
as President in May 1977. One of the issues which emerged from the
national committee's reflection upon these events was described as 'A
concern that the contribution of women to the thinking and activity
of the Movement be less muted'. And they went on to quote a letter

from a member who wrote, 'I would wish to stress that we should give more emphasis to women – at present the gay world seems very much in the general image a man's world, and this is unbalanced.'[26]

One area of debate which seemed to confirm the charge of andro-centrism within LGCM concerned the ordination of women to the Anglican priesthood, an issue which assumed greater prominence with the creation of the Movement for the Ordination of Women in July 1979. An early campaigning objective of LGCM was to end the exclusion of men from the priesthood on the grounds of their sexual orientation and practice, but by no means all of the members saw the exclusion of women because of their gender as a related or comparable matter. As one Anglican priest from the northeast of England wrote in February 1980, 'It seems to me that GCM is going well beyond its own bounds – it is a divisive doctrinal matter within the Church of England.' It was not, he concluded, directly linked to gay liberation.[27] The same stance was adopted by John Brewer in a letter published in Gay Christian the following February in which he argued that 'the problems of gay Christians and the suitability of the ordination of women are two quite separate matters', and he also confessed himself to be 'distressed because a number of groups, organised to help with the legal, social and emotional problems of gay people are giving so much time and thought to other problems'.[28] Letters such as these came in response to a process of debate begun at the AGM in March 1979 when a resolution was passed which asked the national committee to prepare a statement 'on the place of women within the ministry of the Church, including the compatibility or otherwise of gay liberation with opposition to the ordination of women'. In preparing this document Kennedy Thom solicited a response from Sara Coggin, who drew attention to the direct link between homophobia and sexism since 'Gay men are treated as inferior because they are treated as women, who are regarded as inferior.'[29] In its statement for consideration by the members before they debated the issue at the AGM in 1981, the national committee accepted this connection:

> Gay Christians have a responsibility to be in solidarity with other Christian minorities oppressed by the established church structures. Above all gay men must avoid making a pecking order that puts them one above women seeking ordination. A gay man can conceal his sexuality, a woman cannot conceal her sex. The Church refuses ordination to both, because of their nature, what they are. This, as much as anything else,

reveals the necessary link between gay liberation and the ordination of women.[30]

When the subject was debated at the AGM on 8 April 1981, a motion in favour of supporting the struggle for women's ordination was passed by a large majority, but many women within the movement were nevertheless shocked by the indifference or hostility towards them which surfaced during the debate. Immediately afterwards Laurie Roberts aired these feelings in a letter to Richard Kirker. The movement needed, he argued, a massive educational programme to affirm to its women members that they are valued, and he pointedly warned that 'If GCM is to be yet another exclusive club for Anglo-Catholic misogynists, then I for one, must reconsider my commitment to it.'[31] Richard Kirker replied, agreeing with him 'without reservation'.[32] Corinna Smart argued in a similar vein that 'If GCM is to remain a mixed organisation, then the male members are going to have to become more radically-minded than at present over the issue of lesbian matters', and she went on to stress that 'lesbians suffer a double oppression both as women and as gay people'.[33] In a memorandum written before the meeting of the national committee in October 1981 to finalize its thoughts on these issues, Michele Barrat and Elaine Willis also criticized the lack of statements or positive support for issues of importance to women. One way of addressing this was the decision taken by the AGM in 1983 to accept a proposal for co-equality of nominations to the national committee which at that time consisted of nine men and three women, though it was subsequently reported that 'the debate suggested it was a hot issue'.[34]

However, the issues surrounding women's participation in LGCM at this time cannot simply be reduced to questions of voting rights and equality of access to agendas, important though these were. The 1981 memorandum went on to articulate a new kind of relationality and spirituality which was a product of the feminist movement and women's experience within it:

> Women have learnt to organise in a different way, in a collective and cooperative way, without exploiting or putting down one another. I know I can control, exercise authority and power over other people. Why should I? This is not what I want as a woman, or as a Christian ... I wish to be loving, caring, compassionate, assertive, strong, gentle, empowered not to the detriment of men but for the good of humanity ...

> Where is the message of Gospel, where is the theology of
> liberation in GCM?[35]

How far LGCM could succeed in transforming itself in this way was
another matter.

Also of great importance was the development of a distinctively
lesbian theology born out of women's experiences. As Women's Liaison
within LGCM, Sue Jex coopted a subcommittee which organized a
conference in November 1980 addressed by Sara Coggin on the subject
of 'Gay Women and the Bible'. This examined the kinds of alienation
which women as lesbians might feel in reading Scripture and how that
tradition might be reclaimed. A further conference on the theme of
lesbian lifestyles followed. This was part of an ongoing process of
exploration amongst women within the movement, and its significance
was appreciated slowly. It would not be until 1987 that the movement's
name was finally changed to incorporate the word 'lesbian' in its title.
Nevertheless the lead given by the national committee in aligning the
movement with women's liberation and with the campaign for their
ordination in the Church of England was a crucial one. Had it not done
so, it risked not only alienating most of its women members, but also
identifying LGCM with the gin-drinking lace-frilled fringe of an
Anglo-Catholic subculture, whose furtive guilt-ridden sexuality was
often expressed in an aggressive misogyny scarcely concealed behind
a fig leaf of church tradition. To have gone down that road would have
been a betrayal of LGCM's radical challenge to all forms of sexual
oppression and injustice.

Another significant initiative was the creation in 1979 of a separate
Evangelical Fellowship within LGCM. A meeting of 25 evangelicals was
held in Wellingborough in May 1979, and a further one in London in
October. The formation of the new group arose partly out of a sense
that the evangelical voice was not adequately heard in a movement
which was understandably dominated by less conservative theologies.
At the same time it was recognized that evangelicalism was one of the
bastions of opposition to gay and lesbian liberation, and for that reason
evangelical Christians faced particular difficulties in seeking to reconcile
their faith and their sexuality. As Brian Stone, its first chairperson,
recorded, 'The group would be well fitted to work amongst the gay
movement's many arch-enemies in the evangelical church as a whole.'[36]
What that hostility meant in practice was only too evident at a
conference held at Offchurch in November 1982 on the theme of being
both gay and evangelical. Here the Fellowship heard of the treatment

meted out to some of its members by churches, which included being expelled, exorcized or sworn to secrecy after they had revealed their sexual orientation.[37] In December 1984 the Fellowship published its own theological manifesto titled 'The Challenge of Freedom'.

A further constituency which was encouraged to develop separately within the movement was the Young Gay Christian Group which was founded on 17 January 1982. Writing to Richard Kirker the following year, Edward Bell welcomed its creation, having previously been a member of the Friends Homosexual Fellowship and finding very few young people taking part in its activities. He also drew attention to the gulf which existed between the institutional churches and the young: 'I think so many young people who are gay feel so totally rejected by the Church – a religion which is so wholly incompatible with the love of Christ – that they enter a spiritual limbo.'[38]

Relations with the wider gay community

Ecumenical in its outlook and in its own constituency, LGCM sought to maintain cooperative relations with other lesbian and gay Christian organizations. In 1980, for example, the movement was joint organizer with the Friends Homosexual Fellowship, the Roman Catholic organization Quest and the Scottish Homosexual Rights Group of a conference held near Pitlochry in Scotland on the theme of 'Pastoral Approaches to Homosexuality', the papers from which were subsequently published.[39] It also sought to establish links with overseas groups and established a committee portfolio to further this objective. In January 1979, Richard Kirker established links with gay men in South Africa to offer support and to foster gay consciousness.[40] In the summer of that year he undertook a speaking tour in America including a talk at the national convention of Integrity at a time when the American Episcopal Church was embroiled in controversy over the issue of ordaining practising homosexual clergy. At the AGM in March 1980, it was reported that one of LGCM's publications had been translated into Norwegian by the Norwegian Open Church Group, and that the statement of conviction and aims had been made use of by gay Christian groups in Australia, New Zealand, South Africa, France, Switzerland and Germany.[41]

The aim of encouraging members to witness to their faith in the gay community also presented some stiff challenges. Many members of the gay world had little time for religion and regarded the Church, not without reason, as one of the prime generators of homophobia in British

society. The efforts of LGCM to effect change from within were seen as
at best quixotic, and at worse as a blatant instance of bad faith. The
Open Church Group's Newsletter described the way in which its
members and those of LGCM had taken part in the 1976 Gay Pride
march and had given out leaflets, but admitted that Peter Elers' attempts
to speak to the rally held at the end of the day had encountered 'a rather
hostile crowd'.[42] Getting a hearing continued to be difficult in other
ways too. In January 1981 Ray Appleby wrote to Gay's the Word
bookshop describing their refusal to stock the movement's literature as
'a blatant policy of discrimination against Gay Christians'. The reply
was uncompromising. Amanda Russell and John Duncan stated that
'we receive the unambiguous message that people do not want
pornography and do not want religion'. Given the moral obscenity of
many of the Christian churches' pronouncements about the lives of
gay people this was understandable, and they went on to drive home
the point:

> We believe very strongly indeed that the oppression of gays
> which religion has inspired has been more cruel, more
> pervasive and more persistent than that generated by any other
> institution of our society. We feel that it is humiliating for gay
> people to seek acceptance from institutions which have
> consistently abused us in this way.[43]

As one LGCM member commented, the letters columns of *Gay News*
provided ample evidence of how widespread such attitudes were in the
gay community at large.[44] They were unlikely to be changed merely by
professions of goodwill, and LGCM had to earn the trust of those
suspicious of religion by making common cause with their struggles.

There were several early opportunities to do so. In September 1976
LGCM made a submission to the policy advisory committee of the
Criminal Law Revision Committee arguing for an equal age of consent
for homosexuals and heterosexuals, and reinforcing the arguments put
forward by the Campaign for Homosexual Equality. LGCM was also
sharply critical of the restrictions on gay people contained in the 1967
Act which it described as 'very much a half-way house' leading to
toleration within limits but not full acceptance of gay people in British
society.[45] The following year a further occasion to show solidarity with
other parts of the gay community arose when Mary Whitehouse of the
fundamentalist Nationwide Festival of Light brought a successful action
for blasphemy against *Gay News* and its editor Denis Lemon for printing
a poem by Professor James Kirkup which described a centurion's erotic

feelings for Christ on the cross. Opinion amongst gay and lesbian Christians was divided. The Open Church Group issued a press statement describing the poem as distasteful and offensive, and condemned *Gay News* for its irresponsibility in printing it. This led Giles Hibbert, who had spoken in Denis Lemon's defence at the trial, to resign from its committee, arguing that such a stance would only further reinforce the gay world's jaundiced view of Christianity. Not only did LGCM not follow suit in issuing such a condemnation, but a collection was raised for the defence fund. In 1978 LGCM lobbied Anglican bishops who sat in the House of Lords in support of Lord Willis' unsuccessful attempt to abolish the arcane offence of blasphemy and defended *Gay News* in the process:

> *Gay News* can in no way be considered an anti-Christian paper. The publication of the poem, for which the blasphemy charge was brought, was not to vilify Christ, but to express devotion to him through imagery meaningful to homosexuals. The prosecution has been seen by homosexuals as a manipulation of an outdated law to attack them through the one responsible and sympathetic journalistic medium open to them.[46]

In view of the strongly expressed opinions of Gay's the Word bookshop quoted earlier, the events of 1984 showed in the most striking way possible that Christian and non-Christian gay and lesbian people did in fact have a commonality of interests in a homophobic society. Between April and October of that year Customs and Excise seized books, newspapers and magazines which had been imported from abroad for sale in the bookshop. In November the action was extended and resulted in the seizure of 15 copies of *The Joy of Gay Sex* which LGCM had ordered as part of its mail order service. The two organizations joined together in raising funds and preparing to mount court actions before Customs and Excise finally climbed down and returned the books.[47]

Campaigning

The movement's stated aim of changing the Christian Church's understanding of human sexuality in such a way that lesbian and gay Christians could become fully accepted participants in its life, continued to run up against the censorship imposed by those too frightened or too hostile even to consider the arguments. For example in October 1977, when LGCM organized a day conference on the theme of the

Bible and homosexuality, the *Baptist Times* refused to carry an advertisement for the event. When in 1979 a subgroup of the Manchester branch of LGCM organized a day conference on homosexuality in the Church and in society under the auspices of the Christian Institute, an ecumenical organization which was housed at the Northern Baptist College, a number of congregations withdrew their support for the college.[48] In the same year the venue for the March AGM had to be changed from the Westminster Cathedral Conference Centre to Notting Hill Methodist Church after Canon Kelly, its administrator, cancelled the booking, which had been made the previous July, at only three weeks' notice on the grounds that LGCM's stance was contrary to Catholic teaching. Canon Kelly did reimburse the movement for the costs involved in relocating the AGM, which subsequently passed a resolution condemning the Cathedral's action as a blatant example of discrimination and injustice, and warned that it made it even harder to convince non-Christians 'that the Church is anything but a mask for repression'.[49] Also in March, the leading Catholic newspaper the *Universe* refused to carry an advertisement for LGCM which the Rev Derek Reeve tried to place there on the grounds, as its editor put it, that homosexuality was a sin and 'like any sin, it can be overcome by an effort of the will and with the assistance of God's grace'. Reeve replied that homosexuality was not a failing like alcoholism but a natural sexual orientation, and went on to point out that 'The Holy Spirit is not the unique preserve of the hierarchy or theologians.'[50] The Church of England took a characteristically more muddled attitude towards advertising LGCM. *Crockford's Clerical Directory* at first refused to carry an insert, but subsequently modified its stance provided the aim of bringing gay liberation to the Church was left out of the wording. In 1979 it was reported that the *Church Times* had received letters from people threatening to cancel their subscriptions if LGCM advertisements continued to be published.

One of the most obvious ways of countering this conspiracy of silence was for LGCM to produce its own publications. It began distributing its bulletin, the forerunner of *Gay Christian*, in May 1976, the year which also saw the appearance of the first of a series of pamphlets covering topics such as the Bible and homosexuality, gay ethics, and the Church's past and future attitudes to gay people. One other important initiative was the setting up of the Michael Harding Memorial Fund to provide funds for the establishment of an annual address which the movement subsequently published. Michael Harding had been a priest in the diocese of St Albans, and a founding member of the national committee. He was tragically killed in a motor accident in February 1977, and the fund not only provided a fitting memorial to his life but became the means by which a succession of distinguished speakers discussed a wide range of issues relating to the Christian theology of sexuality and gay liberation. The addresses were ecumenical and international in their scope, contributions including Rabbi Lionel Blue's 1981 talk 'Godly and Gay', and that of the distinguished American historian John Boswell in 1982 on 'Rediscovering Gay History'. Another significant publication was *Towards a Theology of Gay Liberation* which appeared under the SCM imprint in 1977. It was edited by Malcolm Macourt, and contained chapters by Jim Cotter and Giles Hibbert. Macourt made clear in his introduction that the book was a product of the new, open and confident assertion of gay identity which characterized the post-Stonewall era. As he put it, 'The "problem" of homosexuality is no longer the "problem" of those who have or seek same-sex relationships; it is the problem of those who cannot, or will not, understand that reality.'[51] But as Macourt and his fellow authors were only too aware, a considerable proportion of those who thought this way was to be found inside the churches, as the publication of reports by the Anglican, Methodist and Roman Catholic churches in 1979 made abundantly clear.

The tensions, ambiguities and discord which surrounded the preparation and reception of the two Protestant reports can only be understood in the context of long-standing theological divisions over the nature and sources of authority within Protestantism. In essence these stemmed from the intellectual and social changes of the late eighteenth and early nineteenth centuries. Faced with the challenges of biblical criticism, Darwinism, and the claims of other religions, liberal Protestants followed the lead given by the German pioneer, Friedrich Schleiermacher, whose influential book *On Religion: Speeches to its Cultured Despisers* appeared as early as 1799. This had sought to reformulate Christian doctrine in the light of contemporary knowledge, and argued that only by doing so would its essential message remain credible. Conservatives had a vision of the timeless authority of Christian truth as residing in either Scripture or tradition in a form which transcended culture, and they viewed liberal attempts to reformulate doctrine as exercises in demolition rather than reconstruction. In Britain, the result of this theological divide was a series of acrimonious and highly public rows which greeted the publication of a long list of revisionist theological works from *Essays and Reviews* in 1860, down to Don Cupitt's *Taking Leave of God* in the 1980s.[52]

What gave an increasingly hard and uncompromising edge to these disputes as the century wore on, was that both positions were responding to the perceived decline in Christian belief and commitment in British society, particularly evident since the 1960s as Church membership and attendance figures, already at a low ebb, began to spiral downward. Both liberals and conservatives offered prescriptions to stem this decline, each accusing the other of being part of the sickness rather than the cure. Homosexuality was an issue which brought these differences into sharp focus. Advocates of change argued that traditional readings of Scripture and tradition had to be revised in the light of modern scientific knowledge, whilst their opponents claimed to find in the biblical texts and past practice of the Church a non-negotiable condemnation of homosexual practice. The fact that the debate involved sex raised the stakes still further. As the highly charged rows over contraception, divorce and remarriage, and premarital sex made plain, whilst many Christians were unmoved by some of the more esoteric theological debates occasioned by post-Enlightenment modernity, the issues were readily understood when translated into questions of social values and individual conduct.

The Methodist report *A Christian Understanding of Human Sexuality* was published on 24 April 1979, and was the result of three years of work by a committee appointed by the Methodist Church's Division of Social Responsibility and the Faith and Order Committee. It was chaired by the Rev David Stacey. The document was brief and only one relatively short section dealt with the question of homosexuality. Nevertheless its conclusions marked a significant step forward in the Methodist Church's acceptance of gay and lesbian people. Same-sex relationships were to be judged by the same criteria of love as heterosexual ones, which meant that those based upon mutuality and permanence could be appropriate for Christians. The report also drew attention to the complexities involved in the process of making moral decisions. There were, its authors argued, six witnesses to be taken into account: the biblical evidence, human reason, the traditional teaching of the Church, the personal and corporate experience of modern Christians, the insights of the human sciences and what was called 'the spirit of the age'. In giving the report a broadly favourable review for *Gay Christian*, Diarmaid MacCulloch rightly saw that it was this question of the sources of authority in ethical decision-making which was the nub of the argument. The difference between liberals and conservatives was, he observed, that whereas both inevitably made moral judgements which were influenced by contemporary culture, only the former were willing to recognize the fact.[53] In the event, traditionalists proved unwilling to accept that Christian decision-making might be as fallible as MacCulloch claimed, and the report was sent back for further work and reconsideration by Conference the following year. This followed a strong attack on its exegesis and interpretation of biblical evidence by the retiring President of the Conference, the Rev Donald English. Two subsequent reports presented in 1980 and 1982 did not substantially alter the conclusions of the original document, and provoked sufficent conservative opposition for the 1982 Conference merely to take note of the report and commend it for further study. This was after speakers from the floor claimed that many Methodists would leave the Church if the report was formally adopted. It was clear, however, that the issues, particularly that of opening the way for the ordination of practising homosexuals in the Methodist ministry which the 1982 report supported, were not going to go away.

The new situation created by the 1967 Sexual Offences Act had also prompted the Church of England's Board of Social Responsibility into set up a working party in September of that year. This set out two opposing views of homosexual relations as being either always wrong, or sometimes the best of a bad job, but it created no public stir since it was only privately circulated. In 1974 a much larger working party chaired by the Bishop of Gloucester, John Yates, was set up by the Board of Social Responsibility. This was done at the request of the Principals of Anglican Theological Colleges who were in the front line in respect to changes of attitude and behaviour in the era of gay liberation. Two questions were particularly pressing. What response should be made to men who came forward for ordination training and who revealed that they were practising homosexuals; and perhaps even more alarming to college principals, what should their attitude be to those who engaged in such behaviour whilst undergoing training? Inevitably the report became a discussion of the whole issue of the acceptability of homosexuality within the Church. The committee was given impressive intellectual ballast by an array of academics, theologians and other experts, but neither LGCM nor any other gay Christian organization was given a place on the body which was to determine their members' future. Attempting to reconcile opposing views within its membership, and conflicting expectations from the Church at large, the report was confused and satisfied no one. It argued cautiously, but to the chagrin of conservatives, that scriptural texts which condemned homosexual acts were not necessarily binding on Christians in the present, and that there were circumstances in which homosexuals were justified in entering into sexual relationships. It disappointed liberals by suggesting that any clergyman living in such a relationship, or any ordinand intending to do so, should offer his resignation to his bishop. What view the bishops were expected to take in such cases was not made clear.[54]

The air of uncertainty and confusion surrounding the Gloucester Report was further heightened by its manner of publication. Four years in the making, it was presented to the Board of Social Reponsibility in 1978 which referred it back for revision. The revised text was then considered by the Board in October amidst mounting speculation that it might never see the light of day. This led the Board's chairman, the Bishop of Truro, Graham Leonard, to assure Synod in February 1979 that it would appear in full. What was being sought, he explained, was a means of presenting it as a contribution to discussion rather than the final word on the subject – a coded way of stating that desperate attempts were being made to distance the Board from the report's more radical proposals whilst diffusing the row that these were certain to provoke within the Church of England.[55] It was finally published on 19 October 1979 with a series of observations by the Board of Social Responsibility. These stressed that its members were deeply divided over the questions which it raised; were not sure that it had taken the passages of Scripture which condemned homosexual activity seriously enough; and that in any case the report did not commit the Church of England to anything.[56]

LGCM responded to the report in the November 1979 issue of *Gay Christian*. Sara Coggin criticized the way in which it encouraged the clergy and potential ordinands to be dishonest about their sexuality, and its assumption that gay relationships were only second best. It was, according to Anthony Coxon, a deeply disappointing and conservative document, and one in which the criterion of love as the basis for evaluating human relationships was largely ignored. As Jim Cotter put it, the report 'was timid and cautious, like maiden aunts opening the door a little but keeping the thief chain in place'.[57] But what was timid to LGCM was radical heresy to its opponents as a number of irate responses to the *Church Times* makes clear. Predictably, Raymond Johnson, the Director of the Nationwide Festival of Light, was particularly vehement in his response. The report had, he claimed, 'done irreparable damage to the fabric of Christian ethics in the minds of the people in the pews and of our increasingly puzzled fellow-citizens'.[58] It was, in his view, just one more in a series of damaging liberal distortions of Christian doctrine of which the Bishop of Woolwich's *Honest to God*, and *The Myth of God Incarnate* edited by Denis Nineham, were two particularly flagrant recent examples. Practising homosexuals, he urged, should be barred from taking communion like any other 'notorious evil-liver'.[59] Humphrey Whistler, a member of the Community of the Resurrection at Mirfield, weighed in with the comment that he would rather change his church allegiance 'than receive the Body of Christ from the hands of a so-called "gay" priest'. Lieutenant Colonel Walton managed to abuse two disadvantaged minorities at once by claiming that homosexuals had 'no more reason for flaunting their abnomality than they should, say, a withered arm'. It was not altogether clear, though, that he was on the same moral wavelength as the Director of the Nationwide Festival of Light since he was prepared to concede that homosexuals, like men who kept mistresses, had often made valuable contributions to public life. What was required of such people was primarily that they should 'keep the thing in a decent obscurity'.[60]

It was not until 27 February 1981 that Synod finally debated the report, and by then it was apparent that the bishops intended to curtail what had become an increasingly polarized discussion. This they did by refusing to allow any amendments to the motion that Synod should merely take note of the Gloucester Report. This meant that Canon Douglas Rhymes's motion, which LGCM supported, that the report should be commended for discussion at diocesan and deanery level was ruled to be out of order. Introducing the document, the Bishop of Gloucester commented on the way in which the atmosphere surrounding the issues had become 'more fraught, more tense'. The aim of the working party, he went on, had been the very Anglican one of combining the claims of Scripture, tradition and reason, including experience – which was a way of stating but not resolving what was at issue between the liberal and conservative wings of his church. Peter Elers continued to do sterling service for the movement. In a powerful speech he drew attention to the evils of homophobia in British society, and rejected the demand that all homosexuals should remain celibate since celibacy was itself a specialized and freely chosen form of religious vocation, whereas most gay people needed love in just the same way as heterosexuals. The Archbishop of Canterbury, Robert Runcie, opined that homosexuality was not a sin but it was nevertheless a handicap. In considering whether or not to ordain a homosexual, the Archbishop explained to Synod that what he called one of his rule-of-thumb tests 'would be if a man was so obsessive a campaigner on this subject that he made his ministry unavailable to the majority of Church people'. Discretion was definitely the better part of valour it seemed.[61]

LGCM subsequently issued a statement attacking the Archbishop's insensitivity in likening homosexuality to a handicap, but one of the most effective reflections upon the significance of the debate came in a letter of Sara Coggin to the *Church Times* on 20 March. After describing the selfless and devoted lives of many lesbian and gay couples she had known, she went on:

> This, however, is the face of homosexuality which the Church does not want to see. It is wriggling with embarrassment at its strangely large percentage of homosexual clergy, but it would like to think that it had a 'compassionate' attitude to 'pastoral problems'. It prefers 'care' to justice, and dislikes stridency on any topic. But can it still hear the still small voice of homosexual lives lived with integrity and love? Or does it need the voices of gay liberationists to go before to cry in the wilderness?[62]

Sara Coggin made two telling points. First she drew attention to the fact that the Church of England's stance of impartial and uninvolved aloofness was in fact a sham. It was not, as it liked to present itself, the objective moral arbiter judging on behalf of society the behaviour and character of an alien minority, for there were significant numbers of practising homosexual clergy within its own ranks. Second, she drew attention to the question of injustice. Once again members of LGCM who highlighted the discrimination and prejudice which they suffered in both Church and society were accused of flaunting their behaviour and of unhelpful militancy. No doubt a number of bishops and clergy who regarded themselves as sympathetic towards the plight of gay Christians, and who were attempting to steer a deeply divided Church towards a more moderate stance, would have claimed that a more softly softly approach was needed. Yet there was no evidence that the churches would ever have been prepared to change their traditional attitudes without such pressure. As for the charge that such advocacy was pastorally damaging, was this to imply that congregations were never to be challenged and made uncomfortable in the cause of justice? Were, for example, clergy who spoke out against racist attitudes within the churches and society at large to be silenced on the grounds that their concerns were obsessive?

In fact the debates surrounding Christianity and homosexuality in 1979 were an indication that LGCM was making significant progress in its campaigning agenda. Even in the Roman Catholic Church, which had not altered its fundamental teaching, there were some signs of movement. In December, the Catholic Social Welfare Commission published its report *An Introduction to the Pastoral Care of Homosexual People* which highlighted the evils of homophobia in British society. The same theme was taken up at the National Pastoral Congress held at Liverpool in May the following year, where the topics group devoted to the subject of human rights and social justice at home discussed the issue of discrimination against homosexuals. Here the ambiguity inherent in the Catholic Church's position was laid bare as the report strove to condemn the high levels of prejudice and discrimination evident amongst employers in Britain, whilst at the same time endorsing the Church's traditional condemnation of homosexual practice which helped to promote such attitudes in the first place. Made uneasy by what it called 'the demands of the campaigning homosexual', the group recommended that 'a clear distinction be made between, on the one hand, the unavoidable and morally neutral fact of homosexual orientation and, on the other, homosexual activity; this would lessen both fear and condemnatory attitudes towards homosexual men and women'. In practice, this would further worsen the situation of those men and women who saw no reason to follow the Catholic Church's teaching. Nevertheless the group concluded that for the future 'a continuing re-evaluation of attitudes is essential'.[63] That was precisely what LGCM intended to promote, and it went about the task with increasing self-confidence and optimism. As Diarmaid MacCulloch wrote in *Gay Christian* in 1981, reflecting upon the first five years of the movement, 'we've an immense amount to thank God for, and a stimulating and exciting task ahead'. LGCM, he quipped, had made enough of a mark to have the mickey taken out of it by the satirical television programme *Not the Nine O'Clock News*.[64] Few could have realized how much harder that task was to become in subsequent years, and how much more aggressive the opposition to gay and lesbian rights would reveal itself to be both inside the churches and beyond.

Notes

1 J. Fortunato (1982) *Embracing the Exile: Healing Journeys of Gay Christians* (San Francisco: Harper & Row).
2 *Bulletin of the Gay Christian Movement*, 4 February 1977, p. 5.
3 M. Johnson (1994) *Outside the Gate: St Botolph's and Aldgate 950–1994* (London: Stepney Books) p. 144.
4 Contract of Employment between the Gay Christian Movement and the Rev Richard Kirker, undated.
5 Letter of Kennedy Thom, 3 May 1977.

6 GCM Branch Convenors Survey, September 1978.

7 *Gay Christian*, 29 September 1983, pp. 26 and 34.

8 S. Thistlethwaite and M. Engel (1990) *Lift Every Voice: Constructing Christian Theologies from the Underside* (San Francisco: HarperSanFrancisco), p. 1.

9 HCA GCM/4/2/14. I have quoted here and elsewhere from the closed files of correspondence of LGCM in the Hall Carpenter Archives at the LSE which are not open to the public without permission. To ensure the anonymity of the correspondents, in these cases I have not given any details which might identify them.

10 HCA GCM/4/18/118.

11 Minutes of the Ninth Meeting of the Committee of the Gay Christian Movement, 29–31 July 1977.

12 *Church Times*, 20 January 1978.

13 *Church Times*, 3 February 1978.

14 S. Coggin, J. Cotter, and M. Johnson (1980) *Exploring Lifestyles: An Introduction to Services of Blessing for Gay Couples* (London: GCM), p. 4.

15 *Ibid.*

16 *Daily Express*, 29 October 1976.

17 Kennedy Thom to John Trillo, 1 November 1976.

18 *Church Times*, 5 November 1976.

19 *Church Times*, 4 March 1983. At national level the Mother's Union was in fact developing a more constructive approach issuing in July of the same year a pamphlet *Understanding Homosexuality*. This concluded that it was 'better to accept it as one of the factors in the make-up of certain individuals, and to learn to live with the limitations this will impose'. Parents were told that homosexuality was not a disease which could be cured. If not exactly a breakthrough in the affirmation of gay lifestyles, this was a step in the right direction from a traditionally conservative source.

20 Committee Minutes of the Gay Christian Movement, 29–31 July 1977, p. 2.

21 N. Pittenger (1978) *Some Notes on an Ethic for Homosexuals* (London: GCM), pp. 7–11.

22 *Gay Christian*, 28 May 1983, p. 4.

23 *Ibid.*, p. 22.

24 *Ibid.*, p. 1.

25 There are discussions of the impact of gender upon the unity of the Gay Liberation Front in J. Dixon, 'Separatism: A Look Back in Anger', in R. Cant and S. Hemmings (1988) *Radical Records: Thirty Years of Lesbian and Gay History* (London: Routledge), pp. 69–84 and J. Weeks (1977) *Coming Out: Homosexual Politics in Britain, from the Nineteenth Century to the Present* (London: Quartet Books), pp. 200–1.

26 *Bulletin of the Gay Christian Movement*, 6 August 1977, p. 3.

27 HCA GCM/4/18/165, 4 February 1980.

28 *Gay Christian*, 20 February 1981, p. 26.

29 Sara Coggin to Kennedy Thom, 11 July 1979.

30 *Should GCM Be Concerned About the Ordination of Women?*, p. 3.

31 HCA GCM/4/19/99, 6 April 1981.

32 HCA GCM/4/19/98, 3 June 1981.
33 *Gay Christian*, 22 August 1981, pp. 9–10.
34 *Gay Christian*, 28 May 1983, p. 4.
35 *GCM and Women*, HCA GCM/8/1/2.
36 HCA GCM/2/10/12.
37 *Gay Christian*, 28 May 1983, pp. 8–9.
38 HCA GCM/4/2/5, 27 January 1983.
39 I. Dunn (ed.) (1981) *The Pitlochry Papers* (Edinburgh: The Scottish Homosexual Rights Group).
40 HCA GCM/4/20/412.
41 Minutes of the AGM, 22 March 1980.
42 HCA GCM/11/100/16–19.
43 HCA GCM/4/1/20, 28 January 1981.
44 *Gay Christian*, 20 February 1981, p. 12.
45 *Bulletin of the Gay Christian Movement*, 4 February 1977, pp. 25–7.
46 Kennedy Thom to the Lords Spiritual, 16 February 1978.
47 *Capital Gay*, 9 November 1984.
48 *Gay Christian*, **13**, June 1979, p. 12.
49 AGM Emergency Resolution, 31 March 1979.
50 HCA GCM/4/19/210–11.
51 M. Macourt (1977) *Towards a Theology of Gay Liberation* (London: SCM Press), p. 2.
52 For a detailed discussion of this theme, see K. Clements (1988) *Lovers of Discord: Twentieth-century Theological Controversies in England* (London: SPCK).
53 *Gay Christian*, 13 June 1979, pp. 19–21.
54 P. Coleman (1989) *Gay Christians: A Moral Dilemma* (London: SCM Press), pp. 149–55.
55 *Church Times*, 23 February 1978.
56 *Church Times*, 19 October 1979.
57 *Gay Christian*, **15**, November 1979, pp. 5–7.
58 *Church Times*, 19 October 1979.
59 *Church Times*, 26 October 1979.
60 *Ibid.*
61 *Church Times*, 6 March 1979.
62 *Church Times*, 20 March 1981.
63 Official Report of the National Pastoral Conference, Liverpool, 1980.
64 *Gay Christian*, 20 February 1981, p. 1.

THREE

Backlash 1985–88

*Behind prejudice there is also fear. We reject that which
we cannot manage. We condemn what we do not understand.
We set up a means of control to render powerless those
dynamic realities we know to be powerful. No aspect of our
humanity is invested with more anxieties, yearnings, emotions,
and needs than is our sexual nature. So, sex is a major arena in
which the prejudice of human beings finds expression.*

John Spong[1]

Internal crisis

On several occasions since the movement's inception, tensions had
been caused by the disjunction between the need to provide a focused
and rapid public response to campaigning issues and an effective
national organization on the one hand, and the desire to sustain more
democratic and diffused structures of decision-making through the
national committee on the other. Inevitably, the role of the administrative secretary and his relationship with the national committee who
employed him, were pivotal in ensuring that these contradictory
objectives did not pull the movement apart. In 1985 as a result of a
financial crisis, the national committee decided to make the secretary
redundant after he was unwilling to accept a drastic reduction in his
working hours. Financially LGCM's position had always been perilous,
since it offered help and support to thousands of people, many of whom
never subscribed to the national organization, and this was even true
of considerable numbers of those who attended local group meetings.
Many, too, joined at a particular time of crisis and left after a short

period. Thus whereas over 2000 people had belonged to LGCM since 1976, the membership averaged about 600–700 in the early 1980s.[2] Nor did all members of the national committee regard the employment of a full-time worker as sustainable or indeed necessarily desirable given LGCM's limited income. As one put it rather sharply in 1980, 'I am spending all my time raising money for ... the Kirker show.'

As this comment indicates, issues of personality and style of leadership which had arisen with Peter Elers in 1977 also played a part in the national committee's decision. Some of them in 1985 made little secret of the fact that they had lost confidence in Richard Kirker and saw the financial crisis as an opportunity to remove him. The committee minutes in March 1985 indicate their unhappiness with some of the remarks he had made on behalf of LGCM, and record their attempts to reassert their control over any written statements made in the movement's name in the future.[4] The fall in membership which had precipitated the financial crisis also appeared to suggest a general sense of malaise and a lack of clear objectives. Not everyone shared this view of the situation, nor thought that the secretary was being treated fairly. At an extraordinary general meeting held in Birmingham on 1 June 1985, the national committee resigned after its analysis of LGCM's financial position and proposed remedy were rejected by 51 votes to 39. A new committee was elected which reaffirmed its commitment to maintaining Richard Kirker as a full-time employee, and issued a new declaration of purpose.[5] There is no doubt that this was a critical decision in the history of the movement. In some ways the aftermath was made easier by the upsurge of prejudice within British society at this time, to which the new committee referred in its declaration. This had the effect of recreating a sense of unity and direction. It was also to show in the next few years the necessity for effectively coordinated national campaigning, as LGCM along with all other sections of the gay and lesbian community strove to combat an increasingly virulent homophobic discourse which sought to curtail its rights and put back the clock on even the limited gains which had been won since 1967. The Christian Right, and its fundamentalist component in particular, played a significant part in the articulation of that discourse which LGCM, itself the target of attack, set out to counteract.

The Christian Right and the assault on lesbian and gay rights

From the beginning, LGCM had been engaged in what was in many respects a sterile and deadlocked debate with conservative Protestants over the exegesis and significance of a small number of biblical passages relating to homosexuality, the meaning of which they regarded as clear and whose moral imperatives, they asserted, were binding upon the late twentieth-century Church. True, it was not too difficult to expose the intellectual incoherence and moral inadequacies of those clinging to a fundamentalist hermeneutic. Evangelicals who did so had to deny that the churches had ever made significant changes in their understanding of Christian morality – as had manifestly been the case on a whole gamut of issues ranging from slavery to contraception and divorce. Equally importantly they had to deny that those changes were evidence of the impossibility of credibly maintaining any kind of literalist interpretation of Scripture. Within the Church of England the divisions within the evangelical camp over the question of women's ordination were further proof, if any were needed, that such a position was untenable. The resulting tensions led to the emergence of what are now pronounced and sometimes acrimonious differences between those who, whilst claiming to uphold a version of the inerrancy of Scripture, have nevertheless found ways of putting aside the clear Pauline prohibitions on women exercising authority in the Church, and those, such as the conservative group Reform, who claim that if inerrancy is to have any meaning the original Pauline view must be upheld. Whilst many of the latter have attempted to preserve their moral credibility in staying in the Church of England by asserting that the issue of women's ordination is merely a secondary matter of ecclesiastical organization, whereas homosexuality is a first-order moral question, this is hardly a sufficient ploy to disguise their intellectual and ethical nakedness from those not within the fold.

Yet in an important sense much of this is to miss the point. As studies of Christian fundamentalist movements have repeatedly made clear, they cannot simply be explained at the level of ideas which can then conveniently be dismissed as irrational.[6] Fundamentalism arose in the nineteenth century as a reaction against both intellectual and social change. Its aim has been a comprehensive rejection of modernity, and its appeal has been to those either socially marginalized or psychologically discomfited by the pluralism and fragmentation of modern life. It is important to note, too, that because fundamentalism has been a broad cultural response to the insecurities of contemporary society, its appeal has not been restricted denominationally to Protestants.[7] For the same reason, the attractiveness, viability and significance of such movements have been crucially influenced by their social context. As the American historian Nancy Ammerman has observed, fundamentalism has been most politically active and culturally visible following periods of major social dislocation.[8] The rise of the Christian Right, which began with the creation of Jerry Falwell's Moral Majority in 1979 as a reaction against the moral and political ferment of the 1960s, would seem to bear this out. Arguing that American society was morally and socially endangered by a tide of abortion, feminism, homosexuality and secularism, the born-again Christian Right made a significant contribution to the support which swept Ronald Reagan to power in 1980. A similar process, though on a much smaller scale, occurred in Britain with the creation in the 1960s of Mary Whitehouse's National Viewers' and Listeners' Association, and the Society for the Protection of the Unborn Child. They were followed in the early 1970s by groups such as the evangelical Nationwide Festival of Light, which set out to combat what it called 'the moral pollution' in British life, and CARE (Christian Action Research and Education).[9]

The pluralism of American society, against which the Christian Right was reacting, in the end limited its chances of success, and its identification of the Bush Presidency with an anti-abortion stance lost him more votes than it won. In Britain the likely political impact of the Christian Right was even less, and its organizational structure far less impressive. Mary Whitehouse's successful prosecution of *Gay News* on a charge of blasphemous libel in 1977 was an indication that the appeal of Christian moralism in Britain was by no means negligible, but it did not herald the beginning of significant legislative change. This was because in Britain levels of religious participation were lower; the opening of the media to tele-evangelism had been resisted; and the federal system of devolved political power, which made it possible for Christian groups to score significant political successes at local level in America, did not exist. It is also clear that not all of those who could be described as seeking to provide a Christian underpinning for Thatcherite policies subscribed to biblical literalism or moral fundamentalism. This was true, for example, of Brian Griffiths, a Methodist and head of Mrs Thatcher's policy unit. It is, however, important to note that the emphasis placed by writers such as Griffiths upon the primacy of the traditional family in providing for its members many of the social support systems regarded by the postwar political consensus as functions of government, dovetailed smoothly both with long-held Tory values and with the moral agenda of Christian fundamentalist groups.[10] The demonization of all alternative family units, including both single parent families and lesbian and gay partnerships, could thus be given both an economic and a moral rationale. Yet as Martin Durham has shown in his study of sex and politics in the Thatcher years, no straightforward alliance of the Christian moral lobby and the government was ever established.[11] This was partly because of the high level of secularization in British society which made Mrs Thatcher wary of identifying her party with sectarian moral stances which might lose votes. Thus rates of abortion, divorce and illegitimacy continued to rise despite the rhetorical exhortation to return to Victorian values, and the government's unwillingness to legislate in these areas was far from satisfactory to moral crusaders such as Mary Whitehouse and Victoria Gillick. Mrs Thatcher's doubts about the agenda of Christian fundamentalism were also partly the result of opposition within her own party from free market libertarians who were suspicious of state regulation of private life in the moral as well as in the economic sphere. This of course merely reflected the tensions and contradictions inherent within Thatcherism which promoted an unrestrained free market individualism – there was no such thing as society as she once famously remarked – but shied away from the social and moral consequences of the pursuit of greed and competitiveness.

Yet where the concerns of fundamentalist Christian groupings could be used to political advantage, they were not unwelcome and might gain publicity as a consequence. There were two main areas where this was the case. First, in order to counter the charge that rising rates of poverty and crime in the 1980s were the consequence of government policy, an attempt was made to blame these upon what it was claimed had been the collapse of traditional family values and moral standards in the 1960s – a collapse which was laid squarely at the door of progressive left-wing policies. Here was politically convenient over-simplification on the grand scale. The restoration of supposedly traditional morality, rather than targeted government expenditure to help the poor – which would have involved higher rates of taxation for the rich – was to be the universal panacea for social breakdown. Such a stance chimed in well with fundamentalist Christian anathematizing of the 1960s as a period characterized by liberal attitudes in both theology and social legislation, and increasing secularization and decline in Church attendance. Second, the Thatcher government whipped up hostility to gays and lesbians – a task made easier by the anxiety aroused by AIDS – to gain direct political advantage. The proposals by a small number of Labour councils that children should be given sex education in a form which did not denigrate sexual minorities was used to portray the Labour Party as a threat to the nation's moral fabric.[12] As early as 1979 LGCM had been seeking support from teachers' organizations to provide more effective educational material about the emotional needs of gay and lesbian people, and it later came to the defence of councils such as Haringey which tried to do so.[13] This was of little avail. The momentum generated by the Thatcher government's policy of attacking the more sensitive and honest forms of sex education pioneered by some London authorities was more than sufficient to ensure the passage of Section 28 of the 1988 Local Government Act which prohibited local authorities from engaging in what it called the 'promotion of homosexuality' or its acceptability as 'a pretended family relationship'. This again was a stance which accorded closely with that of Christian fundamentalists within the churches.

Yet even allowing for these areas of potential agreement, it is important to note how circumscribed the alliance between Thatcherite political opportunism and conservative Christian moralism actually was. For example, the Rev Tony Higton's Action for Biblical Witness to Our Nation, which was founded in 1984, and which sought no direct involvement in politics, was fully in tune with the government's anti-pathy towards homosexuality and with its call for a return to traditional values which Higton interpreted as being identical with his conservative evangelical exposition of biblical teaching. But this correlation was not one made by many Tories who showed little interest in, and even less understanding of, ABWON's diatribes against theological liberalism. Moreover, one of ABWON's other major obsessions turned out to be politically problematic. Higton's concern to combat what he called interfaith compromise, and to assert the unique salvific efficacy of Christianity, was a sensitive and politically damaging policy to pursue in a multicultural society. Not surprisingly, despite gathering a petition with some 76,965 signatures and presenting it to Buckingham Palace in 1991, ABWON was unable to prevent either a multifaith service of worship at the annual Commonwealth Day Observance in Westminster Abbey in 1991, or the Queen's participation in the service. Nevertheless, Higton was to take full advantage of the homophobic backlash of the Thatcher years to cause immense suffering, hardship and insecurity for gay and lesbian Christians within the churches – a fact of which LGCM was to become only too aware.

The group which approximated most closely to the political aims and methods of the American Christian Right was the Conservative Family Campaign which was founded in March 1986 under the chairmanship of Graham Webster-Gardiner, and which numbered ten Tory MPs and one Anglican bishop amongst its sponsors. It also claimed to have the support of 24 MPs in Parliament. In its literature it painted a lurid picture of Britain in the previous 25 years as a country suffering from unremitting moral decline which had resulted in serious political and economic consequences. In case anyone missed the link, the CFC argued that periods of national influence and prosperity had also been eras of strong Christian commitment and it cited Victorian England as a prime example. It condemned laws which had made abortion and divorce easier, and the support given to minority groups which had encouraged what it called 'the spread of abnormality and perversity'.[14] One of its sponsors, Dame Jill Knight, played a major part in the enactment of Section 28, and Webster-Gardiner went on to boast with some exaggeration that his had been the only pressure group which had campaigned vigorously for the clause. Yet not all of its initiatives were equally successful. During the passage of the Education Bill through the Lords early in 1986, Lord Buckmaster, one of the CFC's sponsors, introduced an amendment designed to ensure that sex education was taught only 'in the context of enduring family life', and that parents be given the right to withdraw their children from such lessons. In the Commons it was another of the CFC's sponsors, the Tory MP Peter Bruinvels, who emerged as the leading proponent of the amendment. During the Tory Party conference, the CFC put further pressure on the government by distributing a pamphlet titled *Sex Education and Your Child* which stated the CFC's aim as being 'to save a generation of children from the immoral propaganda for promiscuity, homosexuality, contraception, anti-marriage views, fornication, and encouragement of children to experiment with sex, which has passed in too many schools during the past two decades as health education'.[15] Yet in the crucial debate on 21 October 1986, the government successfully defeated Bruinvels' amendment allowing children to opt out of sex education if their parents wished, by putting forward its own proposal to create new regulatory school bodies made more answerable to parents. As the CFC realized, it had been outmanoeuvred by Kenneth Baker who had revealed what it called 'the full cunning of the government's approach' in the area of sex education, since the CFC had no more faith in the new school bodies than it had had previously in the control exercised by local authorities.[16] But even though the CFC did not succeed in implementing its agenda, the use which it attempted to make of fears over the spread of AIDS in pursuing its aims, was a good example of the potential threat of Christian fundamentalist homophobia in an area which was to pose one of the most significant challenges which LGCM was to face.

AIDS

In LGCM's office in Oxford House there is a picture on the wall of a banner-waving elderly man at a fundamentalist Christian rally in America. A kindly looking figure, he could be anyone's grandfather. The placard he is carrying reads 'Thank God for AIDS'. In Britain, too, the onset of the disease, at first described by an ignorant and prejudiced press as the gay plague, fuelled Christian homophobia in several ways. Here, for those who had always feared and hated gays and lesbians, was evidence of divine wrath poured forth upon them, and comforting reassurance that the wages of sin was indeed death. A lethal disease, whose aetiology and mode of transmission was at first uncertain, also provided ample scope for ostracizing its victims. For example, might not the chalice, the symbol of Christian unity and solidarity, be a source of infection? More generally AIDS could be used emotively to deny the validity of gay lifestyles, and to denigrate gay people as a threat to the fabric of society – for some a sufficient threat to justify the recriminalization of homosexual acts. There can be no doubt that the fear and irrational prejudice aroused by the disease played a major part in the passage of Section 28 and in the sustained attempts to prevent the development of more positive images of gay and lesbian people in the school curriculum. It also, as the Rev David Holloway, the evangelical Vicar of Jesmond and leading Christian homophobe made clear, intensified the debate over homosexuality within the Church of England and provided new opportunities for those intent upon driving practising gay and lesbian clergy and laity out of the Church.[17]

Homophobic Christians attempted to exploit the tragedy of AIDS in all of these ways. Thus Paul Johnson wrote in the *Spectator* in 1985 that the epidemic was 'the direct result of the relaxation of criminal sanctions in Western countries' – sanctions which he believed the majority of Christians wished to see reimposed.[18] The CFC made just such a proposal. In November 1986 its Executive Council, describing itself as 'the Christian Conscience of the Conservative party', wrote to Lord Whitelaw urging the repeal of the 1967 Sexual Offences Act; the compulsory isolation of all AIDS patients in Christian hospices where their life was to be made 'as dignified as possible'; and the ending of government support for the Terrence Higgins Trust, the Family Planning Association and what were described as 'other anti-family organisations'. Instead, resources were to be given to evangelical Christian counselling services such as Turning Point, Pilot and True Freedom Trust which were in the business of providing spiritual 'cures' for those tempted to commit homosexual acts. The government's attempts to limit the spread of AIDS by the provision of information and safe sex campaigns were denounced as offensive and a waste of taxpayers' money. This was of course to be a major faultline within the government itself. The fundamentalist Christian belief that the government should be advocating sexual abstinence rather than facing up to the reality of the nation's sexual behaviour coincided with Mrs Thatcher's own instincts. It was a view which nevertheless had to give way to the dangers posed by a major threat to public health. The CFC statement ended with an apocalyptic claim that without the implementation of the kind of measures it had suggested 25 per cent of the population might be affected within a few years. Finally fundamentalist Christians, having argued for the recriminalization of homosexual acts and the incarceration of AIDS patients, and having denigrated gay people as sinful, were called upon to show compassion and 'care for all the sufferers regardless of any unrighteousness'.[19]

AIDS was also a powerful weapon with which to undermine the human worth and dignity of gay men. In a further leaflet titled 'The Truth About AIDS', the CFC denounced homosexual practice as morally wrong and condemned by the Bible since Sodom, and went on to criticize both the churches and the Department of Health and Social Security for their refusal to condemn it. In fact at the time the Department was desperately anxious to avoid the kinds of hostility and condemnation which the CFC advocated, for fear that it would make the task of helping those at risk of infection or in need of treatment much harder. Tony Higton also jumped on the homophobic bandwagon. Seizing upon the publicity surrounding cases of AIDS amongst the clergy, he sent the *Church Times* a vindictive lament about 'how degrading it is to have the Church of England's name linked day after day in the world's media with such a disease, which has overwhelming connections with active and promiscuous homosexual practice'. The Church of England, he went on, had got what it deserved because of its 'unbiblical toleration of homosexual acts which are an abomination in God's sight'. In a foretaste of what was to come, he called upon the hierarchy to remove unrepentant gay clergy from office.[20] A particularly effective rhetorical discourse used by Higton here and subsequently, was the opportunity which concern over HIV and AIDS gave to suggest that since the disease could be portrayed as being the consequence of promiscuity, and since the majority of its British victims were gay men, homosexuals were inherently promiscuous. The effectiveness of this ploy lay in the fact that the witch-hunt which Higton promoted within the Church of England made it almost impossible for gay clergy who lived in faithful and committed sexual relationships to counteract the stereotype which he tried to disseminate. The climate of fear and hatred which surrounded AIDS sufferers within some parts of the churches was also conducive to Higton's campaign. Speaking at a conference on 'AIDS and Pastoral Care' at King's College, London in April 1986, at which LGCM was represented, Professor Michael Adler took as his starting point the not unreasonable assumption that the clergy and the medical profession shared a common ideal of compassion and would not succumb to bigotry and seek to isolate sick people. In the afternoon Richard Holloway, the Bishop elect of Edinburgh, urged the Church 'to rediscover the theology of the outcast to enable us to minister adequately'. Yet the discussion did not pass without some disagreement and anger being expressed. Not everyone saw compassion as the overriding moral imperative. As one clergyman put it, 'I am in the business of presenting certainties, and one of these is that sin and God don't keep company together.'[21] In August the Churches' Council for Health and Healing issued a working party report which attempted to counteract the growing homophobic exploitation of AIDS. It argued that AIDS and homosexuality were not logically linked, and that although promiscuity encouraged its spread, it was ultimately a medical and not a moral issue.[22] Not everyone was persuaded. As one doctor wrote to the *Church Times*, 'Surely here commonsense and medical science combine with God's Word to scream at us that homosexual activity is completely unacceptable.'[23] The screams of those who were suffering might, it seemed, be drowned out by those who hated and feared them.

LGCM first discussed the issues surrounding AIDS in 1983, but Richard Kirker admitted that the movement should have acted more quickly than it did, though in this its record was no better or worse than other institutional responses to the crisis.[24] In June 1985, after promptings from the membership, the national committee issued a declaration of purpose which included as priorities the care of AIDS sufferers and the combating of the hostility and prejudice which the disease had aroused.[25] LGCM then set up a working group on AIDS chaired by Michael Workman to implement this agenda. In December a joint initiative by LGCM and the Roman Catholic gay group Quest led to the founding of the AIDS Faith Alliance which received financial support from the Terrence Higgins Trust. Barnaby Miln, an LGCM member, was invited to join the planning group, and he and Richard

Kirker attended the National Episcopal Church Conference on AIDS held in San Francisco in March 1986. One of the Alliance's first tasks was the publication of a pamphlet sponsored by LGCM, Quest and the Metropolitan Community Church titled *Is AIDS God's Wrath?* This set out to expose the illogicality and theological obscenity of regarding the disease as some kind of divine retribution. LGCM itself devoted the June 1986 issue of *Gay Christian* to the crisis. In an article on the Christian response to AIDS, Canon Douglas Rhymes, a long-standing LGCM member employed on the staff of Chichester Theological College, attacked the churches for contributing to the problem by their refusal to encourage stable gay relationships.[26] Paul de Fortis, Assistant Chaplain of the Middlesex Hospital, set out what was then known about the illness, emphasizing that from a world-wide view there was no justification for regarding it as some kind of homosexual disease. He also tried to dispel misinformation about modes of transmission which had resulted in some churches resorting to intinction (dipping the bread into the wine) rather than using the common cup.[27]

As a result of a conference on AIDS supported by the leaders of all the main Christian denominations, in July 1986 a more broadly based organization, Christian Action on AIDS was set up with Barnaby Miln as its first chairman, and LGCM subsequently channelled its main efforts into supporting this body which set out to provide education, theological reflection and practical support for those affected. It did not, however, stop its own campaigning against the prejudice and discrimination surrounding the disease. In November 1986 the Synod of the Church of England held a major debate on AIDS at which Barnaby Miln made a powerful speech. In preparation for the occasion LGCM's Evangelical Fellowship wrote to all Synod members pointing out that punitive and condemnatory moralizing were counter-productive:

> Sadly, the traditional church view that all forms of homosexual expression are wrong is one that in practice encourages rather than discourages promiscuity. This is most starkly demonstrated in the Roman Catholic confessional, where a person may receive absolution for a casual homosexual encounter of which he repents, but is denied absolution when he or she is living in a loving committed relationship.[28]

Many gay couples, the letter went on, had nevertheless sustained such relationships 'in spite of all the obstacles created by a society in which gay women and men are isolated, ignored and often ostracised'. As

Higton was about to demonstrate, there were many in the churches still hell-bent upon wrecking their lives.

The Higton affair

In April 1987 Higton wrote to all Anglican diocesan bishops seeking from them a public statement that homosexual genital acts, like those committed by heterosexuals outside of marriage, were the moral equivalent of adultery and fornication. Only 20 out of 44 replied, and only eight gave what Higton regarded as the required answer. This was an indication that the episcopal hierarchy of the Church of England was anxious to avoid a full-scale debate, and still less a definitive pronouncement upon such a contentious subject. Already alarmed by the growing divisions within the Anglican Church's ranks over the ordination of women, and fearful that any synodical condemnation would lead to a witch-hunt directed against practising gay clergy, most bishops preferred to stave off a debate on the grounds that an enquiry chaired by the Rev June Osborne was already underway. Building upon the momentum generated by the Thatcher government's assault upon gay and lesbian rights, and upon public anxiety and prejudice surrounding the spread of AIDS, there is no doubt that Higton's private member's motion debated by the Church of England's Synod on 11 November 1987 wrong-footed both LGCM and the liberal wing of the church. As a result, Synod embarked upon a short and highly emotive debate undertaken in the full glare of the media, rather than considering a carefully prepared and well balanced theological report, which would have brought out the complexities surrounding the interpretation of biblical texts in the light of modern knowledge, and would have allowed some genuine engagement with the reality of the lives led by lesbian and gay Christians.

Higton's motion argued that sexual intercourse should take place only between a man and a woman who were married to each other; that fornication, adultery and homosexual acts are sinful in all circumstances; and that Christian leaders are called upon to be exemplary in all spheres of morality including sexual morality as a condition of being appointed to, or remaining in, office in the Church. Taken at face value, and in the broader context of the Church's debates about the theology of sexuality in contemporary society, the most striking feature of the Higton motion was the way in which it highlighted once again the extent to which the Church of England's teaching was at variance with the actual behaviour and attitudes of the overwhelming bulk of the heterosexual population of the country including many of its own younger members. But at the time, it was correctly taken to be an attack upon gay and lesbian rights within the Church of England, and one which set out to repudiate the more liberal recommendations of the Gloucester report. Reflecting the views of LGCM, Malcolm Johnson spoke in favour of an amendment which would have led to the full acceptance of gay and lesbian relationships. He was sharply critical of the Higton motion:

> This motion seems to me to be a sort of moral M1, an open road, a motorway, down which we are being invited to drive at speed, recklessly knocking down everyone in the way and particularly those who are the most vulnerable in our society. So we hit the single parent with condemnation and calumny; we injure the divorced; we maim the remarried, for in biblical terms they are adulterers. Many in this Synod and beyond have fought hard to recognise second marriages – how can we now say that adultery is sinful in all circumstances? Then finally we knock homosexuals into the gutter, for that is, I believe the hidden agenda of this motion, once again to heap abuse on a minority group who in my view have suffered enough at the Church's hands. This motion is a negative piece of work, lacking in faith, lacking in hope and lacking in love.[29]

In his speech the Archbishop of Canterbury, Robert Runcie, sought not altogether successfully to take the heat out of the debate. Reminding Synod that the Osborne report was at that time in preparation, he warned against giving way to either of what he dismissively called two lobbies who 'do not like to face up to complexities', and urged the need for what he called 'reasoned, persistent, patient work on the issues'. This was not so much a case of sitting on the fence as refusing to climb on it at all. The Archbishop also indicated his support for an amendment by the leading evangelical bishop, Michael Baughen, which moderated the tone and substance of the original motion but did not undo the damage which it had done. Like fornication and adultery, homosexual genital acts were said to fall short of the ideal of sex within marriage, and were to be dealt with by a call to repentance and by the exercise of compassion. The clause stipulating that it was a condition of office that all clergy should be exemplary in all areas of their lives including sexual morality was modified in such a way that the exhortation remained in force whilst the disciplinary threat was removed.

Ill prepared, and divided in their opinions, Anglican bishops had gone into the debate with as much enthusiasm as men asked to cross a minefield wearing magnetic boots – and with much the same result. Both LGCM and their opponents claimed a partial victory. Malcolm Johnson's amendment was heavily defeated, but on the other hand ABWON was far from happy about the amendment which was passed, describing it as 'rather weak concerning disapproval of homosexual acts', and admitting that it retained the *status quo ante* in the matter of clerical discipline.[30] In practice, in the atmosphere prevalent at the end of 1987, Synod's decision provided justification for a hardening of attitudes and a witch-hunt against gay clergy. Emblazoned across the front page of the *Daily Express* at the end of December was the headline 'Bishop Bans Gay Vicars', a reference to a much publicized radio interview by the Bishop of Ripon, David Young, in which he said that practising homosexuals would not be sponsored for ordination or offered a post in his diocese. The controversy surrounding his statement also revealed that different dioceses would continue to treat candidates for ordination in different ways. The Venerable Roger Sharpley, who was director of ordinands for Stepney, warned that the Church was going down what he called 'a very dangerous road', and he made it clear that it was not his policy to enquire about the sexual practices of potential ordinands since he was more interested in their other qualities. Some gay clergy whose work he admired were, he said, 'very rounded, responsible people in stable relationships'.[31] The Bishop of Durham added further to the evident disarray amongst the bishops when he told the *Independent* that in his experience practising homosexuals made good clergy provided they avoided scandal and promiscuity – adding for good measure that a number of senior clergy thought as he did but were unwilling to say so in public. Never one to avoid controversy, David Jenkins further enraged conservatives by pointing out that notwithstanding the Higton motion passed by Synod, the pastoral care and disciplining of the clergy remained the responsibility of individual diocesan bishops. Supposedly backing the Ripon rather than the Durham line, the Bishop of Peterborough, Bill Westwood, only made matters worse in a revealing comment that if a parish were to 'get lumbered with a chap who has got his boyfriend living round the corner' then that was life, but it was quite another matter if the situation had the official sanction of the bishops. Kiss but don't tell was, it seemed, the approach adopted by a number of bishops. In a statement LGCM seized upon the hypocrisy evidenced here and elsewhere in the Church of England's contortionist writhings. Robert Runcie's claim that the Bishop of Ripon's statement did no more than reiterate the Church's official teaching sat uneasily, LGCM pointed out, beside the fact that he and other bishops had knowingly ordained and employed homosexual clergy in the past. Attention was also drawn to the plight of such clergy who were now being driven to deceit and concealment.[32] This was a theme that was taken up in an article by the religious affairs correspondent of the *Independent*, Andrew Brown, titled 'Voices from the Wilderness'. Through LGCM he was put in touch with a number of gay clergy who were living in relationships and who now felt increasingly vulnerable.

Dissatisfied by what they rightly regarded as the unwillingness of many bishops to embark upon a McCarthy style crusade against gay clergy, conservatives pressed the issue again in the meeting of the General Synod in February 1988. The context of this debate in the House of Laity is significant. It followed an earlier one on Christian values in Britain, in which the Tory Minister for Agriculture, John Selwyn Gummer, accused the Church of England of failing to give a strong moral lead to the nation. He went on to single out the Archbishop of York, John Habgood, for particular censure for not supporting Section 28 in the House of Lords the previous November. The scapegoating of both gay and lesbian Christians and of liberal theology as being somehow responsible for the increasing marginalization of the Church of England in society was also a powerful subtext in the debate in Synod. According to one speaker, the devoted efforts of both clergy and laity during the past 35 years had led only to a decline in church attendance and influence – a trend which he believed could only be halted by a confident reassertion of traditional values and teaching.

In the subsequent debate on sexual morality, an amendment was passed calling upon the bishops to issue a clear statement on where the Church of England stood on all aspects of the question including homosexuality and lesbianism. This was despite a speech by Barnaby Miln commending the pastoral work done by gay clergy, and urging the Synod to wait for the publication of the findings of the Church's own working party. However, demands for an explicit statement on the disciplining of gay clergy were rejected, and the bishops reiterated their right to make their own judgements in this area.[33] Tony Higton's attempts to find out if active steps were being taken by bishops to detect if candidates for ordination were homosexuals were also resisted. As the *Independent* concluded, the upshot was that the Church remained divided over the selection of homosexuals for the priesthood.[34] One of the most eloquent if unintentional comments upon its confusion and embarrassment over the gay issue was a photograph published in *The Times* of Robert Runcie responding to demands for greater disciplining of homosexuals within the Church. He was flanked by one of the Church's highest ranking officials. That this person was himself a practising homosexual remained, of course, unsaid.[35] As Geoffrey Thompson commented in LGCM's *Journal*, the bishops had engaged in an exercise in damage limitation and instead of expelling gay clergy they had been content to insult them. The price in terms of integrity, he went on, was high:

> Individuals are expected to engage in lying and concealment so that bishops and Diocesan Directors for Ordination do not have to lie if they are asked if they ever knowingly ordain practising homosexuals. 'Don't embarrass us and we will ordain you.' The system works rather well. Thousands of people have been trained and ordained under it and are now exercising ministries every bit as effective or disastrous as their heterosexual colleagues.[36]

In the same edition of the *Journal*, LGCM member Diarmaid MacCulloch made it clear how costly honesty could be in the new Higton-style regime. Sponsored by the Bishop of Bristol, Barry Rogerson, and after training at Cuddesdon Theological College, he was ordained to the diaconate where he served for a year in a Bristol church. His refusal to lie about his committed relationship with his partner resulted in the bishop refusing to ordain him to the priesthood. The Church of England lost a man of outstanding intellectual and pastoral gifts; others who were economical with the truth were ordained in the same diocese. The bishop had kept the rules.[37]

Yet to accuse the Church of England of division, confusion and hypocrisy at this time, though true, does not go to the heart of the matter. Peter Tatchell made this clear in his own inimitable style when, in an interruption from the public gallery during Synod's tortuous deliberations, he accused the Church of England of fanning the flames of prejudice and discrimination. As a number of contributors to the debates in Synod in both November and February made clear, the issue of gay clergy and the condemnation and expulsion of unrepentant gay and lesbian Christians from the Church was only part of the wider assault on gay and lesbian rights which had culminated in the passage of Section 28. Whatever their protestations to the contrary, the bishops' refusal to challenge the belief in the sinfulness of homosexuality more vigorously, and their pretence that the supposed sin could be separated from the obligation to love those who committed it, could only play into the hands of those who condemned the extension of gay and lesbian equality before the law, and whose ultimate agenda was to recriminalize homosexuality in the name of Christian morality. The dangers inherent in this stance were evident, for example, in a comment made by Lord Coggan, Runcie's predecessor, in support of what he called the firmer line now being taken by the Christian churches. It had originated, he correctly pointed out, in 'a reaction against a certain license of the Sixties, and that is welcome as long as it is a reaction pursued in love, understanding, and pastoral care'.[38] Others were much clearer about the implications of reacting against the liberalism of the 1960s, and on the links which could be drawn between sin and the criminal law. The same article in the *Daily Telegraph* which reported the Bishop of Ripon's diatribe against gay clergy, carried as a footnote a report of an interview on Irish radio given by the then Chief Constable of Greater Manchester and devout Christian, James Anderton. He described the decriminalization of homosexuality in 1967 as 'one of the worst changes in legislation ever enacted in this country', and went on to state that it was beyond his comprehension 'how anyone could say it is not sinful or against the law to engage in practices of that kind'.[39] In the climate of moral panic and prejudice in which such views could gain ground, LGCM was now to find itself the target of attack.

Taking leave of one's faculties: the eviction from St Botolph's

As we have seen, the siting of LGCM's office in the tower of St Botolph's Church, Aldgate, was the result of the Rector Malcolm Johnson's wish to provide pastoral care for London's gay community – a concern which led him to offer his church and the adjoining Sir John Cass primary school as venues for the movement's inaugural meeting. Subsequently LGCM entered into an arrangement whereby its first administrative secretary worked partly for the movement and partly for the Rector. When the post of administrative secretary became full-time, LGCM continued to have the use of the tower room as its office, for which it paid rent to St Botolph's. As a founder member of LGCM, Malcolm Johnson obviously wished to help in a practical way. He also saw the offer of a base for LGCM as part of the social outreach to disadvantaged minorities which was a major part of the work of his church. A large part of this endeavour centred upon the provision of food, clothing and accommodation for London's homeless. He had not, however, sought to obtain a Faculty from the Diocesan Chancellor to permit

LGCM to use the tower room as its office. This was a somewhat technical matter. Normally a Faculty is needed when any proposals are made to make alterations to the fabric of a church or to install a new work of art or other fittings. Johnson says that he did not realize until January 1987 that a Faculty should have been obtained for the change of use involved in letting part of the tower to LGCM.[40] When he did, the PCC decided that a draft lease should be drawn up to regularize LGCM's position. The PCC had in fact always strongly supported the use of St Botolph's by LGCM and it worked harmoniously with its administrative secretary, Richard Kirker, who reported regularly to it on the work which the movement was doing. Although a certain amount of discretion was used, such as LGCM having its own box number and not using the church's address in its material, Malcolm Johnson is also clear that the existence of the movement at St Botolph's for over eleven years was known to the diocesan authorities.

The highly charged and widely publicized debate on the Higton motion in Synod in November 1987 drew the attention of the Diocesan Chancellor, George Newsom, to the fact that LGCM had its office at St Botolph's, and he informed the diocesan Registrar that an application for a Faculty should be made at once. This was done on 16 December 1987. As Malcolm Johnson was aware, in the hostile climate which the Higton debate had generated, the application was likely to prove controversial. Following up his action in Synod, Higton mounted an attack on LGCM urging that it should no longer be allowed to retain its office on Church premises.[41] The main thrust of his argument was the charge that pornographic material was being sold by the movement on Church property. On 14 December 1987 Malcolm Johnson made one of a number of attempts to discuss the matter with the Archdeacon of London, George Cassidy. In his letter he expressed concern that opposition to the granting of a Faculty might result in a court case which could jeopardize the extensive programme of social work undertaken at St Botolph's, and he sought to arrive at a pastoral rather than a legal solution to the dispute. To achieve this he undertook to regularize the legal position of LGCM, to exercise reasonable control of its literature and publicity material, and to discuss with LGCM its future use of St Botolph's.[42] The Archdeacon proved to be unwilling to respond to this overture and opposed the application.

In his final judgement the Chancellor of the Diocese insisted that the case had only been about the rule of law. In fact the Act on Petition made to the court by the Archdeacon of London, as well as some of the media coverage of the events, makes it clear that a concerted attack was made upon the integrity of LGCM, and that the case can only be understood in the wider context of the politically charged debates about gay rights and the promotion of homosexuality which were occurring at the time. Making use of material provided by Higton, who was ready to give evidence in court, the Archdeacon's Act on Petition to the Consistory Court unleashed a torrent of invective against LGCM which went far beyond what would have been needed to secure its removal from St Botolph's on legal grounds. LGCM was accused not only of occupying Church premises without permission, but of condoning sexual acts involving promiscuity, pornography, paedophilia, sado-masochism and proscribed drugs.[43] This onslaught was justified by identifying without reservation or qualification the views expressed in publications such as *The Joy of Gay Sex* and *The Gay Guide to London* with those of the movement. No attempt was made to indicate that these were only a tiny fraction of the books, mostly of a theological character, which LGCM offered through its mail order service, or that some secular literature was stocked not because it necessarily reflected the views of the movement, but because it might be helpful to some of the many enquirers who contacted LGCM with sexual and psycho-logical problems. *The Joy of Gay Sex* was not the kind of book to put into the hands of one's grandmother, and some within LGCM itself thought that it had been unwise to stock it, but what was often overlooked was that no one was going to stumble across it on sale in St Botolph's since LGCM's mail order stocks were kept under lock and key in its private office. More potentially damaging was the charge that the movement condoned paedophilia. This serious charge was based on the fact that LGCM advertised for sale copies of Parker Rossman's book *Sexual Experience between Men and Boys* and, as the Petition put it, 'this book does not condemn illegal paedophile practices'. What this failed to make clear was that Rossman's work was a highly respected academic textbook on its subject for use by those who had to deal with paedophiles in the legal and caring professions, and that it in no way condoned such practices. The case against LGCM was backed up by drawing upon part of the wider campaign against gay rights and freedom of expression which culminated in the passage of Section 28 of the Local Government Bill earlier that year. In support of the contention that LGCM condoned 'contact with children in association with homosexual acts', Richard Kirker and the movement were said to support 'Education Authorities which encourage school teachers to project favourable views of homosexuality in their teaching of children', and went on to charge that one of LGCM's leaflets argued that 'school children should be taught that homosexual feelings are not sinful but should be developed'. The critical point that this was meant to aid and support those of a homosexual orientation, and to lessen prejudice and discrimination against them, was concealed by the depiction of LGCM as part of a left-wing campaign to corrupt the morals of school children – the same accusation which was used to good political effect against Labour councils by the Thatcher government in the 1987 election. What was really at issue in the ejection of LGCM was nowhere made more starkly evident than in the inclusion in the Petition of the claim that the movement was in opposition to the criminal law of England in that it supported the Labour Campaign for Lesbian and Gay Rights which sought further changes in laws which discriminated against gay and lesbian people. LGCM, as the Petition made clear, supported the aims of the gay rights movement. Archdeacon Cassidy and his supporters did not.

Faced with legal advice that the application for granting a Faculty had no chance of success, and that to proceed would involve crippling legal costs, St Botolph's – not without some dissent from within its Parochial Church Council – withdrew from the action three days before it was due to be heard in court. As the price of doing so, the Rector had to promise to evict LGCM from his church by 15 September. Was this decision, which effectively conceded the case and left the movement standing alone, the right one? Malcolm Johnson maintains that it was, though he admits that it left LGCM not only on its own, but also less able to refute the charges brought against it.[44] Speculation at this point is unavoidable. In a full contested hearing the biased and one-sided nature of the Petition might have been damagingly exploited. It remains doubtful whether in the climate of the time LGCM would have won its case.

What it did win was nevertheless substantial. At the full hearing on 16 May, the Chancellor accepted – with regret as he put it – counsel's argument that LGCM should not have been part of the action in the first place since it was not a person in law. This meant that although the Archdeacon was free to pursue costs against individuals it was not clear that he could do so against LGCM itself. This was a vital victory. It left the diocese to pay total costs which could have been as high as £80,000, a figure which would certainly have ruined the movement. The whole affair also won LGCM considerable sympathy in the Church and in the press. On 18 May 1988, under the headline 'A Scandal to the Faithful', the *Independent* denounced the proceedings as a heresy trial, concluding that 'the whole process looks like simple, vindictive bullying', a charge which the Archdeacon attempted to deny in a letter to the paper the following day.[45] Rowan Williams, then Lady Margaret Professor of Divinity at Oxford, and a widely respected priest and theologian, took the same line, writing to the *Church Times* that 'The deliberate will to humiliate which seems to be evident in the way this case has proceeded is very scandalous for the Church.' [46] Perhaps the most telling comment on the whole affair came in a statement sent by 70 clergy in the diocese of London to both the Bishop and the Archdeacon:

> Most of us have no link with LGCM and may not support all its aims, but we believe that the resort to law in this way was an inappropriate response to a pastoral problem. Members of LGCM are our brothers and sisters in Christ and the rest of the Church should listen to them with respect and love, especially at this time of increasing hostility to gay people. But again the Church has been seen as intolerant and rejecting, driving gay people out both physically and symbolically. [47]

Reaction from a far less supportive quarter is also telling. Iain Walker's article in the *Mail on Sunday* on 10 July 1988 was a vintage example of the way in which a hostile press dealt with gay rights issues.[48] Under the headline 'Scandal of Gay Clergy – Truth about the Church that is used for Peddling Pornography', the paper printed an extract from a sexually explicit pamphlet available at St Botolph's, without making it clear that it was part of a safe sex leaflet designed to combat the spread of HIV.[49] Offering no evidence, it continued with the remarkable suggestion that 'many of the ancient City churches are open pick-up joints'. Whether this led to any dramatic increase in either visitors or worshippers to churches in the City of London is not recorded. Walker's article then went on to reiterate one of the leitmotifs of those who opposed LGCM and other gay and lesbian rights groups: 'If St Botolph's had remained reasonably discreet counselling the homosexual community in the same way as the Roman Catholic Church does, no one would have complained.' The example – though the irony was wholly unintended – could not have been more apposite. The Catholic Church was commended for providing 'pastoral care' for those whose problems were caused in large part by the Church's own attitudes and teaching – rather as if the SS doctors of the concentration camps had offered to provide counselling to alleviate the distress of their inmates.[50] Organizations like LGCM, which were not content to accept a discriminatory legal toleration which left unchecked the ravages of homophobic prejudice, were once again accused of being strident and unreasonable, and of being the cause of their own troubles. Recognition of the achievement of LGCM and of its administrative secretary from such a source was therefore all the more impressive. As Walker admitted, Richard Kirker had 'spearheaded a mission, which in terms of new membership has been the most successful in the recent history of the Church of England'.

Those who attended LGCM's celebration of thanks and farewell at St Botolph's on 10 September, which took as its theme Passover and Exodus, heard an inspirational sermon from the Rev Kenneth Leech. They left with good reason for optimism. As a result of the eviction, LGCM had gained a tremendous amount of goodwill for its cause, including some from figures such as the conservative Anglican Church historian the Rev Edward Norman, which they could not previously have expected. Like the rest of the gay community in the 1980s, LGCM had endured some pretty dark times, but had gone on to see its opponents lose public sympathy as a result of what many people felt to be their manifestly pathological vehemence, whilst the issue of full equality and acceptance for gay and lesbian people within both Church and society had been placed even more prominently within the realm of public discourse. Even Section 28 and Tony Higton had their uses.

Notes

1 J. Spong (1990) *Living in Sin? A Bishop Rethinks Human Sexuality* (San Francisco: Harper & Row), p. 23.
2 *Gay Christian*, **39**, February 1986, p. 4.
3 Letter to Kennedy Thom, 22 April 1980.
4 LGCM Committee Minutes, 2 March 1985.
5 *Gay Christian*, **36**, July 1985.
6 See on this subject, C. Liebman, and R. Wuthnow (eds) (1983) *The New Christian Right: Mobilization and Legitimation* (New York: Aldine Publishing Co.) and S. Bruce (1988) *The Rise and Fall of the New Christian Right: Conservative Protestant Politics in America 1978–1988* (Oxford: Clarendon Press).
7 These points are well made for the earlier manifestations of Christian fundamentalism in the 1960s and 1970s, such as the National Viewers' and Listeners' Association and the Nationwide Festival of Light, in D. Cliff 'Religion, morality and the middle class', in R. King and N. Nugent (1979) *Respectable Rebels: Middle Class Campaigns in Britain in the 1960s and 1970s* (London: Hodder and Stoughton) pp. 127–52.
8 N. Ammerman 'North American Protestant Fundamentalism', in M. Marty and R. Appleby (1991) *Fundamentalisms Observed* (Chicago: Chicago University Press), pp. 1–65 (56).

9 There are helpful overviews of these groups, and of the context in which
they emerged, in two essays by Gerald Parsons, 'From consensus to
confrontation: religion and politics in Britain since 1945', and 'Between
law and licence: Christianity, morality and "permissiveness"', in
G. Parsons (ed.) (1994) *The Growth of Religious Diversity: Britain from 1945*
(London: Routledge), pp. 123–59, and 231–66.
10 See for example B. Griffiths (1982) *Morality and the Market Place: Christian
Alternatives to Capitalism and Socialism* (London: Hodder and Stoughton),
p. 94.
11 M. Durham (1991) *Sex and Politics: The Family and Morality in the Thatcher
Years* (London: Macmillan).
12 This episode is perceptively analysed in D. Cooper (1994) *Sexing the City:
Lesbian and Gay Politics Within the Activist State* (London: Rivers Oram
Press).
13 In January 1979 LGCM wrote to Terry Casey the General Secretary of the
National Association of Schoolmasters and Union of Women Teachers
unsuccessfully seeking his support for the distribution in schools of the
Campaign for Homosexual Equality's tape slide kit, 'Homosexuality: A
Fact of Life'. HCA GCM/4/20/384.
14 *Conservative Family Campaign: Bringing the Family Back into Focus* (n.d.)
(Epsom: Conservative Family Campaign).
15 M. Durham (1991), p. 109.
16 *Family Matters* (Epsom: Conservative Family Campaign), vol. 2, no. 1
(February 1987), pp. 4–5.
17 D. Holloway 'The Recent Debate on Homosexual Relationships in the
Church of England', in T. Higton (ed.) (1987) *Sexuality and the Church: The
Way Forward* (Hockley: Action for Biblical Witness to Our Nation), p. 59.
18 The *Spectator*, 17 August 1985, p. 16.
19 *Ibid.*, pp. 2–3.
20 *Church Times*, 15 March 1985.
21 *Church Times*, 18 April 1986.
22 *Ibid.*
23 *Church Times*, 26 September 1986.
24 *Gay Times*, April 1986.
25 *Gay Christian*, **36**, July 1985, p. 23.
26 *Gay Christian*, **40**, June 1986, pp. 4–6.
27 *Ibid.*, pp. 13–16.
28 Letter of the Evangelical Fellowship within LGCM to all Synod Members,
10 October 1987.
29 Quoted in P. Coleman (1989) *Gay Christians: A Moral Dilemma* (London:
SCM), p. 167.
30 Higton (1987), p. 2.
31 The *Daily Telegraph*, 30 December 1987.
32 The *Guardian*, 31 December 1987.
33 *The Times*, 9 February 1988.
34 The *Independent*, 9 February 1988.
35 *The Times*, 9 February 1988.
36 *LGCM Journal*, **48**, November 1989, p. 12.
37 Ibid., pp. 8–9.

38 The *Guardian*, 31 December 1987.
39 The *Daily Telegraph*, 30 December 1987.
40 M. Johnson (1994) *Outside the Gate: St Botolph's and Aldgate 950–1994* (London: Stepney Books), p. 158.
41 Higton (1987), p. 79.
42 Letter of Malcolm Johnson to George Cassidy, 14 December 1987. Copy in possession of the writer.
43 I have taken the text of the Act on Petition from the Rev Norman Boakes's thesis 'Sexuality and Embarrassment: A Critical Analysis of the Response of the Church of England to Lesbian and Gay People Through A Case Study of the Eviction of the Lesbian and Gay Christian Movement from St Botolph's Church, Aldgate, in 1988', submitted in March 1996 in part-fulfilment of the requirements of the M.Th. in Applied Theology in the University of Oxford. I am very grateful to Norman Boakes for allowing me to read his thesis and for discussing it with me. The interpretation which I have put upon his work is entirely my own.
44 Johnson (1994), p. 163.
45 The *Independent*, 18 May 1988.
46 *Church Times*, 20 May 1988.
47 Statement by London Diocesan Clergy, 29 May 1988. Copy in the possession of the Rev Malcolm Johnson.
48 For this subject see T. Sanderson (1995) *Mediawatch: The Treatment of Male and Female Homosexuality in the British Media* (London: Cassell).
49 The *Mail on Sunday*, 10 July 1988.
50 This parallel is even more pertinent when one remembers that such bizarre inversions of the hitherto accepted social and moral order were commonplace within the concentration camp universe. For example inmates were forced to play Mozart and Beethoven for their own and their guards' edification. One should also remember that a significant minority of those who died in the camps did so because they were gay.

FOUR

From strength to strength 1988–97

*Gay men and lesbians need to know how much everyone in
society will benefit from the gains in their own struggle.*

James Nelson[1]

Organizational change and growth

LGCM emerged from a bruising few years and set about strengthening
its organizational structures and redoubling its campaigning work. As
a start, a new office was established at Oxford House in the East End of
London in June 1989. There was a certain degree of irony in being
located here, for Oxford House had once been the flagship of High
Church social reformers in their endeavours to reach the poor and
marginalized, whereas LGCM now found itself the victim of persecution
by some of their successors.

Another fruitful development in the same year was the establishment
by LGCM of the Institute for the Study of Christianity and Sexuality.
Its primary aim was to facilitate education and discussion of all aspects
of human sexuality within the Christian community, and in further-
ance of this objective it produced its own bulletin, edited by its national
coordinator, Alison Webster, who was based in LGCM's office. LGCM
also had the sole right to appoint the Institute's trustees. ISCS was also
important for LGCM in that it had charitable status and ran the
movement's telephone counselling service. Increasingly, its primary
focus upon theological reflection and education came to its members
to seem distinctive from the wider aims of LGCM, and whereas in 1992
there was talk of the relationship between the two bodies as being one
of mutual enrichment, by 1994 there were clear signs of tension. By

then LGCM was investigating the possibility of becoming a limited company and registered charity in its own right, which was effected from 17 August 1995. This change of legal status allowed the movement for the first time to benefit from covenanted tax-free giving. These changes did not involve any major alterations in the management structure of LGCM, which continued to be vested in a national committee whose officers took on particular responsibilites and employed the general secretary. The principle of gender parity on the committee was reaffirmed.

The need for LGCM to become a registered charity, and thereby maximize its income, reflects the ever-present challenge to balance the books. As a campaigning organization LGCM has achieved national prominence, a fact which is even grudgingly admitted by its opponents. Yet it has accomplished this feat with a national membership of under 1000 and an overall membership of some 3000 to 4000. Even allowing for the generosity of such a small number of supporters there is an inevitable gap between subscription income and the movement's expenses. In 1995, for example, subscription income amounted to some £25,000 which was barely 50 per cent of expenditure. Generous donations and bequests, such as that made by the late Brian Smith, have to make up the bulk of the rest.[2]

Financial stringencies notwithstanding, the movement continued to develop its denominational organizations. In 1988 the Roman Catholic caucus was set up, and by 1991 it had 120 names on its mailing list. In 1989 Iain MacDonald founded the United Reformed Church caucus and edited its first newsletter which appeared in February 1990. Other caucuses continued to flourish. In 1991 the Evangelical Fellowship had approximately 100 members, whilst the Young Lesbian and Gay Christian Group reported that it was attracting people who would not otherwise be in contact with LGCM.[3] With the creation of new groups, the task of maintaining inclusivity and diversity within an overall unified structure has not become any easier. In a letter of 1994, responding to criticism that LGCM was not doing enough to meet the needs of its women members, Richard Kirker spelt out the challenge:

> It is terribly difficult for an organization such as ours when it tries to say 'yes' to all types of people – some of whom are, frankly, in disagreement about what are held by some to be the 'fundamentals'. But we are determined to continue to try to provide a meeting point for that type of diversity, and the full

range of experiences that people have of God and the Church, regardless of their starting (or finishing?) point.[4]

The context of this letter indicates that the relationship between men and women within the movement was still one of the central elements in this tension. In December 1994 Liz Bodycote reflected upon the issues in an article in *LGCM News* titled 'Daunted by Diversity?' She wrote of the sensation felt by many lesbians 'of being rendered invisible by the predominantly male culture of the organisation'. The discomfort which many women felt in LGCM was, she pointed out, more than simply a matter of structures. Women did not identify with much of the androcentric core symbolism of Christianity, which made it harder for them to remain in either the churches or organizations such as LGCM. The discovery of diversity was not necessarily comfortable for everyone. For example, white women within LGCM were being challenged by their black lesbian sisters to face up to the nature and extent of exclusionary white assumptions. If an exodus of women from the movement was to be avoided, she warned, LGCM would need to be evolutionary and dynamic in both its theology and praxis.[5] Similar points were also made by Rosie Miles in the exchange of letters with Richard Kirker from which I have already quoted. Reflecting upon the anger that many women had felt during the 1994 AGM, she suggested that 'women who are trying to come to terms with their sexuality and their spirituality will be wrestling with all sorts of issues that some gay men don't see at all as issues, or indeed may find offensive'. She hoped that LGCM could function as a supportive environment in which lesbian and bisexual women could do their theology, and not as 'something I have to fight all the time in order to get my needs and the needs of others like me heard and met'.[6] In reply, Richard Kirker described LGCM's relationship with its women members as the issue which had probably taken more time and energy than any other in the movement's 17-year history, and which continued to engage the attention of a not inconsiderable proportion of men as well as women.

As a result of such concerns, 21 women met in London in September 1994 to explore what lesbian and bisexual women were seeking from their faith, and this was followed by the setting up of Lesbian Matters as the coordinating group for women within LGCM. In 1995 the keynote address at the annual conference was given by the theologian Grace Jantzen who took as her theme 'Off the Straight and Narrow – Towards a Lesbian Theology'. In January 1996 the group held a national gathering at Charney Manor in Oxfordshire which took as its subject lesbian sexual ethics. By the middle of the year Lesbian Matters had established 11 regional contacts, though the north of England still remained relatively under-represented.[7] Its minutes for February 1996 recorded that the profile of women and of issues relating to lesbianism had been raised and that adequate resources were being provided. These continued to be sensitive matters, however. In response to requests from Liz Bodycote, the national coordinator, Richard Kirker agreed that the national office would send out a letter of welcome to women enquirers and would distribute its journal *Sophic Voices*.[8] But he explained that not all of the problems surrounding women's participation in LGCM were that easy to solve. Out of a membership of 930, 653 were men and 277 were women, and in 1993 60 per cent of the latter were concentrated in London and the Home Counties.[9] In its November 1996 edition of *Sophic Voices*, the group made clear the ambivalence which some women felt in belonging to LGCM, and the pull of women's networks for those struggling to survive in a heteropatriarchal society. One of the group's aims was not separatism, but a commitment to the future of women in the movement – a goal which will require in the future as in the past the highest degree of structural flexibility and intellectual and theological openness and empathy.[10]

Tensions between the centre and its constituent parts have not been confined to women's issues. In January 1996 the Rev Peter Colwell, a member of the URC caucus, resigned from LGCM on the grounds that it spent a disproportionate amount of time and money campaigning within the Church of England and provided inadequate funds for other denominations.[11] Richard Kirker replied that funds had and would continue to be forthcoming for special activities or campaigns mounted by the caucuses. The reality of the situation was that LGCM had some 500 Anglican members as against 31 current and 45 former members of the URC caucus, and he welcomed any suggestions for increasing that percentage.[12]

Issues of inclusiveness took other forms too. In March 1996 John Matthews wrote an article to the newsletter expressing his concern that the movement had never really engaged with the situation of its bisexual members who were on the receiving end of what he called a kind of gay fundamentalism. Amongst gay men, he noted, this often took the form of stigmatizing bisexual men as homosexuals who lacked the courage to face up to their true orientation.[13] The fact that LGCM was anxious to give a hearing to the widest possible range of views by publishing comments such as these in its newletters and journal was evidence of its desire to take the challenge of inclusivity seriously. It has also succeeded in remaining true to its initial vision of embracing human sexuality in all its richness. Its list of those willing to state publicly their membership of LGCM in 1997 included 244 gay men, 65 lesbians, 15 bisexual men and women and 54 heterosexuals.[14]

The movement has also continued to maintain and strengthen its international links. In May 1990 the European Forum of Lesbian and Gay Groups elected LGCM member Paul Scroxton as its President at its meeting in Strasbourg which was attended by delegates from 12 countries. His successor in 1992, Aasmund Vik from Norway, was also an LGCM member.[15] In 1995 the European Forum held a major international conference titled 'Changing Church Attitudes?' at Dreibergen in the Netherlands, at which Elizabeth Stuart gave the keynote address. In a wider arena, in January 1991 at the World Council of Churches Assembly in Canberra, a Lesbian and Gay Caucus was formed at which LGCM member Alison Webster was one of the key speakers. The movement has continued through its journal and newsletter to keep members informed about issues of gay and lesbian rights throughout the world. A particular recent concern has been the decision of the World Council of Churches to hold its 1998 fiftieth anniversary General Assembly in Zimbabwe despite the virulent homophobia evidenced by both the churches and the government in recent pronouncements. At the 1996 meeting of the Forum in Oslo in May, a statement was issued by LGCM urging that the WCC relocate its meeting to South Africa, a call which went unheeded. LGCM in conjunction with other groups is fighting to turn this damaging decision to advantage by ensuring that the issue of gay and lesbian rights finds a prominent place on the agenda.[16]

Care and support

Local groups continued to be what Richard Frost, their Coordinator, and Bob Liston, the national Honorary Secretary, called in 1989 the bedrock of the movement. In their survey of the 21 formal and 12 less formal groups, an impressive range of activities was revealed, which included campaigning against Section 28, the publication of newsletters, and cooperation with other gay and lesbian organizations at local level. All regarded welcoming and supporting anyone who needed their help as one of their primary functions. This was often a daunting task given the huge geographical areas which they sometimes had to cover. From 1988 LGCM nationally began to offer grants on a per capita basis to help with this work.[17] In 1994 the national committee introduced a special grant of up to £100 to help local groups engaged in projects of outreach in their local areas.[18] In 1997 LGCM had 31 formally constituted groups and a further five contact persons. The coverage was national but inevitably there are still many isolated people in need of support who cannot be helped in this way, particularly in rural areas.

One dimension of LGCM's work which continued to expand, and which as we have seen was part of its outreach from the start, was the provision of services of blessing for gay and lesbian couples. By 1996 LGCM was receiving about 500 enquiries a year and kept a confidential register of some 40 clergy who were willing to conduct such services.[19] Most of those who sought LGCM's help in this way saw it as a means of strengthening their commitment to each other. Typical was this letter:

> Myself and my partner have been together for over 3 years. We have bought a house just over a year ago. We know we both love each other, care for each other and want to remain with each other. We both know we need a blessing as a final part of our lives that only God can give.[20]

Others were aware of the lack of social as well as spiritual support which resulted from the Christian churches' refusal to help. As two women who had lived together for seven years and were bringing up a teenager explained:

> We only want what any other couple in love wants. We want to declare our love for one another in front of God, family and a few chosen friends. That will give the respect that any normal marriage demands.[21]

LGCM, in conjunction with ISCS, produced a factsheet which considered the theological issues raised by such requests, and argued that both marriage and gay and lesbian partnerships shared a common basis grounded in relationality and friendship rather than in legal contract.[22] Such considered discussion was much needed. When the *Daily Mail* denounced a service of blessing for two women conducted in Bolton by the Metropolitan Community Church in the summer of 1996, it described the event as a complete travesty of the marriage rite on the grounds that 'marriage is for the procreation of children' – which was to say the least a rather misleading oversimplification of the Christian Church's theology of marriage.[23] The attitude of the mainstream churches was, as so often, to engage in victim blaming.

They continued to denounce the supposed promiscuity of gay men and lesbians, and to preach the desirability of permanent relationships whilst promoting attitudes which discouraged their creation and maintenance. When, for example, Canon Michael Woods, a clergyman in Norfolk, spoke on a BBC television programme in March 1996 of his experience in carrying out such services, the Rev David Holloway called for his removal from office.[24] The Bishop of Thetford, Hugo de Waal, issued a statement stating that the Canon's actions had been wrong, as had been his decision to discuss them publicly, since the bishops believed that 'the discussion of these sensitive issues is better conducted away from the glare of publicity'.[25] Although no further action was taken, and the value of Canon Woods's ministry was acknowledged, once again the majority of bishops in the Church of England had shown themselves to be desperate to avoid public debate and controversy, and willing to put expediency before the pastoral needs of their gay and lesbian members.

They continued to do so. In December of the same year LGCM member Derek Rawlcliffe was dismissed as Honorary Assistant Bishop in the diocese of Ripon for publicly conducting a service of blessing.[26] The Church of England also found itself once again in a contradictory position in one other important respect. It professed itself to be committed to combating homophobia and discrimination, yet its refusal to acknowledge or validate same-sex relationships provided powerful ammunition for those seeking to prevent the establishment of legal equality for gay and lesbian partners in areas such as inheritance and pension rights. It was in fact partly because these issues were being widely debated in Britain at the time, that services which had been conducted without controversy for many years suddenly came to prominence.[27] Not everyone in the Church was unaware of these inadequacies and contradictions, and as so often when facing the agenda of gay and lesbian rights, the attempt to confine discussion behind closed doors was doomed to failure. In the same month that Derek Rawlcliffe was dismissed, the Bishop of Bath and Wells, Jim Thompson, suggested that both the State and the Church of England should recognize stable homosexual partnerships. Such recognition, which would not be marriage, would, he believed, act to bind people together.[28] In August 1997 the Bishop of Jarrow, Alan Smithson, agreed.[29] Both aroused the fury of the evangelical member of Reform, the Rev David Holloway, who again took the opportunity to denounce homosexual practice as unbiblical. In lurid terms he went on to assert that the gay issue was 'the motor for the whole programme of destabilising the sexual culture'.[30] It was a clear message to LGCM that its fight for an inclusive and caring Anglican Church was far from won.

One particular matter which has exercised the movement from the start has been to counteract the influence of so-called 'support' groups run by homophobic evangelical churches which claimed to offer 'cures' for the sickness of homosexuality. In 1992 LGCM set up a commission of enquiry into the ex-gay movement under the secretaryship of Tony Green. Its report, written by Tony Green, Brenda Harrison and Jeremy Innes, was published in May 1996 and was highly critical of the failure of such ministries to meet professional standards of training, supervision and self-understanding. It also asserted the right of homosexuals to explore their own sexuality and make their own choices in a safe and non-threatening counselling environment – something which the ex-gay groups conspicuously failed to provide.[31]

LGCM's telephone counselling service also continued to increase its work. In 1992 the counselling coordinator, Mark Davies, reported that the 16 volunteers running the service had received 228 calls, a 50 per cent increase on the previous year, and that the hours of operation had been extended. The fact that the number of referrals to one-to-one counsellors had been reduced was an indication of the increasing effectiveness of the helpline.[32] In 1994 the base for its operations was moved to Oxford House where it continued to be staffed by unpaid volunteers. Since the national office has also continued to run a large mail order book service, LGCM can justly claim to provide the most comprehensive and effective support and advice service for gay and lesbian Christians of any organization in the United Kingdom.

Challenging the churches

It is a measure of the success of LGCM's caucuses that they have borne an increasing part of the burden of confronting prejudice and attempting to transform attitudes within their respective denominations. It therefore makes sense to survey LGCM's campaigning work in the years since 1989 in a more denominational framework than in the previous period. The Roman Catholic caucus was operating in a climate of opinion and pastoral practice which was inevitably dominated by the Vatican's hardline stance in 1986 that: 'Although the particular inclination of the homosexual person is not a sin, it is a more or less strong tendency ordered towards an intrinsic moral evil; and thus the inclination itself must be seen as an objective disorder.'[33] It followed of course that any physical expression of such an inclination was sinful. The caucus had as one of its primary objectives the task of contesting this theological tradition by ensuring that the experience of lesbian, gay and bisexual Catholics should be heard. In such a hostile ecclesiastical environment the job of 'being the Church for each other' was also vital.

Apart from engaging in the general and ongoing debate with the Vatican over its view of human sexuality, the caucus has also responded to a number of specific issues. One of these was the publication by the Congregation for the Doctrine of the Faith in July 1992 of the notorious document titled 'Some Considerations Concerning the Catholic Response to Legislative Proposals on the Non-Discrimination of Homosexual Persons'.[34] This was a comment upon proposed anti-discrimination legislation in the United States, and it rejected the claim that lesbian and gay people were a deserving minority comparable to racial or ethnic groups. It went on to argue that discrimination was both morally and legally justifiable – for example in the employment of teachers, athletic coaches, in military recruitment and in the placing of children for adoption or foster care. Whilst the document conceded that as human beings gay and lesbian people had rights, it contended that these could be legitimately limited in cases of 'objectively disordered external conduct'.[35] In seeking to justify discrimination in employment and in fostering, the CDF argued that a parallel should be drawn between gays and lesbians and 'contagious and mentally ill persons'. LGCM's Catholic caucus was quick to respond. Its co-convenors, Jerry Walsh and Elizabeth Stuart, drew up an open letter to the English and Welsh Catholic bishops which castigated the document as 'riddled with homophobia', pointing out that the statement was not compatible with the bishops' 1979 'Introduction to the Pastoral Care of Homosexual People' which had pledged to eliminate injustices perpetrated against homosexuals. They also criticized the CDF for perpetuating atavistic stereotypes of gay people as presenting a threat to children and young people. The letter was then sent to a number of prominent English Catholics, both gay and non-gay, and the caucus was able to publish it with 108 supporting signatories including priests and nuns as well as members of the laity. Quest was equally sharp in its critique of the document, and their combined reaction strengthened the liberal wing of the English Catholic Church in rejecting the CDF's prejudiced assumptions. According to the *Catholic Herald*, the differences between the English bishops' pastoral approach in 1979, and the much harsher tone of the new pronouncement pointed to a dangerous if not unprecedented mixing of messages by the Catholic Church on the question of homosexuality.[36] The *Tablet* agreed, depicting the Vatican as attempting to square an impossible circle.[37] Once again pious platitudes about the Church's responsibility to love and affirm its gay and lesbian members were at odds with its moral and social denial of their worth. Moreover as in other instances, such a contradiction could have serious political and social consequences – a fact of which many bishops were only too aware. For example in the state of Oregon, its two Catholic bishops William Levada, the Archbishop of Portland, and Thomas Connolly, the Bishop of Baker City, gave a strong lead in opposing a constitutional amendment in November 1992, which was sponsored by Pat Robertson's Christian Coalition. This characterized homosexuality as 'wrong, unnatural and perverse' and required the state's government to declare that homosexuality was a moral offence similar to paedophilia, sadism and masochism. Such language, Connolly argued, was an incitement to hatred and violence.[38] It was also, of course, the language of the Vatican itself.

Cardinal Basil Hume was fully aware of concerns of this kind, and of the furore generated by the CDF document both inside and outside his Church. In September 1992 he produced a draft document which was published on 22 July 1993, titled 'Some Observations on the Catholic Church's Teaching Concerning Homosexual People'. He admitted that the CDF statement had caused distress and anger, but claimed that it had been taken out of context, and as a result had led to misunderstanding of where the Catholic Church stood on the issue of homosexuality. But it was clear from his subsequent remarks, that there had been no such misunderstanding over the Church's fundamental teaching. Homosexual inclination was not of itself sinful, but genital acts were in all circumstances. At the same time, the Cardinal was at pains to stress, nothing in the Church's teaching could be taken as supporting any victimization of homosexual men and women.[39] LGCM's Roman Catholic caucus replied by giving the statement a cautious welcome and commending it for at least being pastorally sensitive if theologically inadequate. It welcomed Hume's condemnation of homophobic violence and prejudice, and his insistence that a homosexual orientation was in itself morally neutral. On the latter point Elizabeth Stuart detected a softening of the line taken in the Vatican's 1986 'Letter to the Bishops of the Catholic Church on the Pastoral Care of Homosexual Persons'. At the same time she argued that although the Cardinal was to be thanked for going as far as he could within the bounds of the Vatican's official teaching, so long as he continued to disseminate its more derogatory implications, lesbian and gay Catholics would always feel unwelcome in their Church, whilst homophobic Catholics would be confirmed in their prejudice and hate. She was also sharply critical of the dualistic distinction which the Church drew between sexual acts and orientation, arguing that it actually encouraged irresponsible and immature behaviour by many of the Church's own clergy.[40]

It is interesting to note that one of the other sources of criticism of Basil Hume's statement was the gay activist group represented by Peter Tatchell, OutRage!, and that it, and LGCM's Catholic caucus, did not altogether see eye to eye over the implications of the Cardinal's stance. Partly this was because OutRage!'s concern was less with the finer nuances of theological restatement, and more with what it saw as Hume's refusal to unequivocally support full legal and social equality. On Palm Sunday 1993 members of the group confronted the Cardinal during a procession at Westminster Cathedral, protesting over what they saw as his inadequate response to discriminatory Vatican policy and teaching. It was this point that they returned to in a letter four days later, criticizing what they regarded as a crucial ambivalence in the Cardinal's words that the Church opposed discrimination 'where a person's sexual orientation or activity cannot reasonably be regarded as relevant factors'. Confirmation that this was a legitimate cause for concern came in a reply on the Cardinal's behalf from his Assistant General Secretary, Nicholas Coote, who stated that because of the Church's commitment to supporting the institution of marriage, it was unlikely that it would support lowering the age of consent to 16 because of what he called the susceptibility of the many young people who were passing through a homosexual stage at that age. The illogicality of this pronouncement was so blatant that it did not even commend itself to Catholic MPs when the following year 25 voted in favour and 19 against Edwina Currie's amendment proposing 16 as the age of male homosexual consent.[41] LGCM found itself, not for the first time, in a slightly uncomfortable position as it sought to build bridges and transform attitudes from within the churches. In a letter to OutRage! the caucus was anxious not to appear to have 'sold out' on gay and lesbian rights by welcoming the Cardinal's statement. The letter also likened the position of liberal Catholic bishops to that of dissidents in the former Soviet Union and highlighted what was, within admittedly narrow confines, a significantly more tolerant and sympathetic tone from that expressed in earlier Vatican statements.[42]

Contextualizing the Cardinal's response was one thing. Defending or endorsing it was quite another. In 1995 Basil Hume issued a revised and longer version of his original text. In some ways this reinforced the condemnation of injustice and homophobia in the original, and in a sentence which attracted much attention argued that 'To love another, whether of the same sex or of a different sex, is to have entered the area of the richest human experience.' Yet rhetoric of this sort served only to heighten the paradoxes and ambiguities which characterized the Catholic Church's response to gay and lesbian Christians, as a number of members of the caucus made plain. One priest welcomed what he called the Cardinal's willingness to go the extra mile with the gay community, some of whom were his own clergy; but another caucus member could not see why if to love was the richest area of human experience that love was automatically nullified if it was expressed genitally. Several others drew attention to the credibility gap which existed because of the contrast between the Catholic Church's professions of love and pastoral concern towards its gay and lesbian members, and the stark reality of its hostile or, at best, ambivalent attitudes towards ending legal and social discrimination. Above all it was realized that the Catholic Church's negative evaluation of homosexuality could not be divorced from its overall teaching about human sexuality, and its implications for heterosexuals as well as for gay men and lesbians. One correspondent to the caucus's newsletter tellingly encapsulated this insight:

> The weakest part of the letter is the assumption of the two
> fundamental principles of the Catholic Church's teaching on
> sexual matters – that the sexual expression of love is exclusively
> permissible within marriage, and that this expression must be
> open to the possible transmission of new life. It is time that the
> official teaching church took a new look at these principles.
> The faithful of whatever sexual orientation are ignoring them.
> Our understanding of love is changing. God's will for human
> beings in the area of sexual relationships is not as clear or set in
> stone as the church might want to make out.[43]

This was to recognize that Catholics would have to continue to do battle with a Vatican hierarchy whose theology and teaching had grown increasingly sclerotic and hermeticized, but it was also to proclaim that they would increasingly be empowered to do so by drawing upon their own experiences and spiritual resources. The mountain that remained to be climbed was evident enough in the agenda for change put forward in 1996 by Jubilee People, the UK Coalition of Catholic Groups for a Liberating Church, of which LGCM's Catholic caucus was a founding member. The long overdue reforms for which it called, included the admission of women to the priesthood, the right of clergy to marry, a far greater role for private conscience in matters such as birth control, and a Church which would affirm the human rights of all its members irrespective of sexual orientation.[44] As the caucus's coordinator Elizabeth Stuart suggested, for Roman Catholics the work of LGCM was only just beginning.[45]

Debate within the Church of England at the start of the decade was dominated by dissection of the findings of the Osborne Report named after its Chairperson, the Rev June Osborne, at that time a deacon in Tower Hamlets in London. This was a splendidly surreal situation of the kind which Anglicans are particularly adept at creating, since the report itself was never officially published. The working party of seven began meeting in July 1987, and their brief was to advise the House of Bishops on the subject of homosexuality and lesbianism. It received written submissions from a number of sources including LGCM, but carried out its work in a secretive manner. When Richard Kirker wrote to June Osborne late in 1987 urging that there should be direct public involvement in its work, he was told that unlike the earlier Gloucester working party, which reported in 1979, its scope was merely to advise the bishops. As a result it was felt necessary that it should remain 'a confined and confidential piece of work'.[46] In fact in an earlier letter, the Rev John Gladwin, who was the working party's secretary, had already indicated that in the highly fraught atmosphere of the time there were other reasons for the secrecy, and he hoped that 'growing openness about the issues raised will mean that in the future we shall not have to proceed in this kind of way'.[47] The Church of England's refusal to publish the report, and thereby to allow a full-scale debate in Synod, was explicable given the highly polarized atmosphere which had been created by the Higton motion. But as a strategy designed to lower the ecclesiastical temperature it was a resounding failure since the findings of the report were leaked to the media and widely discussed in the press. For example, in an article under the headline 'Mystery of Church's Gay Report', the *Independent*'s religious affairs correspondent, Andrew Brown, claimed that although as a result of the Higton debate a number of bishops stated publicly that they would refuse to ordain practising homosexuals, 'those who made a practice of knowingly ordaining them continued to do so quietly'. After reading a copy of the report, Judith Judd in the *Independent on Sunday* in February 1990 seemed to confirm this, when she quoted from the results of a survey of episcopal opinion by the working party indicating that most bishops would not ordain a practising homosexual – which of course was to admit the possibility that some might. The report also made it clear that in dealing with gay and lesbian ordinands a variety of strategies were adopted, one of which it described in this way: 'If the person declares their intention to remain very discreet in their sexual activities, those in authority have to judge whether this seems a likely option and to assess whether a clandestine sexual life will be detrimental to their moral and spiritual ministry.'⁴⁸ This was a far cry from the inquisitorial disciplinary regime demanded by Tony Higton, and it led to immediate demands in Synod for Robert Runcie to deny that the bishops ever knowingly ordained practising homosexuals. His studied reply that, 'Decisions about ordination are the responsibility of each diocesan bishop, but I have no reason to think that the statement is correct', was not likely to appease the Anglican Church's homophobic tendency.⁴⁹

In fact, had the Osborne Report been published and debated in full, rather than been concealed under a transparent cloak of secrecy, most of its findings and recommendations would have appeared a good deal less sensational than the media implied. It quoted from the experiences of a number of gay and lesbian Christians, and then gave a succinct summary of the opposing views on the morality of same-sex relationships which existed within the Church. It also provided an unexceptional account of the way in which Anglican theology and ethics rested upon the dual foundations of biblical and traditional teaching on the one hand, and contemporary experience on the other – unexceptional, that is, since the report made no attempt to assess the weight to be given to each. Its conclusion that the bishops needed to find ways of handling conflict which were inclusive and creative, was also to define rather than to resolve the problems facing the Church of England. This was not, the report concluded, the time for any change in its traditional theological understanding of homosexuality. Before that could become a possibility, much more work needed to be done. Lord give me theological vision and courage – but not yet, seemed once again to be the Anglican plea.

LGCM responded to the inadequacies of the report, and of the Church of England's more general failure to address the needs of lesbian and gay Christians, by publishing in conjunction with the Stonewall Group a reply titled *Call to Action* drawn up by Austin Allen, Tim Barnett, Richard Kirker, Alison Webster and Elaine Willis. A comparison of the two throws into sharp relief the fundamental differences between LGCM's approach and the line adopted by the Church of England in the early 1990s. Although the latter made reference to the need to do theology by taking contemporary experience into account, the former calls for much more use to be made of the insights of liberation and feminist theologies which take such experience as their starting point, rather than simply relying upon the traditional theological appeal to *a priori* theoretical frameworks.[50] In effect this was a call for the Church to completely re-envision its sexual theology and to move away from a model based exclusively upon the norm of male and female complementarity. One of the widest chasms separating the two positions concerned the question of gay and lesbian rights and the need to combat homophobia. According to the Osborne Report:

> The church also has a critical role in the public realm of bearing witness to the Gospel by seeking to defend the civil rights of homosexual people against those who would discriminate against them. We do not need to share other people's convictions and lifestyles in order to defend their human dignity as members of a particular society. We believe that it is possible and essential for people of all theological and moral persuasions on this issue to unite in opposing the forces of homophobia in society and all attempts at denying homosexual people their basic civil rights.[51]

This was an extraordinarily naïve, confused and evasive statement. It failed to acknowledge that the origins of homophobia lay largely, if not exclusively, in the Christian churches' own traditional teaching; and that Christians who regarded gay and lesbian relationships as sinful, sick and harmful to society provided powerful justification for limiting their civil rights. As LGCM and Stonewall pointed out, the report also commended support for basic rights but without defining them. It did not, for example, appear to include equal employment rights within the Church itself, nor the right of freedom of sexual expression within the law for those who sought to be members of the Church of England. Reference was also made to resolution 64 of the 1988 Lambeth Conference which had addressed the issue of human rights, and had urged the churches of the Anglican communion to examine this question with regard to their gay and lesbian members.[52]

In December 1991 the bishops of the Church of England published *Issues in Human Sexuality* which, despite its title, was almost entirely given over to the questions raised by homosexuality.[53] It was a tortuous document, since it attempted to express a common mind which the bishops simply did not have, and also tried unsuccessfully to square several theological and pastoral circles. LGCM was, however, able to recognize and welcome the unequivocal rejection of the Higton attempt to drive all gay and lesbian Christians in committed sexual relationships from the Church. Such relationships were, it was recognized, a blessing both to those involved and to society at large.[54] It was left to the conscience of individual Christians to decide on the appropriateness of such lifestyles. On the other hand, a model of male/female complementarity was appealed to in order to suggest that same-sex relationships fell short of the monogamous heterosexual ideal. Given the degree of love, spiritual growth and benefit to society which it was admitted could be found in them, the reasons for their second-class status were far from clear. Most seriously, whilst such relationships were permissible for the laity, they were forbidden amongst the clergy. This created a puzzling and ethically ruinous distinction between clergy and laity. It also side-stepped the issue of justice in the interests of expediency, by arguing that the clergy must not engage in any behaviour which might embarrass or alienate members of their congregations. If taken seriously this would seem to imply that no prophetic and therefore uncomfortable stance was ever to be adopted by the clergy.[55] In sum, *Issues in Human Sexuality* represented some tangible gains for LGCM, but fell far short of the theological and practical liberation which it sought to effect within the Anglican Church. Its temporizing equivocations also gave plenty of scope for those still seeking to push the Church in a hardline homophobic direction.

If any further evidence were needed of the established Church's ambivalence towards its gay and lesbian members, this was forthcoming in March 1992 with the decision by the Church's own publishing house, SPCK, not to print the collection of gay and lesbian prayers and liturgies which it had commissioned from LGCM member Elizabeth Stuart. This followed the intervention of the Archbishop of Canterbury, Dr George Carey, who threatened to resign as SPCK's patron if the book went ahead. Limpid clarity of thought was not his forte and the reasons which he gave for acting in this way were both disingenuous and confused. Since the book contained prayers both for those with AIDS and those struggling to come out, the Archbishop claimed that it might further encourage the myth that AIDS was confined to the homosexual community. Since, as he put it, its assumptions and liturgical provision ran counter to *Issues in Human Sexuality*, he did not feel that it contributed to the process of education and discussion which the bishops' statement called upon the Church to begin.[56] How that process of education was to be promoted if the Church of England set out to suppress the experiences and spirituality of its gay and lesbian members was not made clear. The *Independent*'s assessment of what it considered to be an ill-judged intervention was severe: the Archbishop had emerged from the affair 'looking intolerant, heavy-handed and homophobic'.[57] Since the book contained nothing more subversive than prayers of blessing for those embarking upon committed relationships, as well as for those facing death and bereavement caused by AIDS, the censure was richly deserved. The Bishop of Durham, David Jenkins, agreed, saying that he was worried and distressed at what appeared to be ecclesiastical censorship. Two other Anglican bishops, the Bishop of Edinburgh, Richard Holloway, and Peter Coleman, the Bishop of Crediton also publicly expressed their support for the book.

The bishops' confusion and embarrassment was further increased in September 1994 when it was revealed that Michael Turnbull, the Bishop-elect of Durham, had been cautioned for commiting an act of gross indecency with another man in a public lavatory in 1968. As LGCM pointed out, Turnbull publicly supported the Church of England's official teaching which condemned homosexual activity amongst the clergy. This was in itself an act of hypocrisy, but what was really at fault was a policy which seemed to allow the promotion to the highest office of a man guilty of 'cottaging' provided he repented, but condemned clergy who sought to build the kinds of faithful sexual relationships which would have prevented or discouraged such casual sexual contacts in the first place.[58] Following the bishop's enthronement, LGCM kept up its attack, demanding that all other clergy who had been required to resign for this and other similar offences should be given the chance of reinstatement. Summing up the whole episode, Richard Kirker reiterated LGCM's view that 'the greatest indecency is homophobia, not a responsible sexual relationship'.[59]

The need to challenge the kinds of prejudice within the churches which made the creation of such relationships so much harder, was again in evidence in the same week with the announcement by the Church of England's Children's Society that it would no longer accept gay and lesbian applicants for either short- or long-term fostering. This flew in the face of the best working practices set out in the government's Children Act of 1989 which stated that it would be wrong to arbitrarily exclude any groups from consideration. The Society's own Council could in fact offer no evidence that the employment of lesbian and gay carers had in any way been detrimental to the children's best interests. It fell back instead on the argument that it was difficult for them to employ people in direct contravention of the Church of England's teaching.[60] Yet as we have just seen, it was far from clear in the case of lay people just what that teaching was.

The tactics of OutRage! never gained LGCM's official endorsement. But the naming in 1994 of ten Anglican bishops as being homosexual, and the pressure which forced the then Bishop of London, David Hope, to declare his sexuality to be ambiguous and a 'greyer' area than for most people, further discomfited the Church of England and added impetus to LGCM's campaign.[61] Lord Runcie's admission in a BBC radio interview in May 1996 that he had never knowingly ordained a practising homosexual clergyman when the fact was directly presented to him, but that there had been occasions when he had acted in a 'don't want to know way and why should I enquire way', was further proof of the Church of England's desperate attempts to adjust reality to meet the exigencies of ecclesiastical politics. Runcie also made the damaging admission that the distinction made by the bishops in 1991 between what was permissible in this respect for the laity and the clergy was untenable.[62] When the former Bishop of Salisbury, John Austin Baker, who had chaired the 1991 committee which produced *Issues in Human Sexuality* agreed, such coherence as the Church of England's stance still possessed was clearly in ruins.

The Methodist Church found the subject no more comfortable to handle. In 1988 it set up a Commission on Human Sexuality, and it was partly in response to this that the Methodist caucus within LGCM was created in 1989. One of the key issues which emerged from the report, which was published in 1990, concerned its recommendation that the Methodist Church should not produce new and more explicit instructions on whether or not practising homosexuals should be accepted as candidates for the ordained ministry. Instead the matter should continue to be left to the discretion of individual candidating committees. The report was received but not endorsed by the 1990 Conference and then sent for study and reflection at local level. As part of that process, in January 1992 three Methodist clergy wrote an open letter to the *Methodist Recorder* making it clear that in their view acceptance of the report's recommendation on candidating procedures amounted to an endorsement of gay lifestyles, and they proposed instead to draw up a conference resolution which would condemn homosexual genital acts as contrary to God's will.[63] Three weeks later almost 200 Methodists, including several former Presidents and Vice-Presidents of Conference, attacked the proposed resolution as too rigid and called upon Methodists to respond to the report 'in a spirit of openness and of willingness to struggle to understand something of the vast diversity of experience and of conviction in matters of human sexuality which is to be found within the church in our time'.[64] It was clear from these reactions, and from those expressed in the correspondence columns of the *Methodist Recorder*, that the Methodist Church was becoming increasingly polarized over the question. One correspondent, writing under the headline 'Hold fast to our heritage', expressed relief at the publication of the conservative open letter, commenting that although premarital sex and adultery were contrary to God's will 'at least they are between a man and a woman', whereas 'homosexual acts are (to use an old but very valid word) an abomination'. This was very different from the view expressed by another writer who urged that those examining candidates did not require explicit instructions 'lifted from the Bible by dinosaurs' such as those who had drawn up the open letter.[65]

Further confirmation of deep divisions within Methodism came from the results of two surveys of opinion. An analysis of replies to a questionnaire from local churches, circuits and synods, revealed that in response to a question about whether the Church should tighten up on its selection procedure for the ministry, 99 circuits were in favour and 74 against; in the case of individual churches the figures were 191 in favour and 53 against.[66] A second survey of 300 local preachers, carried out by the Department of Theology at Nottingham University in May 1992, revealed that 51 per cent of respondents agreed that sexual orientation should not be a bar to ordination, whilst 28 per cent thought that it should and 21 per cent were undecided. On the question of whether or not sexually active gay and lesbian Methodists should be barred from ordination, 66 per cent felt that they should, 16 per cent disagreed, and 18 per cent were undecided. Not surprisingly, there was a direct correlation between answers to these questions and the view which respondents held about the nature of biblical authority: the more fundamentalist a view taken of the biblical text and the more weight given to its place in determining contemporary doctrine and ethics, the more hostile respondents were to homosexual practice.[67] Taken together, the two surveys suggested that the leadership of the Methodist Church was more supportive of gay and lesbian rights, and less homophobic than opinion at grassroots level.

The crucial debate on the report took place at the Methodist Conference held at Derby in June 1993, and LGCM's Methodist caucus was active both before and during its deliberations. Denied the right to be listed in the Conference Directory, or to set up a stall on the grounds that it was of a 'lobbying nature', the caucus held a public meeting in Derby Central Library on 28 June. It also sent information packs which included accounts of the lives of Methodist lesbians and gay men to all Conference representatives, at a cost of some £1500 which the caucus had to raise.[68] The deliberations predictably mirrored the kinds of divisions within Methodism already mentioned, as well as a fair sprinkling of homophobic outbursts. One delegate likened homosexuality to what he called other blights upon creation which were consequences of the Fall, such as AIDS, spina bifida and cystic fibrosis;[69] another compared it to incest, adultery, rape and crime.[70] Against such prejudice Peter Smith, convenor of the LGCM caucus, spoke of the necessity for gay and lesbian Christians to affirm a vital part of themselves and in so doing to create the possibility of their falling in love and sharing their lives with another person. What they hoped for was a fully inclusive Church.[71]

This was never likely to be the outcome of such a polarized debate and in the end the Conference accepted a series of highly contradictory resolutions. On the one hand, it reaffirmed the Church's traditional teaching in favour of chastity for all outside of marriage, and directed that all candidates for ordination and membership be made aware of this. On the other, it accepted that Methodism's existing procedures for assessing candidates for the ordained ministry were adequate. This was a major defeat for conservatives, and taken with the passage of a further resolution that 'Conference recognizes, affirms and celebrates the participation in ministry of lesbians and gay men in the church', it meant that the LGCM caucus had good reason to be pleased with the outcome. The resolution welcoming the contribution of gay and lesbian Christians to the life of the Methodist Church was one of the most affirmative statements by any English denomination to date – far more so than the hesitant and contradictory language of the Anglican bishops in 1991. Not surprisingly, it was a target for attack by conservatives whose motion to revoke the resolution was discussed and defeated at the 1994 conference. At the same time a resolution was passed which acknowledged the pain of those who had sent over 30 memorials to the Conference expressing their opposition to the Church's affirmative stance towards homosexuality, and assured them that 'the continuing expression of their convictions is vital to the life of our Church'.[72] This was to signal that homophobic theology was still sanctioned, but it is an indication of how far the Methodist Church had come in its acceptance of gay and lesbian inclusivity, that those who opposed a re-envisioning of the tradition were beginning to feel the discomfort of marginalization.

In April 1995 the Methodist Council reaffirmed the decisions taken in the two preceding years, and acknowledged that despite the departure of a relatively small number of members over the issue, the Church had achieved what it called 'a delicate and fragile accord'.[73] It was particularly concerned that no changes should be made to the rules governing the acceptance of candidates for ordination, which it rightly recognized was the crevasse which had been bridged only precariously by the contradictory resolutions accepted in 1993. When the Council's recommendations were accepted at the 1995 conference, some circuits expressed their disappointment that a more explicit form of wording had not been adopted which would have spelt out in the clearest possible terms that all lesbian and gay clergy within the Methodist Church were required to be celibate.[74] This was a foretaste of things to come. At the 1996 Conference in Blackpool, further attempts were made by evangelicals to 'clarify' the meaning of the resolutions passed in 1993, and after the Church declined to institute proceedings against a Methodist minister living with his partner, two evangelicals took private disciplinary action which ultimately proved to be unsuccessful. As John Cooke reported, the atmosphere at the Conference was extremely tense with threats of schism hanging over the proceedings. This led the new President of the Conference to appeal to the Church 'to behave and think and pray together as people who respect one another and realise that we are on a difficult journey together'.[75] The task for the LGCM Methodist caucus in the future is to defend the gains made by the passage of the affirmative resolution of 1993, and to facilitate dialogue within the Church so that the final outcome of that journey will be the unconditional acceptance of its gay and lesbian members.

Change within the United Reformed Church has followed a very similar pattern to that within Methodism. A sampling of letters written to the denomination's magazine *Reform* in 1988 is indicative of a comparable range of views on the subject of homosexuality. One gay man wrote of his sense of isolation and despair, and of the lack of support which he had received from his minister – a situation which he believed had been made worse by the backlash created by AIDS. The Rev John Price agreed, urging the URC to consider whether the biblical writers 'were they living today, would have made the same judgments about the homosexual condition or the gay relationship of mutual care and fidelity which I believe most Christian homosexuals are seeking'. Yet on the same page,

Brian Rose, a URC Elder, argued that 'Sodomy is clearly recognised as a sin in the Old Testament and there is nothing in the New Testament to change that'; and in what was presumably a veiled reference to AIDS, he went on to describe homosexual acts as risking physical or emotional damage to the partner and therefore incapable of expressing love.[76] Less hostile in tone, but no less offensive, was the comment of another writer, that the URC should make efforts 'to cure those handicapped by sexual abnormalities rather than suggest that sufferers be put in touch with other sufferers'.[77] As this correspondence rumbled on into 1989 and 1990, divergent views on the issue of same-sex orientation and relationships were often focused on the possibility of 'curing' or 'healing' those deemed to be sick or in thrall to sin as advocated by groups such as the True Freedom Trust. As convenor of the newly formed URC caucus, Iain McDonald was able to offer much needed support for those within the Church who felt threatened and demeaned by such attitudes.[78]

Three caucus members also contributed to the work of the URC working party which in November 1991 published its report *Homosexuality: A Christian View*. This was described as a contribution to an ongoing debate and as setting out a particular view on a contentious matter. It was not intended to define a common policy for the Church, which the working party concluded was not feasible given the divergence of views on the subject which existed within it.[79] Its most significant conclusions were that the biblical writers could have made no judgements about homosexuality as a given sexual orientation, and that the working party was not prepared to describe homosexual activity as inherently sinful.[80] Persuading grass-roots members to agree was another matter. In response to the report, one URC minister recommended resort to the Courage Trust which offered a Christian ministry 'to those wanting to overcome homosexuality in their lives'; another member wrote somewhat confusingly that even if homosexuality was genetically determined, he was still anxious about what he called 'the possible dissemination of the homosexual/lesbian 'habit' to the young and impressionable'. But he had no doubts about the cure: 'Penicillin for influenza, the word of God for sins, irrespective of origin.'[81] Iain McDonald spoke for all those within his Church whose lives were being blighted by this kind of bigotry:

> I am tired of the Bible being misused as a weapon to undermine my life. I am tired of being told that all the wonderful things that have happened in my life are the result of an illness for

which Christ is the cure. I am tired of being told that the depth of love that I have experienced is sinful and that I must repent of it. In fact, I am tired of justifying my entire being to those who are not prepared to listen.[82]

He was soon called upon to dig further into his reserves of optimism and stamina. In 1994 as an openly gay man living with his partner, he was unanimously recommended for ordination training by the Muswell Hill congregation where he had been an Elder. This decision was confirmed at district level and by national assessors after a 48-hour selection procedure, but the provincial ministry committee withheld its approval, arguing that a point of principle was at stake which needed to be resolved by the General Assembly. Ultimately he was able to appeal successfully against the decision and begin his training.[83] McDonald was one of two openly gay men accepted for training in 1994, decisions which led conservatives within the URC to attempt to force two resolutions through the General Assembly in 1995. Conservative opposition was expressed through the organization Gear, the Group for Evangelisation and Renewal, which in 1993 had produced its own report *Homosexuality and the Gospel*. This condemned homosexuality on traditional fundamentalist lines, and argued for the Church to offer 'healing' – even including in its report the testimony of what it called 'a healed homosexual adulterer'. In the event, its arguments failed to persuade the General Assembly, which declined to allow Gear's motions to be put to the vote. These sought to place a moratorium upon the acceptance of further homosexual candidates for ordination training and to reaffirm what were called traditional standards of holy living.[84] All of this was a prelude to the crucial debate in the July 1997 General Assembly, and for which the LGCM URC caucus campaigned vigorously which, given its size, placed a considerable burden upon its members. Early in 1996 the caucus sent a letter to all URC churches and organized a network of people willing to speak at church meetings. It also produced a video in which David Evans and the Rev Janet Webber spoke about their lives. At the York Assembly in 1996, all 600 delegates received copies of a specially prepared booklet *Voices from Within* which drew upon articles from the caucus newsletter.[85] All of this bore fruit in the July 1997 Assembly in which the URC agreed not to change its existing selection procedures, and thereby rejected hardline conservative attempts to exclude lesbian and gay candidates from the ministry. The task of breaking down prejudice and discrimination in parts of the URC remains, however, a very real one.

Celebrating at Southwark

The outcome of such hard-fought battles, although partial and uneven, gave LGCM plenty of cause to celebrate the achievements of its first 20 years. When it became public knowledge that it planned to do so by holding a service of thanksgiving in Southwark Cathedral on 16 November 1996, the reaction of homophobic fundamentalists was predictable. Tony Higton attempted to prevent the service from taking place by resorting to the same tactics which he had used to secure the expulsion of LGCM from St Botolph's in 1988. On 5 May 1996 he wrote to the Cathedral's Provost, Colin Slee. Disclaiming any of the sort of 'gut-revulsion' to gay and lesbian people which some Christians held towards them ('I can relate to them perfectly normally', he wrote), he condemned LGCM as 'an undesirable and pernicious organization'. As before, he quoted from a misleadingly small selection of books stocked by LGCM, implying that the opinions they contained were representative of the movement's own views. He then went on to refer to an investigation by the Obscene Publications Squad into charges that LGCM was making available copies of the banned poem 'The Love that Dares To Speak its Name' on the Internet. He concluded with a scarcely veiled threat:

> If the Cathedral goes ahead with allowing this celebration the true nature of the LGCM will inevitably be revealed and those involved would be damaged by it. I don't want that to happen. Furthermore there would be extreme embarrassment if around that time the police investigation led to a court case.[86]

To his credit, the Provost did not respond well to this kind of pressure. He admitted that LGCM might have made mistakes in the past over the kinds of literature it had stocked, but, if so, these had been corrected and were scarcely grounds for refusing to work with it or any other organization. Although, he continued, LGCM had been aware of the existence of the poem on the Internet, so now was he 'because it seems to have been very widely publicised in Fundamentalist Evangelical circles'. He also accepted the movement's assurance that the poem had not been put on the Internet by them, concluding that 'I am sure you will agree with me that repeated and unjustified or untrue allegations are not a proper way to oppose something however much one may disagree with its objects'. As for the possibility that LGCM might be charged with an offence (in fact they were not), this revealed in the Provost's mind 'a clear intention of convicting LGCM by innuendo which is, I have to say, a very poor way for Christians to behave in the interests of truth'.[87] Undeterred by such a rebuke, Higton tried the same tactics again, urging all bishops to boycott the service and quoting passages from Terry Sanderson's book *The A–Z of Gay Sex* which LGCM stocked, but which made no claims to be written from a Christian perspective, as if these represented the views of the movement. One particularly pernicious form of blackmail advocated by both ABWON and Reform was the threat to withhold payments to diocesan quotas if the service went ahead. When it was suggested that the money might be donated instead to AIDS charities, the country's leading Christian AIDS organizations were quick to denounce the suggestion. Tessa Sowerby, the chair of the Catholic AIDS Link, issued a statement on behalf of their coordinating group:

> The acceptance of any monies which arise as a result of
> attempts to deny lesbian and gay people their right to meet and
> be met by Christ in prayer and worship would contradict our
> core values. Furthermore, it would be an insult to the memory
> and lives of those with whom we journey, day in, day out.[88]

A further attack on the service which attracted much attention came from an unexpected source. In a broadcast on BBC Radio 4's *Thought for the Day* on 10 October, Anne Atkins, the wife of a London clergyman, condemned the service, sneering that 'soon no doubt we'll have an adulterer's Christian fellowship, a sex-before-marriage Christian fellowship'. She seized upon a report issued earlier that week which disclosed that numbers entering the Anglican ordained ministry were falling, to claim that 'In an age in which bishops are supporting a cathedral event celebrating 20 years of gay sex we should hardly expect anything else.' This was too much even for the temporizing mentality of the Church of England, whose director of communications complained to the BBC's head of religious broadcasting that the piece was factually inaccurate, and described as preposterous the claim that the decline in vocations could be attributed to the Church's position on homosexuality.[89] But in a duplicated letter sent to those who wrote to her after the broadcast, Mrs Atkins continued to impugn the motives of LGCM, making some extraordinary charges against it:

> The situation is both a lot worse and a lot better than we had
> realised till we received your letters. The corruption is far
> deeper, more widespread, and more evil than I had any idea of
> when I gave my broadcast. I also now believe, from what I can

gather, that the movement to make homosexuality acceptable within the church is driven not so much by confused – but genuine – Christians, as by a secular pressure group cynically using the church to gain a socially acceptable face. (And the ultimate philosophy of this movement is that promiscuity is a positive lifestyle, and that there should be no minimum age of consent.)[90]

The canard that the movement was secular rather than Christian in inspiration had a familiar ring: it was the same charge repeatedly levelled at the Movement for Women's Ordination by its conservative opponents. In fact as we have seen, LGCM had spent a great deal of time and energy over the previous 20 years seeking to develop a specifically Christian theology and ethic for gays and lesbians within the Church. LGCM's philosophy had never been to condone promiscuity or to advocate no age of consent. On the latter point its stance was to fight for an equal age for both heterosexuals and homosexuals. The insinuation of paedophilia here continued to do service in the absence of proof or reasoned argument, although by 1996 – given the overwhelming evidence that child abuse was predominantly a crime committed by heterosexuals, often family members – it was beginning to wear a little thin.

The controversy surrounding the service continued unabated with a stream of letters to *The Times* and considerable media comment, much of which suggested that outside the churches LGCM was winning its case rather easily. For example in *The Times*, Libby Purves argued that LGCM's members were asking no more than the right to pray and 'to give thanks for their lives, their human and divine loves, the spiritual richness of religion'. She went on to attack the evils of gay-bashing and discrimination, suggesting that the Southwark service was both right and important if homosexuals were to be fully integrated into the mainstream of British society.[91] Like some latter-day Laocoön writhing in the serpents' coils – though perhaps he cut a rather less heroic figure – the Archbishop of Canterbury felt obliged to issue a statement which in four short paragraphs managed to agree both with Purves's line and with that of LGCM's opponents. The decision to hold the service had not been taken either collectively or individually by bishops, he emphasized – perish the thought that any of *them* might have the courage to give such a lead. To have done so was not wrong, since a service would highlight the faith that Christians hold in common, but neither did it amount to an endorsement of LGCM. Pressure group tactics were to be avoided on either side, and the Archbishop ended with the hope that the Church of England should not become preoccupied with these issues but should continue to study them. This cut little ice with the Anglican fundamentalist evangelical group Reform, which issued its own statement arguing that the bishops' duty lay not in affirming what 'we all have in common', but in the case of LGCM, their task was 'to banish and drive away'. Just for good measure the statement went on: 'Would Dr Carey think that Southwark Cathedral should be available for pro-apartheid or neo-Nazi groups who claim to be Christian and "our brothers and sisters in Christ"?'[92] Even the pretence of loving the sinner but hating the sin seemed to have become more than a little threadbare in this instance.

In the event, the Cathedral service proved to be a fitting climax to the workshops and lectures held in the adjacent Glazier's Hall which discussed the first 20 years of LGCM's history. These included an address by the retired Bishop of Iowa, Walter Righter, who had been accused of heresy for ordaining a man who lived with his same-sex partner.[93] Later 2000 people packed the Cathedral and heard the Bishop of Guildford, John Gladwin, condemn the evils of prejudice and discrimination from which lesbian and gay people had suffered. His sermon was a carefully nuanced one which included a lengthy reiteration of the importance of marriage and family life to society, something which few in the congregation had ever doubted. His real audience at this point was the media and LGCM's opponents, who would have been quick to seize upon anything controversial in the bishop's address. In the circumstances, his decision to accept the invitation to preach, and to attend the reception later, was a brave one for which he received a good deal of criticism. In his welcome, the Provost, Colin Slee, recognized what he called the deep spirituality of many members of LGCM. At the Day of Judgement, he suggested, we would not be asked whether we were heterosexual or homosexual but rather how much we had loved one another.[94] But in the end it was not the controversy which had surrounded the day which really mattered, but the sense of community and strength which it engendered in those who participated. As Amanda Price put it:

> The evidence for the power of such a gathering can be seen in the strength of the opposition to the service. Why was it so important for our opponents to prevent the service? Because by gathering, community is created: community builds confidence and gives strength; community destroys the invisibility (our

opponents seek to deny our very existence) and community
builds identity. [95]

Writing in the *URC Caucus Newsletter*, Susan Durber reinforced this view
of the significance of the day, reflecting that 'As someone who has had
her own struggles and defeats and failures with sexuality, I was grateful
to be in such a supportive and affirming community and to join in
praise and celebration of the God who made us all and who simply loves
us'.[96] There was not much sign here of either the secularism which Ann
Atkins claimed to find at the heart of the movement, or the ethically
irresponsible freewheeling portrayed by Reform.[97] Even though these
voices of prejudice and discrimination continued to be heard, Jim Cotter
made clear in his foreword to the order of service, that this was much
less the case than 20 years before partly as a result of the work done by
the members of LGCM – work which had not been without cost:

> Many of us have struggled mightily – even lovingly – with the
> ecclesiastical 'powers that be', refusing to let go and claiming
> that we too are part of the rainbow people of God. Not a few
> gay and lesbian Christians have risked their ministries; many
> more have either had their membership withdrawn or have
> themselves drawn away in sorrow and in anger. But
> understanding has grown. Even the closeted live in larger
> rooms than they did, and some have taken the locks off their
> doors. So the events today mark an affirmation, even a 'coming
> home', to find it less forbidding than the last time we passed
> this way. [98]

It was a fair assessment of what LGCM had achieved in its first 20 years,
and a recognition that much still remained to be done.

Notes

1 J. Nelson (1983) *Between Two Gardens: Reflections on Sexuality and Religious
Experience* (New York: The Pilgrim Press), p. 127.
2 LGCM Statement of Accounts, 31 December 1995.
3 LGCM Annual Report, 1991, pp. 4–5.
4 Richard Kirker to Rosie Miles, 14 July 1994.
5 *LGCM News*, December 1994, pp. 9–10.
6 Rosie Miles to Richard Kirker, 11 July 1994.
7 *Sophic Voices, Newsletter of the Women in LGCM*, June 1996, p. 8.
8 Richard Kirker to Liz Bodycote, 27 August 1996.
9 Richard Kirker to Liz Bodycote, 25 April 1996.
10 *Sophic Voices, Newsletter of the Women in LGCM*, November 1996, p. 8.

11 The Rev Peter Colwell to Richard Kirker, 18 January 1996.
12 Richard Kirker to the Rev Peter Colwell, 5 March 1996.
13 *LGCM News*, March 1996, p. 11.
14 *LGCM Newsletter*, Spring 1997, pp. 11–12.
15 *LGCM Newsletter*, June 1992, p. 3.
16 *LGCM Newsletter*, Spring 1997, p. 3.
17 *LGCM Journal*, **48**, November 1989, p. 18.
18 LGCM Annual Report, 1994, pp. 3–4.
19 Richard Kirker to the Rev Michael Woods, 14 March 1996.
20 Letter to LGCM, 31 May 1995.
21 Letter to LGCM, 13 February 1997.
22 E. Stuart (1994) *Christianity and Sexuality Factsheet 1: Lesbian and Gay 'Marriages'* (London: LGCM/ISCS).
23 *Daily Mail*, 21 August 1996.
24 *Daily Mail*, 14 March 1996.
25 Press release by the Rt Rev Hugo de Waal (n.d.). The question of same-sex services was also exercising the Jewish Reform synagogues at this time, and in October 1996 Rabbi Elizabeth Sarah was prohibited from holding a blessing for a lesbian couple. As a result, a working party was set up to consider the issue. See the *Jewish Chronicle*, 4 October 1996.
26 *Gay Times*, December 1996.
27 For example, the decision by the BBC to grant leave to two of its male employees to take part in a service of blessing and then go on holiday together, was widely reported in the press. See the *Daily Telegraph*, 23 May 1996. At a more serious level, the article by Martin Bewley, 'A too fragile social fabric?' in the *New Law Journal*, 22 December 1995, p. 1883, discusses the case for legal change in the context of the recognition of registered partnerships in Denmark, Norway and Sweden.
28 The *Independent*, 16 December 1996.
29 *Church Times*, 15 August 1997.
30 The *Independent*, 16 December 1996.
31 *Church of England Newspaper*, 24 May 1996.
32 LGCM Annual Report, 1992, p. 8.
33 Quoted in E. Stuart and A. Thatcher (1997) *People of Passion: What the Churches Teach about Sex* (London: Mowbray), p. 170.
34 There is full discussion of the document and the debate which it aroused in R. Peddicord (1996) *Gay and Lesbian Rights. A Question: Sexual Ethics or Social Justice?* (Kansas City: Sheed and Ward), pp. 123–40.
35 *Ibid.*, p. 126.
36 *Catholic Herald*, 24 July 1992.
37 The *Tablet*, 1 August 1992.
38 Peddicord (1996), pp. 130–1.
39 'Cardinal Hume's observations on the Catholic Church's teaching concerning homosexual people', *Briefing*, 22 July 1993.
40 LGCM Catholic caucus press release, 21 July 1993.
41 Figures taken from the *Tablet*, 26 February 1994. On the main motion to reduce the age of consent from 21 to 18, 33 Catholic MPs voted in favour and 11 against.
42 LGCM Catholic caucus letter to OutRage!, 5 August 1993.

43 *Roman Catholic Caucus Newsletter,* 20, April 1995, pp. 6–7.
44 'We are Church: A U.K. Roman Catholic Declaration' (London: Jubilee People).
45 *LGCM Journal*, Winter 1996, pp. 18–19.
46 June Osborne to Richard Kirker, 2 November 1990.
47 John Gladwin to Richard Kirker, 29 September 1990.
48 *The Osborne Report* (n.d.), p. 116. Privately circulated.
49 The *Independent*, 28 July 1990.
50 E. Willis (ed.) (1990) *Call to Action* (London: LGCM/Stonewall), p. 6.
51 Osborne *Report*, p. 134.
52 Willis (1990), pp. 5–7.
53 *Issues in Human Sexuality. A Statement by the House of Bishops* (1991) (London: Church House Publishing).
54 *Ibid.*, p. 33.
55 These points were made at the time and in C. Sumner (ed.) (1995) *Reconsider: A Response to Issues in Human Sexuality* (London: LGCM).
56 *Daily Telegraph*, 12 March 1992.
57 The *Independent*, 12 March 1992.
58 LGCM press release, 25 September 1994.
59 LGCM press release, 24 October 1994.
60 LGCM press release, 28 October 1994.
61 The almost universal press condemnation of OutRage!'s methods was a fair index of their effectiveness. Typical of press response was the leader in *The Times* on 14 March 1995 which spoke of a brave churchman resisting persecution, and claimed that those who outed men who preferred their homosexuality to be a private matter showed scant regard for ordinary decency. This of course was to ignore the fact that David Hope was not targeted as a private individual, but in his capacity as a senior representative of a Church which continued to condone discrimination against its gay members.
62 *The Times*, 16 May 1996.
63 *Methodist Recorder*, 9 January 1994.
64 *Methodist Recorder*, 30 January 1992.
65 *Ibid.*
66 *Methodist Recorder*, 18 February 1993.
67 *Methodist Recorder*, 15 April 1993.
68 *LGCM News*, June 1993, p. 3.
69 K. Albans (1993) *The Human Sexuality Debate, The Methodist Conference, Derby, June 1993: A Transcript of the Entire Debate* (Privately printed), p. 16.
70 *Ibid.*, p. 19.
71 *Ibid.*, p. 35.
72 *Methodist Recorder*, 7 July 1994.
73 *Methodist Recorder*, 27 April 1995.
74 *Methodist Recorder*, 20 July 1995.
75 *Lesbian and Gay Christian Journal*, Winter 1996, p. 10.
76 *Reform*, February 1988.
77 *Reform*, April 1988.
78 *Reform*, March 1990.

79 *Homosexuality: A Christian View* (1991) (London: URC Distribution and Supplies), p. 6.
80 *Ibid.*, p. 5.
81 *Reform*, May 1992.
82 *Reform*, June 1992.
83 *LGCM URC Newsletter*, **10**, 1994, pp. 9–10.
84 *LGCM News*, March 1996, p. 6.
85 *LGCM Journal*, Winter 1996, pp. 14–17.
86 The Rev A. Higton to the Very Rev Colin Slee, 5 May 1996.
87 The Very Rev Colin Slee to the Rev A. Higton, 9 May 1996.
88 *Church Times*, 13 October 1996. The threat of prosecution for blasphemous libel hung over LGCM's head for 18 months while the Crown Prosecution Service decided that there was no charge to answer. See the *Observer*, 20 July 1997 for an account of the episode.
89 *The Times*, 11 October 1996.
90 Duplicated letter of Ann Atkins, 5 November 1996.
91 *The Times*, 12 November 1996.
92 Reform press release, 11 November 1996.
93 Their story is told in W. Lecky and B. Stopfel (1997) *Courage to Love: A Gay Priest Stands up for His Beliefs* (New York: Doubleday).
94 Order of Service, Southwark Cathedral, 16 November 1996 (London: LGCM), p. 5.
95 *Lesbian and Gay Christian Newsletter*, Spring 1997, p. 1.
96 *LGCM URC Caucus Newsletter*, **15**, 1997, Supplement A–C.
97 See for example The Rev David Holloway's letter, *The Times*, 15 November 1996.
98 Order of Service, Southwark Cathedral, 16 November 1996, p. 6.

◆

FIVE

Conclusion

We are born to make manifest the glory of God within us.
Not just in some of us, it's in everyone. And as we let our light
shine we unconsciously give other people permission to do the
same. As we are liberated from our own fear, our presence
automatically liberates others.

Nelson Mandela[1]

In the 22 years of its existence, LGCM has undertaken a vast range of activities at national and local level involving many thousands of individuals. Inevitably, I have scarcely touched upon most of these, but have tried instead to highlight within an interpretative framework what seems to me to be a number of crucial and recurring themes. By way of conclusion I would like to assess the significance of these for both the past and future of the movement.

Collective identity and the queer dilemma

As Steven Seidman has recently argued, the advent of queer theory and politics with their emphasis on difference, diversity and the deconstruction of stable sexual and gender identities poses acute dilemmas for activist political movements which appeal to a common experience of oppression. He defines the problem in this way:

> But what happens to a movement when multiple identities are admitted? Does not conceding difference greatly weaken social movements? This then is the dilemma: social movements seem strong when they pivot around a unitary (racial, gender, or

sexual) identity but this same heightened solidarity is purchased at the cost of increased internal repression as well as potential social and political isolation. Admitting multiplicity within a movement, however, seems to threaten its stability and political effectiveness.[2]

Or, as Joshua Gamson asks, must identity movements self-destruct, or do some succeed in avoiding 'the tendency to take themselves apart'?[3]

The history of LGCM has been one of negotiating precisely these kinds of contradictions with a very considerable degree of success. Beginning as a largely male, Anglican-dominated organization, it has grown to embrace a variety of denominational, gender and sexual identities. Crucial stages along this path have included the recognition of the linkages between the oppression of gay men and the exclusion of women from the ordained ministry of the Church of England; changes in the name and the committee structures of the movement designed to make it more gender inclusive; and the recognition that the aspirations and spirituality of gay men and lesbians within LGCM do not automatically coincide. Doubtless these insights have been only imperfectly perceived and their implications only haltingly pursued. Uniting under a common banner of combating homophobia has been easier than honestly recognizing that gay men and lesbians are very differently situated within a heteropatriarchal society from which the former, though stigmatized, still benefit, and in which the latter are doubly disadvantaged. Incorporating the still more marginalized voices of black, disabled and bisexual gay and lesbian Christians into the movement still remains as a major challenge. Yet we should not underestimate what has been achieved. This has required a great deal of goodwill and a willingness to accept innovative structural change. As Gamson recognizes, these are not the kinds of dilemmas which can be transcended in the postmodern era; they can only be coped with by the use of either destructive and self-defeating, or creative and politically significant strategies. LGCM has always tried to pursue the latter and it must continue to do so if it is to remain true to its initial vision of inclusivity.

LGCM and the politics of activism

In her recent analysis of New Right discourse on race and sexuality in the Thatcher era, Anna Smith draws attention to the way in which its hegemonizing agenda depended for success upon the adoption of a

supposedly centred and reasonable position. This was achieved by resort
to a series of rhetorical differentiations and inclusions. Homophobic
discourse, she argues, is more subtle though no less pernicious and
authoritarian than is sometimes supposed. With regard to the promoters
of Section 28 she observes:

> They spoke again and again of a law-abiding, disease-free,
> self-closeting homosexual figure who knew her or his proper
> place on the secret fringes of mainstream society ... They
> argued that they only aimed to restrict the activities of a
> completely different kind of homosexual, the promiscuous,
> diseased, angry, flaunting and militant homosexual – the kind
> of homosexual that we lesbians and gays ourselves call 'queer'.
> This distinction between the acceptable good homosexual and
> the dangerous queer ran through the entire discourse of the
> supporters.[4]

Drawing upon the work of writers such as Fanon and Nandy, she goes
on to draw parallels between sexual and colonial discourses on
oppression. Imperial regimes, she contends, depend for their survival
not only upon the use of force, but also upon the internalization of
colonial values by their victims, of which the most important is the
mapping out in advance of the limits of legitimate resistance. Colonial
discourse thus 'produces forms of "official dissent" which, for all their
oppositional appearance conform quite closely to Western ideals'. The
'good' black is allowed an oppositional stance provided it adheres to
the limits set by his oppressor – limits which of course are designed to
ensure that no fundamental challenge to colonial hegemony is
countenanced.

Insights of this sort, derived from the use of discourse theory and
analysis, are highly relevant to the campaigning history of LGCM. Again
and again lesbian and gay Christians have been asked to accept
definitions of their status, and limitations upon the kinds of protest
deemed legitimate which stop short of challenging or reconfiguring the
current hegemonic sexual discourse. Groups like LGCM who refuse to
do so, are traduced for being strident, aggressive, or unreasonable. Such
a tactic allows ecclesiastical authorities to position themselves on what
they claim to be the moral middle ground between competing extremist
lobbies. This is made possible, however, only by a crucial obfuscation
of the issues of oppression and injustice which sexual, no less than
gender, or racial, apartheid involves. A good example of this process is
a passage from the Anglican report *Issues in Human Sexuality* published

in 1991, in which the bishops attempt to reflect upon the consequences of homophobia:

> One effect is to drive some homophiles underground. This inevitably makes it more difficult for them to build lasting relationships, and increases the temptations to infidelity and promiscuity. In addition the untruths and concealment to which some homophiles are driven for self-protection, and the constant fear that others will sooner or later penetrate the façade behind which much of their life has to be conducted, are corrosive of personal integrity. By contrast other homophiles, who refuse to be trapped in these ways, are driven to protest by taking up a defiant stance, demonstrating their pride in being gay or lesbian, and making exaggerated claims and demands. This further polarises what is already a situation of conflict, and leads others who were sympathetic to be hostile.[5]

There is no acknowledgement here that the Christian churches themselves might be implicated in the creation and dissemination of homophobia, inequality and violence which drive some gay and lesbian Christians to live lives of concealment and insecurity. Even more striking is the way in which organizations like LGCM, which seek to challenge this situation, have been transmuted by the end of the passage into a major cause of their own and of the churches' problems in this area. It has been one of LGCM's greatest achievements that it has never ceased to campaign in the most visible way possible against injustice and discrimination. Nor has it ever succumbed to pressure from the churches to keep silent or to compromise its vision of a sexually inclusive Church and society, something for which Richard Kirker deserves a great deal of credit.

Prospects for the future

How effective has this campaign been, and what still remains to be done? Undoubtedly the question of sexual inclusiveness has been near the top of the agenda of nearly all the mainstream Christian denominations in the past 30 years, something for which LGCM deserves a large measure of praise. Both the URC and the Methodist churches have moved considerably nearer the full acceptance of openly gay and lesbian sexually active clergy. The Church of England's repeated attempts to adjust reality to fit in with the uneasy balance of power within the Church by denying the existence of such clergy within its ranks is no longer sustainable. The unsatisfactory state in which the Church of England now finds itself was acknowledged by all sides at the July 1997 meeting of Synod which passed, by a large majority, Archdeacon David Gerard's motion, suggested by LGCM, which described the 1991 bishops' statement as not the last word on the subject, and called upon the Church of England to reflect further upon the issues which it raised.[6] A further positive sign was the refusal of the bishops to allow amendments by evangelicals which would have condemned sexual acts outside marriage. LGCM backed up its pressure upon Synod with a characteristically well publicized survey which revealed that a significant number of Anglican bishops had knowingly ordained practising gay clergy.[7] With the 1998 Lambeth Conference also discussing the question, and likely to appoint an international commission of enquiry on human sexuality, much of the damage caused by the backlash of the 1980s has been repaired.[8]

There are other grounds for optimism too. Social and political attitudes towards gay and lesbian rights are now changing in a much more constructive direction than was the case in the 1980s. The achievement of an equal age of consent, for which LGCM has long campaigned, and equality of treatment in the armed forces, now both seem likely in the wake of the Tory electoral rout in May 1997. It is also interesting to note that attempts by the Christian Right to influence the outcome of that election by appealing to homophobic religious moralism were totally ineffective. The Conservative Christian Fellowship, which was set up in 1990 with the blessing of Party Chairman, Brian Mawhinney, sought to follow the example of the American Conservative Coalition whose training resources it borrowed. Its scaremongering tactics included claims that Labour would scrap religious education in schools, introduce euthanasia and 'allow homosexual people to marry'. Its Director, Tim Montgomerie, hoped that 'following the pattern of America, more and more Christians will support the Conservatives as the anti-family, pro-abortion character of Labour is exposed'. But strategies which had worked well for the Tories in 1987 now failed totally. One particularly eloquent symbol of the change was the defeat in Exeter of Dr Adrian Rogers, adviser to the Christian Family Campaign and outspoken homophobe, by the Labour candidate, and openly gay Christian, Ben Bradshaw. To the evident discomfort of many traditional Tories, William Hague has been quick to sense the change of public mood. Even the Conservatives, it seems, are now keen to reach out to gays and lesbians and to shed their image as the party of the traditional family and the scourge of those who dare to live their lives in different ways.

Yet a note of caution also needs to be struck. Surveys of public opinion make it clear that Christians remain far more conservative in their social and moral attitudes than the public at large, and in most denominations the growth of evangelicalism at the expense of liberalism has further reinforced that trend.[10] It may well be that providing a refuge for those committed to the preservation of what they perceive to be traditional moral and social values in the face of rapid social and intellectual change increasingly comes to be the primary function of the Christian churches in our society. If so, LGCM should not expect a short or easy ride over the issue of the full acceptance of gay and lesbian clergy for which it has campaigned so hard.

It is also worth asking how important this question really is. As Trevor Thurston-Smith has recently suggested, because the issue has acquired such a high public profile, it may be a catalyst for bringing about an end to the myriad forms of subtle and pervasive discrimination which gay and lesbian Christians encounter in everyday aspects of their faith-lives.[11] But he is also well aware that there are arguments to be won within the churches which are more fundamental than this one. It is these more basic challenges, I would argue, which will ultimately be decisive for LGCM's success or failure in bringing about its original vision of a sexually inclusive Church. The admission of gay and lesbian clergy as honourable exceptions to heteropatriarchal norms will do nothing to undermine their pervasive and discriminatory power. Only a genuine queering of Christian theology and spirituality will be truly liberating, since it alone can deconstruct the hierarchical constructions of gender and sexual identity which imprison us. LGCM is already providing, and must in the future continue to provide, space and encouragement for its members to explore what this might mean for the transformation of their own and the whole Church's life.[12] But neither political campaigning nor theological and spiritual trans-formation can be accomplished at the expense of mutual care and compassion for one another and for those who seek the movement's help. As its national Chair, Geoffrey Thompson, has recently suggested, LGCM should itself seek to be the inclusive and liberated Church in microcosm – a foretaste, however inadequate, of a time when the movement will no longer need to exist.[13] Peter Elers' campaign for justice, truth and love will then finally have achieved its end.

Notes

1 Nelson Mandela, inaugural speech, 1994. Quoted in *LGCM URC Caucus Newsletter*, **15**, Autumn 1996, p. 20.
2 S. Seidman (ed.) (1996) *Queer Theory/Sociology* (Oxford: Blackwell), p. 22.
3 Ibid., p. 412. This issue has been a troubling one within the feminist movement. See, for example, Judith Butler's discussion in J. Butler (1990) *Gender Trouble: Feminism and the Subversion of Identity* (London: Routledge), pp. 142–9. Here she argues that the deconstruction of identity is not the end of radical sexual politics but its essential precondition.
4 A. Smith (1994) *New Right Discourse on Race and Sexuality: Britain, 1968–1990* (Cambridge: Cambridge University Press), p. 18.
5 *Issues in Human Sexuality: A Statement by the House of Bishops* (1991) (London: Church House Publishing), p. 34.
6 *LGCM Newsletter*, December 1997, pp. 3–4.
7 *The Times*, 12 July 1997. The exact number of gay clergy within the Church of England remains unknown. The *Observer Review*, 13 July 1997, puts the figure at 2000 or about 20 per cent of the total. How many adhere to the life of celibacy laid down by the bishops in 1991 is even more conjectural.
8 *The Times*, 15 July 1997.
9 *Church of England Newspaper*, 24 January 1997.
10 When asked in 1996 if being a Christian was compatible with being a practising homosexual 52.5 per cent of members of the Church of England's Synod answered No, and 40.4 per cent Yes according to the *Guardian*, 8 July 1996. Amongst conservative evangelical churches the former figure was 96 per cent in a survey quoted in the *Church of England Newspaper*, 15 November 1996.
11 *LGCM Journal*, Winter 1996, pp. 23–4, 26.
12 A recent outstanding discussion of the connections between queer sexuality and spirituality is P. Sweasey (1997) *From Queer to Eternity: Spirituality in the Lives of Lesbian, Gay & Bisexual People* (London: Cassell).
13 *LGCM Journal*, Winter 1996, p. 4.

PART II

Selected Texts

◆

SIX

From alienation to affirmation

The creation of an inclusive Christian Church in which gay, lesbian, and bisexual relationships will be affirmed and celebrated remains one of the primary goals of LGCM. As a corollary, the movement has set out to oppose all forms of Christian homophobia and sexual apartheid. Sometimes it can appear that pursuing these aims results only in a series of abstract and often abstruse theological debates coupled with a great deal of ecclesiastical political in-fighting. What should never be forgotten is that LGCM is a liberation movement whose theology and praxis are rooted in the pain and suffering of individual Christians. Prejudice, discrimination and injustice are the antithesis of the Christian Gospel, and if unchallenged may diminish and in some cases wreck the lives of those who are subjected to them – facts which pious and self-deceiving platitudes about loving the sinner but hating the sin should never be allowed to obscure. In one way or another all of the extracts in this section illustrate this theme. The first two letters are typical of the many hundreds which LGCM receives every year.

(1)

I am 21 years of age, and gay. I am also a 'born-again' Christian, and have been for the last 14 years. At first I thought that being gay and a Christian were two things that were never meant to go together, but now I am just *very* confused!

I was raised in a Pentecostal church, where I remain at present. I have spoken to my Church Leader about my being gay and he just wants me to see a friend of his who happens to be a psychologist to 'sort myself out' as he put it. He made me feel as though I had some sort of disease.

I do not want to see the friend because I am *not* ill in the head just because I happen to have feelings for men instead of women, and although I can't change my feelings (having tried very hard over the last few months, going into doomed relationships with different girls), I am now quite content with the idea of being gay. At the same time, I do not want to stop being a Christian because I've been one for so long, and it is important to me. Having said this, I am finding my church life very hard going at present; I feel that it would be easier if I 'came out' and was honest, because I'm living a double life and it's killing me!

Basically, I'm just writing to see if you could send me some information (as much as possible) about being homosexual and a Christian. I would especially appreciate the names and addresses of any churches where I would be welcome for being me, not somebody people want me to be. Also, could you tell me the best way of coming out and telling my friends at church that I'm gay in addition to my Christian family who are completely against homosexuality.

I'm sorry for going on so much, but I just have to tell a fellow gay Christian what I'm going through – I hope you understand.

(Source: LSE, Hall Carpenter Archive, GCM closed correspondence)

(2)

I am a young gay Christian who is struggling to come to terms with not only my own sexuality but also with the church's confusing teaching on this issue at the present time.

A small proportion of my friends know that I am homosexual but the majority of these are non-Christians. I don't feel that I can tell my Christian friends because I think that I am going to get a bad and unsupportive reaction from them.

At the moment I just feel really isolated as even though I know other gay people none of them are Christians and therefore cannot understand the difficult position I am in. I feel that I am being torn in two completely different directions, in one direction by my faith and in the other by the way that I feel towards my sexual preference.

Mostly I feel that I have got it sorted with God, but then God is a lot more understanding than I know that some of my friends are going to be.

If you have any literature that would be helpful or a support group that is near me, even though in a couple of weeks I will be moving back to Bath as the University term will be ending, then I would be really grateful if you could help me as at the moment I feel a real lack of support which is making the problem seem a lot worse than it really is.

(Source: LSE, Hall Carpenter Archive, GCM closed correspondence)

In the third extract, Peter Seer, an LGCM member, describes his experience of a typical suburban evangelical church in 1986, and of his determination not to be silenced or excluded. In the fourth, Tim Parry reflects upon the pressures which many gifted gay and lesbian clergy have faced in trying to exercise their ministry with honesty and integrity.

(3)

I came to live in leafy suburban south London nearly two years ago, and I was recommended by a straight friend to try the local evangelical Church of England. This friend knew that I was gay, incidentally, and was himself curate of a similar church about ten miles away.

The whole set-up was really very friendly – especially for a large church with over 500 on the electoral roll – and I quickly found a nearby housegroup for Bible study and prayer, and a host of other groups to which I could belong. I thus made a nice circle of albeit superficial friends.

No one at church knew I was gay, because I had decided it was not an issue I wanted to bring up. If I found a boyfriend and wanted to set up house, then I might change my mind. Or if the subject of homosexuality came up in the course of discussion or study, then I was quite willing to say my bit. But for the moment I could not see that anything could be gained by proclaiming my orientation.

By the time I had been there 18 months, two very nice young ladies had tried to get me interested in romance. I told one of them about my being gay; but although the other one had shared a flat with someone who was gay, she was rather antagonistic about the whole issue, so I merely let her surmise the truth about me.

Next, a well-known convicted 'cottager' appeared in church one evening, got talking to someone about homosexuality, and was promptly told by the vicar not to darken the doorstep again. A lot of people over-reacted to the situation, and the subject of homosexuality began to be discussed with tremendous emotion and prejudice – and total ignorance! The time had come for me to say my piece for the 'cause'.

Before I had the opportunity, two young men in the church both confided in me that they were gay. A third person, walking home from the midweek Bible study, asked me if one could be Christian and gay, because he was gay too. Then he told me about two young women in the church who were lesbians. A week later, one of the women I had been close to revealed that she knew five people who were certainly gay. It seemed like an epidemic!

My chief concern about these people was that they should not be put off by the church's hard-line approach to the question of homosexuality. From what I could gather, the vicar taught that gayness was a psychological condition which could be 'cured' if the person were willing. It was supposedly condemned in the Bible, and certainly a 'degenerate condition'.

So I went to see the vicar, on the pretext that I was concerned about the presence of so many homosexuals in the church, and to ask whether or not we could have some kind of sensitive and positive discussion at a meeting. I told him about the distress and depression suffered by the people who had talked to me, and argued that we had a collective responsibility to be supportive and caring, without making our care conditional on any personal views we might have on the rights and wrongs of being gay. I then told him about my attendance at last November's conference of the Evangelical Fellowship; I expressed a little about my own views, and suggested that if he thought it helpful, we could get somebody from GCM to counsel the distressed.

I should have realised that someone with such fixed views would not respond very positively. We sat down and argued the Bible passages, and I suggested that the situation these gay brothers and sisters found themselves in today was in no way similar to the cases of rape, temple prostitution or corruption described in the Bible.

The vicar suggested that I ought to refrain from mentioning these matters in my midweek homegroup prayer session. (Are some real burdens so unrespectable that we cannot share them?) He went on to say that a discussion group about homosexuality was out of the question, and any further counselling of gays in the church was preferably to be left to the vicar and church staff. I realised that he now saw me in a threatening light, since I had more or less said that I thought one could both live a Christian life and live in a positive relationship with a gay partner. And yet I was in no way condoning promiscuity or exploitation.

The problems and depressions of the gay people at church have continued – and while some are thinking of leaving the church, others are rejecting their faith altogether. Still others are leading a double life, without being honest even to themselves. The spirit of openness seems to be dead; the church seems to be a place where you have to conform in order to be accepted; there is no willingness to learn, or to listen, or to reach out to those suffering from very real problems. It seems totally un-Christian to me. And that is why I am staying on at the church, in the hope that I may eventually be an instrument of education and change.

(Peter Seer, 'On Being Gay in a Suburban Church', *One in Ten. Newsletter of the Evangelical Fellowship within LGCM*, June 1986, pp. 4–5)

(4)

I was ordained deacon at Petertide 1988 by the Archbishop of York in York Minster, and priest by the Bishop of Hull almost exactly a year later. Both were happy and moving occasions, with lots of support from family and friends, and a real feeling that I was embarking on a worthwhile and probably life-long journey in the Anglican ministry. And, at first and generally speaking, I was contented and hard-working as a curate in a suburban parish on the northern side of the city of Hull. I had the encouragement and friendship of a sympathetic and conscientious parish priest, and enjoyed the kindness and warmth of a mixed and growing church community. So what went wrong, and why, at the end of three years, do I now feel unable to return to serve the Church with whom I had invested so much energy and so many expectations? Certainly I feel no sense of bitterness or pique against those to whom and with whom I ministered – ordinary and extraordinary people who in one way or another had found a home in the Church of England. Nor do I feel resentful towards my vicar or the bishops, who were usually helpful and patient. As to my colleagues in the ministry, some I liked and some I found less likeable, as in any profession.

From a personal point of view my underlying anxiety was, I think, expressed in my unease over the role of a priest in the parish and the local community. What was I there for and did I have a real job to do? From the beginning I was extremely self-conscious of the image I presented as a clergyman. Even at the end of three years I found the black suit and clerical collar hard to deal with, as well as the sidelong glances and 'witty' comments it tended to elicit. It's now hard for me to comprehend the thoughts of ordinary people when they encounter a clergyman, but some idea can be gained from the way priests or vicars are presented in films and television; usually as bumbling well-meaning incompetents with their heads in the clouds and little understanding of the way of life of those whom they have been called to serve. They are sometimes painfully shy, sometimes pompous, and often shocked by the slightest moral misdemeanour, as well as being obsessed by politeness and the avoidance of bad language at all costs. They are moreover totally naive and inexperienced when it comes to sex.

As a clergyman working in the city with the lowest church-going population pro rata in the British Isles I was still aware of this perception. The fact that I was young, enjoyed a drink and was not easily shocked seemed a source of endless amazement to people outside the Church itself who couldn't conceive of a priest without white hair and a patronising manner. In the Church it was on the whole better; most in the congregation treated me as an individual, and because I was a very different person from my boss I attracted some whom he didn't, and of course vice versa. And again, many had known a whole series of curates and therefore had no illusions about the lack of frailty in young priests!

As to my homosexuality, however, that was a completely no go area. To be human and have failings was acceptable – to be homosexual was quite out of the question. Or perhaps more exactly to be homosexual and to say so was the real taboo. There's no doubt that some people had their private opinions about my unmarried state at the age of twenty-eight, and probably most of them were not particularly bothered or interested. What would have been shocking would have been for me to proclaim publicly what at most it was believed generally should have remained an intensely personal and private matter – a burden to bear solitarily or with the help of a few close friends. And in the end, for someone who has been brought up to believe (and whose Christian understanding has reinforced) that integrity and honesty are two of the most profound and vital principles, it was ultimately too much to bear.

It is a small comfort to me that I never in fact denied my sexuality in so many words. But neither was I able to contradict the received opinion that I was either hetero or a-sexual. I remember at one time being asked by a visiting worshipper whether I was married, and before I could reply one of our own congregation had chipped in that 'Oh no – Father Parry has only just come out of college', as if I had been kept in holy isolation for years on end and would have not had time yet even to consider the more intimate side of life. My sexuality was in the context of the parish very much my affair; my being gay was very much my problem. It is integral to the person I am, and most probably without it I would never have found myself an ordained man in the first place. But it was almost entirely mine to deal with, and in a situation in which working hours and parish commitments curtailed most socialising which others take for granted, I was thrown largely back on myself for support and reassurance. Although I was not without gay friends, some of the loneliest and most isolating times of my life were spent during my three years as a curate in Hull.

In such circumstances the obvious place to look for friendship and acceptance would seem likely to be amongst those who shared one's sexuality. Yet this was problematical. For one thing many clergymen, especially of an older generation, would simply refuse to admit there was a problem or even an issue here. Sexual desire for members of one's own sex was simply a quirk or divine trick or burden which it was up to the individual to deal with, maybe with the help of a very close friend or two. It had nothing to do with the essentials of the Faith, and 'ordinary' people could not be expected to appreciate or understand it; therefore the primary objective was to keep it under wraps at all costs. At one meeting of the Hull Deanery Synod a prominent and ambitious local rector welcomed the fact that the General Synod had declined a pernicious attempt by a pressure group to have clergy sexuality discussed with a view to outlawing certain gay priests, on the grounds that St Paul had told us to banish all thoughts of 'evil things' from our minds! As far as he was concerned it didn't matter what tactics or reasoning were employed as long as the dreaded subject was kept off the agenda. For him and for many others like him it was just too close to home.

Amongst younger priests attitudes were more mixed. Many are relatively confident and self-respecting on a personal and social level, and use support networks of friends and colleagues in order to counter isolation and insecurities. But beyond that, in their professional capacity, they are almost entirely unable to define themselves as gay, or even to bring the issue into open discussion for fear of the probable consequences. At a time when hardly any of the bishops are willing to even admit the presence of 'practising homosexuals' amongst their clergy, and feel bound increasingly to defend the perceived status quo, a single letter or phone call from a parishioner (or worse, an article in a local newspaper) can cause havoc for a priest's ministry. Whilst a clergyman I myself was asked to appear on a morning television chat show to debate the subject of gay clergy. I could not agree to do so, because of the possible repercussions for my vicar, the parish and for myself. No serving clergyman could be found who would agree to speak openly about his sexuality on such a public stage, and it is symptomatic that the honesty and courage of Michael Peet (*Times*, December 4 1992) has thus been treated with such wonder and applause.

Many gay priests battle courageously on, maintaining a remarkable integrity in the face of prejudice, ignorance and lack of institutional or pastoral support. Many are the Church's most loyal servants, the most conscientious and diligent in their daily work, and the most thoroughly grounded in their prayer lives and theological understanding. Yet the living of a life which near its centre bears such a burden as homosexuality has been made to be by the Church in general, cannot be continued without cost. Dr Ben Fletcher, in his *Clergy Under Stress* (Mowbray 1990) presents disturbing evidence that stress levels are considerably higher amongst gay clergy persons, and that this is directly related to an inability to share a vital and integral aspect of themselves with those to whom they have been called to minister.

After three years 'serving my title' in Hull I no longer felt that I could continue in the ministry whilst there remained such an unresolved conflict between my perceived role as a priest and my own emotional and sexual needs. I felt that, far from living a life of wholeness – holiness – my public and personal lives were radically disjointed. I lacked the basic integrity which could only come from my being able to be myself as a priest and gay man.

The subject of homosexuality and the Christian way of life is one which has generated a great deal of verbiage, and a considerable quantity of anguished debate in public and private. Yet for the average lesbian or gay man the problem is largely incomprehensible. We all know that we make good doctors, lawyers, salespeople, accountants, cleaners, and so on. Most of us know at least one exemplary clergy man or woman whose sexuality is a positive and creative plank in their ministry. Yet the Church, that body of people who are supposed to stand up for Truth, Integrity, Acceptance and so on, cannot bring itself to accept the obvious; that there is nothing integral to being an actively gay person which makes one unfit for Christian ministry. In the eyes of most gay people the Church thus seems ridiculous, outdated and, yes, downright immoral, in the way it treats ordinary men and women who wish to pursue a freely chosen vision and vocation. It is no wonder that most lesbians and gay men have long ago turned their back on an institution which has no real place for them except as 'repentant sinners'.

The Church consistently claims to operate in the world but not to be of the world. Its attitude towards the basic rights of lesbian and gay people shows that it is in total subjection to the prejudices and uninformed opinions which society in general clings to. When it comes to the bottom line the reason many priests and bishops simply will not speak out on the subject has little to do with personal convictions and far more to do with their terror of 'what people will think' and how the world outside will judge them. The question of gay clergy is therefore a deeply moral question, and one which strikes at the heart of what it means to be a Christian and what it *really* costs to stand up for the downcast and oppressed, as opposed to jumping on fashionable bandwagons.

My experience as a gay man and as a clergyman has been painful. I blame myself as well as the Church for not accepting reality; for hoping that things would turn out alright in the end. I am saddened that the Church shows no sign of repenting, of apologising to lesbians and gay men for what it has done to them over the centuries, and of courageously welcoming their precious insights and contributions openly and honestly instead of covertly and deceitfully.

Since the first part of my story was published in the *LGCM Newsletter* two gay men have contacted me to recount how they were denied the chance to test their vocation in the ordained ministry purely because they refused to lie about their sexuality. I am convinced that they are only the tip of the iceberg, and equally sure that such experiences point to the real scandal about homosexuality and the clergy; not of course, that it exists, but that there remains a pernicious policy a) to deny that fact and b) to prevent self-respecting lesbians and gay men from gaining access to positions of authority in the Church. While personally I shall not be returning to full-time Christian ministry, it is my prayer and hope that the Church will begin to cease collaborating in the persecution of my lesbian and gay brothers and sisters, will begin to treat human beings with the respect they deserve, and will in doing so become more open, more accepting and more acceptable to those it has done so much to alienate.

(Tim Parry, 'Parry's Progress', *LGCM Newsletter*, June 1992, pp. 1–3)

The next three accounts illustrate how in different ways membership of LGCM has been a source of empowerment for those seeking to affirm their identities in the face of hostility and prejudice. In the first, Sara Coggin explains the significance in her life of a service of blessing upon her relationship and the reactions to it which she encountered in her church. Such services have continued to be an important part of LGCM's provision of pastoral care to those who seek its help. In the second Jerry Walsh, a member of the Roman Catholic caucus within LGCM, writes of the impact which the movement has made upon his life, as does Judith Weeks, a member of Lesbian Matters, the women's group within LGCM, in the third account.

(5)

'Will I need a hat?' asked my sister over the phone. After all, I'd worn one at her wedding and she wanted to do the 'right thing' on my special day. 'I'm really interested to know what happens,' said a heterosexual colleague at school. Even a gay priest confided, 'I've never been to one of these services before.' Everybody has a good idea of what to expect at a wedding, but gay blessings are still a largely unknown quantity. Because they are always quiet occasions, unofficial and fairly rare, there is no fixed pattern and no one set of social assumptions. Different couples seek a service of blessing at different stages of their relationship and for different reasons. Gay couples also have a unique opportunity to work out their own lifestyles and to design appropriate services for themselves. Our experience is only one example.

Sue and I got to know each other through GCM. Our friendship developed slowly – though telephone conversations got longer and meetings were eagerly awaited. Although Sue had known she was gay since she was in her teens, she was newer than me to gay organisations, and I wanted to give her time to find her feet. Besides, we're both cautious people and neither of us wanted to get hurt. Eventually, however, we began to go out together, and one day plucked up courage to share our feelings with each other. It turned out to be the beginning of a further six months 'engagement' period, fairly unusual in the gay world.

Waiting for a blessing

It was Sue who said a few weeks later, 'Do you mind if we wait until we can have some kind of blessing service?' An inspired question. We both needed time for the relationship to develop before we committed ourselves sexually. It was important to meet each other's family and friends. There were practical matters to be considered if we were going to set up home together.

Waiting was obviously significant, but why have a blessing? Isn't it just aping heterosexuals? Should liberated gay people be seeking 'external validation' for their relationships? Indeed can one properly have a blessing when the Church as a whole doesn't yet approve of homosexual relationships? For Sue the most important thing was for us to recognise at the beginning of our life together that there is a Third Person in our relationship. Far from defying God, she was actively trusting him to bless the very relationship which her Evangelical friends considered so dubious. For me the emphasis was rather different. Although I believe that homosexual equality should include the option of gay marriage, in the sense of a legally recognised institution, it was not quite that framework that I was seeking for myself. In the previous ten years I had moved increasingly to a view of life as a journey, a pilgrimage of development and change. Now, in this new stage of our journeys, I wanted our friends to wish us, in the deepest and most literal sense, Godspeed in our life together.

As soon as we began to study examples of services which had already been used, we found that they all put the emphasis on an exchange of vows, which I found rather alarming. Vows tend to assume a fairly static relationship. They are also assumed to be very exact promises worded in precise language. However, unlike heterosexuals getting married, we were free to make our own service relevant to the particular relationship. As we struggled to find out what we really wanted to say to each other and the right language to express it, two major issues emerged.

Until death us do part?

The first was the question of permanence. Sue had naturally made a direct parallel with heterosexual marriage and was suddenly forced to think about alternative patterns for a gay relationship. Sexual fidelity was not an issue for us as we both assumed it, but I had to ask whether either of us was really in a position to promise to love each other until death. Unlike Sue, I had been in a relationship before, and then it had been me who had insisted on a promise of permanence. I had no desire to face the sorrow of a broken relationship again, yet the previous two years had forced me to accept that loving sometimes involves letting the other go to journey in another direction. So this time I wanted to make an open kind of vow that we should share our feelings, work things out and stay together as long as is right. Eventually we agreed on the formula, 'as long as God wills', and the natural insecurity which Sue felt has been removed by the deepening love of our life together.

With all my worldly goods I thee endow?

The question of property was one which we both wanted to discuss but on which we found no disagreement. We saw it as a vital part of the question how we as a couple could become one flesh but remain two people. Our work is very important to both of us, and it continues to provide us with separate status and separate money. Sue already owned a car and I was in the process of selling my house and buying another. We had seen the negative effects of partners not having separate money in both heterosexual and homosexual relationships. So our solution was to set up a joint account for all running expenses, but to leave ourselves the freedom to give presents spontaneously, decide our own charities, and not feel guilty about the occasional luxury. In practice, of course, we increasingly speak of 'our car' and 'our house', especially as we clean and decorate together, but ownership still defines certain areas of responsibility.

Quiet wedding?

Having approached a priest we both knew, and fixed a date, we found we had a host of practical things to do. We sent out invitations to a small but representative selection of our friends, both heterosexual and gay, but, as we wanted to share our joy with the wider community of our local congregation, we ordered a large cake to take to church on the Sunday after the blessing. As we rushed out on a last-minute expedition to buy rings, and struggled with the refreshments, we realised why the couple's families are so important at a wedding! But our friends were marvellous, giving us practical help and moral support. And we certainly needed the moral support when first Sue's fellow evangelicals proved unable to cope with her entering a gay relationship, then some of my local congregation (to whom I had been 'out' for three years) started to make a fuss about the cake. In the midst of all the hassle, the priest's advice to set aside a quiet time together before the service proved more than necessary.

The blessing itself was a peaceful and loving occasion, both a wonderful start to our life together and a strengthening for the morrow's battles. The service was friendly and personal yet dignified. Everybody hugged us and signed a card. We emerged into the dappled September sunshine, deeply happy. Back at home, my two-year-old niece presented her two 'aunties' with a gift and my brother-in-law photographed us cutting the cake. Romantic memories, reminiscent of many a quiet wedding?

Onward Christian Soldiers

A friend of ours told us, 'I don't think I'd have wanted a blessing service unless it could be at my local church.' I understand his feelings, but pioneers can't have everything. (And when gay people seek to define their own lifestyles and build a social context for their relationships, they are pioneering.) While my previous vicar might well have blessed us happily, I had not sought to force a difficult decision on someone who didn't know me very well. But we had hoped to be remembered in the intercessions, while sharing cake on special occasions is a well-established tradition. Some members of the congregation were coming to the blessing and others had given us a card. There was no hint of opposition until the week before, when I was told by telephone that certain unnamed people were threatening to leave the church. As Christians we did not want to give needless offence to others, but there were clearly moral issues which the congregation had to face. Most of them had known I was gay for three years, yet no one had expressed any negative feelings to me. I had tried to introduce Sue to as many of them as possible, though obviously there was no official announcement like calling the banns to give people time to adjust. They now had to decide whether homosexuality was so evil that they should turn us out of the church (in which case shouldn't they have said something to me before?) or whether homophobia, like racialism, is an unfortunate prejudice which Christians should be seeking to overcome. They could not claim to accept us without accepting our relationship. They might not pray for us publicly (though some did privately), but we would share our cake with those who would eat it.

Gay people who come out have to be prepared to meet prejudice, but it is never pleasant. When it comes from Christians, gay people naturally feel unwelcome in the Church. Indeed one of our church-wardens expressed surprise that we returned the following Sunday after the way we had been treated. But really the attitudes we found were a microcosm of those in the wider Church, and we have to try to change them not just by making a stand but also by giving those who have opposed us the opportunity to change their stereotypes.

Christians usually try to ignore the existence of the homosexual minority in church and society, and the pressure to keep quiet leaves many gay people isolated, unable to find appropriate pastoral care and denied the spiritual and social support of a church blessing. Church leaders are reluctant to make any public stand on what they see as a controversial issue, thus patronising the supposed 'simple faithful' and in effect denying their responsibilities to gay people and to their relatives and friends. However, we are all the Church, and ultimately we have to take responsibility for ourselves and our relationships. Thanks to a few courageous clergy, a service of blessing can be part of the pattern if we wish.

(Sara Coggin and Sue Jex (1980) *Exploring Lifestyles: An Introduction to Services of Blessing for Gay Couples* (London: LGCM), pp. 7–11)

(6)

I have heard that the Journal of the LGCM exists to give a voice to those who otherwise might not have one. I had not anticipated however, how difficult it would prove to write down how LGCM helped end my alienation from the Roman Catholic Church. It is not easy to write openly and honestly as a gay man. The atmosphere of the closet clings rather like the odour of camphorated mothballs clings to clothes left too long in those mysterious wooden wardrobes I remember from childhood days. The fresh air takes a long time to permeate through every fibre!

Forty years old and alienated for some 20 years from RC practice, it is difficult to see why I allowed such a state of affairs to persist for so long. It seems unimaginable that even one year ago there was a barrier which prevented me from participating wholeheartedly at RC services. What brought about this change?

Alienation

Growing up gay in a Roman Catholic family in Southern Ireland in the 50s and 60s was not easy. My parents were not uncaring, nor were they by any stretch of the imagination fanatical about religion. We rarely worshipped together as a family – only at funerals and marriages. Nonetheless support for gay people was non-existent. There was no one to confide in at home, at school or in the Church. No organisations existed which could give positive advice about gay issues. My religious question was simple – I had and have a deep-seated wish for 'Church' approval and support for my loving sexual relationships with other men. The official 'Church' attitude (i.e. that of Hierarchy) was as unhelpful then as it is now. For understandable reasons in my view, the result of all this was quite simply a total rejection of the moral authority of the Church on my part. The outcome of this rejection was unhappiness and loneliness. These difficult emotions led to a deep-seated desire for reconciliation if only the Church could see its way to go some of the way to try to understand.

Some 20 years later, older and hopefully a little more mature, in the midst of the AIDS crisis, the time seemed right to reconsider the problems and difficulties outlined above. Could the unhelpful attitude of the Roman Catholic Church be changed? Could the Church accept lesbian and gay relationships and bless them? Could the Roman Catholic Church come to understand its responsibility to lesbians and gay men? Could the Church come to some appreciation of its contribution to our sufferings? Could the Church ask our forgiveness for the ill-treatment of centuries? Could the Church ever come to consider we might be a valuable asset? Could the Church perhaps realise that human awareness of sexuality had altered? Did the Hierarchy know that new scientific thinking existed regarding homosexuality as a normal variation of human sexuality? Had the Church any idea of their responsibilities towards young lesbians and gay men – particularly during their formative years at Catholic schools? Were any Catholic lesbians or gays speaking up on these issues? How could I find the answers to these questions?

One fact which remained constant for me before, throughout and after my period of alienation was my special personal relationship with God. This developed with my understanding of the Christian faith learned through my Catholic education. An intimate personal relationship with a loving and caring God was right for a lonely gay boy! Nurtured by the Scriptures, by the writings of the great Christian mystics, by the Catholic sacraments and liturgy, by prayer and meditation, this is a deep love and is right for this gay man. It is a mutual love – God loves me as I love God. No matter what the difficulties are God is there and I am with God. Troubles with work and difficulties with love affairs are discussed constantly in prayer. Answers are given – always right! When I love another and another loves me God is with us to bless us! My needs are met – I try to meet God's needs.

Reconciliation

God has given me the lesbian and gay community as a family! I feel privileged to be a member! Therefore, the Lesbian and Gay Christian Movement seemed the best place to find the answers to my questions. I have not been disappointed. I am deeply grateful to a woman member of the Evangelical Fellowship within LGCM for her personal support through letters. I have tried to educate myself with numerous books purchased from the Movement – books not all that easy to find in the shops. I attended the 1989 AGM and met many people like myself. How wonderfully reassuring! I attended the inaugural meeting of the proposed Roman Catholic Caucus within LGCM. I learned of the existence of Catholic AIDS Link and attended a mass of reconciliation. One of the Catholic members of LGCM asked had I approached my local parish. I plucked up courage and started to attend Sunday mass. An approach to the priest resulted in a friendly 'Welcome home!' The local parish have agreed to help raise some money for Catholic AIDS Link and Frontliners. The *Catholic Herald* now seems to have some of the most positive reporting of lesbian and gay issues I have seen in the non-gay press! They have even published a letter from me! I had not anticipated that I would be welcomed as a member of a renewed Church, firmly based on the faith of ordinary people, increasingly intolerant of unreasoning authority, seeking to right the hurts and wrongs of centuries! How nice of God to begin to change the Church so that I could feel at home! Can I ask more than that?

(Jerry Walsh, 'Alienation and Reconciliation', *LGCM Journal*, October 1990, p. 15)

(7)

My first contact with LGCM was soon after its foundation. My partner and I were watching a television programme in which Peter Elers was featured, as a result of which we wrote to him and asked to be put in touch. We were living in Cornwall in those days and very much immersed in caring for children so that our first few years' membership were by post. There were regular journals in those days, small stubby journals full of erudite articles. Some of them I found incomprehensible! Nevertheless it did feel good to be linked up with a wider network of gays and lesbians within the Church.

It seems hard to believe but at that time we had never knowingly met another lesbian couple! It was through LGCM that we made our first contact. This was with an Australian couple travelling in England who had met up with Richard Kirker who had asked us if we would like to offer them some hospitality. I can well remember how scared we were at the prospect of meeting them. Eventually they telephoned to say that they were in the Market Square of our nearest town and as I drove to meet them, I kept trying to picture what they would be like.

I suppose I was as much into stereotyping as everyone else and did really expect to find them in big boots and boiler suits! I then took myself in hand, reminding myself that they were lesbians just like us. When I met them, of course they were, and we had a delightful few days with them before they travelled on. I remember that they told us that Richard Kirker was remarkably young! We were astonished at this, as our telephone conversations with him had given us the impression that he was somewhat elderly!

Our next major contact with LGCM was when a child with whom I had worked in care, having grown up and joined the Coldstream Guards was charged with having indulged in 'homosexual acts' whilst a serviceman. The support that we received from a priest in LGCM at that time was incalculable. He visited David in detention and came with me to the Court Martial. It felt good to have such support around one.

I think it was about that time that we began going to LGCM Annual Conferences and soon after that my partner Pat joined the Committee. We became much more closely involved then and made some very good friends through LGCM who are still close today.

We lived through the eviction from St Botolph's. Pat and I were present in Court on that dreadful day. Perhaps the most moving experience I have had in all my association with LGCM was the service of exodus from St Botolph's. I remember particularly that hymn in which Jim Cotter replaced the ghastly words to 'I vow to thee my Country' with wonderful ones about the 'love that dares to speak its name'.

The other thing for which I have to blame Richard Kirker is my media career! It was back in 1986 that we appeared on the Kilroy programme with him. That was about gay priests. It was in the area of adoption and fostering by lesbians that it really took off however. Richard recommended us for a programme on this issue, and from that time onwards it didn't seem to stop! We made many joint television programmes; I took part in numerous television and radio discussions and we were featured in 'the quality press'. It was an exhausting time but we got to know so many wonderful people who were with us in the struggle and there were many more who had had prejudiced views but who, meeting us and our family and finding that we were in fact quite ordinary and boring, changed their views on this issue.

The whole thing seems to have almost gone full circle and I have little to do with LGCM these days although I try to make it a priority to attend the AGM. I am delighted that the Women's Group seems to have grown so well over the last few years. That has risen and declined all through the time I have been in LGCM. There have been many wonderful women who have tried to keep it going. At the moment I don't have time to be heavily involved with any of those activities but I have only just over two years to go before retirement and then hopefully will be back!

It is hard to express just how important LGCM has been to me over the years. In the early days I was still a member of the Anglican Church so felt very isolated. Around 1980 I became a Quaker and much more at home with my sexuality there. In many ways my own need for LGCM has passed but I remain a member as I feel it is a vitally important organisation both in terms of campaigning and in terms of offering love and support to young men and women who are trying to find themselves as gay or lesbian and as committed, loving Christians in today's tempestuous world.

(Judith Weeks, 'Judith Weeks Remembers', *Sophic Voices. Newsletter of the Women in the Lesbian and Gay Christian Movement,* November 1996, p. 2)

The task of creating an inclusive Christian community is not just a matter of changing minds and hearts outside of LGCM; it also has important implications for its own internal praxis. In this extract Savi Hensman, who was a student member of LGCM in 1982, and the movement's link with Christian Organisations for Social, Political and Economic Change, writes about the double impact of racial as well as sexual discrimination, and the challenge which this poses for what have been predominantly white middle-class gay and lesbian liberation movements.

(8)

Why do I remain a churchgoing Christian?

Christianity was brought to my country, Sri Lanka, and to many others now in the Third World, as the creed of armies of occupation. It has been used over the centuries to justify the plunder and exploitation of my people and to teach us to despise ourselves. We were comparatively lucky: with the connivance of the Church the peoples of North America, Australasia and the Caribbean were simply exterminated.

When Britain was recruiting blacks in large numbers after the war as a source of cheap labour, many were Christians. These were the days of open discrimination; my mother had one job application after the other turned down without a second glance – who could expect a 'wog' to be able to teach English? – and my parents had to hunt for a home until they found a Jewish landlord who did not operate a colour bar. The open hostility that many blacks faced from white fellow-Christians was one of the principal reasons why independent black-led churches were formed.

And today, when blacks are rounded up in dawn raids for passport checks and may be deported without trial, when the police harass young blacks on the streets and turn a blind eye to racist violence, where is the Church? Bishops may say good things but, as far as I know, in the majority of congregations racism is not discussed. Why do blacks in mixed congregations not raise the issue more often? Because some, particularly of the older generation, cling to their chains; others do not want to upset the fragile unity that exists, or feel that white Christians in general are too far gone in their racism to be reached.

Over the centuries the Church has endorsed the oppression of the poor, besides conniving in the murder of millions of Jewish people, blacks, 'witches', 'heretics', gays. Why do I, a black Lesbian, remain? Because of my beliefs, whether I like it or not, I am a member of the Christian community, deeply imperfect and often unfaithful as it is, and God works with and through the imperfect and fallible. Amazingly the Church in the Philippines and Latin America, and to a lesser extent throughout the Third World, has discovered God's identification with the poor and oppressed and is proclaiming the Gospel of liberation. I think that given the chance, the majority of white Christians in this country are capable of coming to understand and oppose racial oppression and injustice.

'But what has this got to do with us?' I can hear white gay Christians asking. 'We have our own battles to fight.' It is true it is not easy to be gay in this society or the Church. Black gay Christians face the same pressures, perhaps more. Many of the older generation clung to 'traditional morality' to preserve their self-respect in the face of the contempt they came across, and we are a threat to that. If we are open we risk being told it is a sign of 'Western decadence'; after discovering the hard way and gradually learning to be proud of our identity as blacks, it is a kick in the teeth to be told we represent the worst aspects of the culture we have just broken away from! On the other hand, perhaps it is easier for me to be the only open gay in my congregation because as a young black laywoman I have little left to lose. In any case, I do not think white gay male Christians can achieve their liberation alone. Unity is necessary, and they cannot unite effectively with

Lesbians and black gays unless they regard us as fully human and oppose all that grinds us down, even if most do not have the time to do much about it. And as Christians we should see our aim of bringing gay liberation to the Church in its overall perspective, as a vital part of the massive task of re-Christianising the Church and bearing witness in our words and lives to God's liberating love at work in the world.

(Savi Hensman, 'Blacks, Gays and the Church', *Gay Christian*, November 1982, pp. 4–5)

SEVEN

Reconfiguring the theological tradition

The following three extracts critically address the inadequacies of the Church's traditional theology of human sexuality in general, and of same-sex relationships in particular. In the first, Brian Thorne examines the harmful consequences of the spirit/body dualism and erotophobia which have informed much of the Church's thinking about sex, and points to the contribution which gay and lesbian Christians can make to the creation of what he calls a gracious sensuousness which is capable of enriching our lives. In the second, Joe Mulrooney discusses one of the most controverted of all issues: the use and abuse of the Bible in our thinking about same-sex relationships. In the third, Kennedy Thom suggests ways in which what are often viewed as transgressive forms of sexuality have the power to challenge and transform the life of the Church.

(1)

'The Word Became Flesh', St John 1: 14

I think it is most revealing that many Christians find it difficult – even abhorrent – to consider Our Lord's sexuality. It is as if for them the incarnation stops short at this point and they prefer to assume that Jesus was a sexless being or, at most, someone who set sexuality effortlessly to one side. Clearly this will not do if we believe that Jesus was true man. Indeed to deny Jesus sexuality is for most people today about the most effective way of saying that he was not fully human at all. But we believe that the 'Word became flesh'.

It is important to say this at the outset and to state it bluntly, for it must be admitted that for the most part the Church through the ages has presented Jesus as sexless and by doing so has detracted from his humanity and made it difficult for many Christians to affirm their own sexuality and to integrate it into their own loving. When we consider further that our sexuality is intrinsically related to our capacity to love, the seriousness of the matter becomes the more apparent. To tell men and women to love their neighbours as themselves while at the same time encouraging them to deny their sexuality is rather like telling athletes to run fast while recommending that they distrust their arms and keep them strapped to their sides.

A favourite trick of moral theologians, of course, is to pose a sharp contrast between *agape* and *eros*. Christians, it is argued, are called to agape and therefore sex does not come into it. But love is not like that. It does not come in neat categories. I am not a sexual being in bed with my wife and a non-sexual being in the office with my secretary. I am me all the time and that means I am sexual all the time. My loving, therefore, will always be a rich unity of different dimensions and my sexuality will underline and inform all my loving. The agape–eros opposition has been a source of endless confusion to those who cannot reconcile the distinction with their experience and then become burdened with needless guilt at their inability to arrive at a form of loving devoid of all desire. The whole business becomes even more baffling when we discover that in the Greek Bible there is no separate word anyway for sexual love – agape is used to describe the divine love, the intimacy of David and Jonathan and the sensuous love of the Song of Songs alike. If that seems fairly scandalous is it not also true to say that the nature of God as revealed in Jesus is itself an unexpected scandal? That Jesus was a sexual being is a not insignificant part of the scandalous humanity of God as revealed in him. Put it another way. God is love and because that love was embodied in Jesus we know that it incorporates the sexual and is nourished by it. If we hold on to that we shall avoid the vain attempt of trying to be more spiritual than God himself. In Christ sexuality and love were radically integrated and this is surely our possibility and challenge. Sex is intended to be a language of love. My direct answer therefore to the question 'Is there a sexual morality?' is 'Yes, there is and that morality demands that our sexual behaviour is shaped in accord with the ethics of love and that it serves and enhances the fuller realization of our divinely intended humanity'.

Immediately we begin to think of our sexual behaviour in this way the need for us as Christians not only to accept our sexuality but to understand its vital role in our sanctification becomes plainly evident. Our job as Christians is to be effective lovers and I would argue that our effectiveness will be mightily reduced if we are fearful of our sexuality and cut off from its life-giving energy. We need to grasp that it is the Holy Spirit who will inspire our sexual experience if we will let him and that sexual intercourse for us can be as much a relationship with God as the most profound contemplative prayer. It is the Holy Spirit, too, who can develop in us a graceful sensuousness (a sensuousness full of grace) which radiates warmth and spontaneity and which, because it is without tension, can be a source of healing for others. And yet how terrified in the past the Church has been of sensuousness. Indeed a cloud of ecclesiastical suspicion still hangs over pleasure when it involves the celebration of the physical. The fear presumably is of self-indulgence and of a selfish destructiveness towards others. But in experience the reverse seems to be true. If I can be properly in touch with my own body instead of cut off from it, if I can enjoy and love my bodily self, if in short I can experience something of my own unity I am the more able to be open and receptive to the other. What is more, as I grow in graceful sensuousness so I shall be released from what has sometimes been called the genital tyranny in relationships. It is a fact that the more we are able to relate lovingly and harmoniously to our own physical selves the more we experience a kind of diffusion of sexuality throughout the entire body. And so it is that our sexuality can irradiate every aspect of our encounters with others and spread its warmth and its healing into our work, our conversations and our many transactions which fall outside the bounds of actual 'love-making'.

If I am right about the desirability of this kind of sensuousness and the creative and healing vibrancy of sexuality when it is spread throughout the body, it follows that Our Lord must have been our example in this as in all else. My own reading of the Gospels strongly supports this view. I see there a man who is totally open to others and totally accepting of himself. What is more, his human tenderness is so pronounced that it is impossible to imagine it flowing from an asexual being. At times Our Lord is so ablaze with compassion that such tenderness is unimaginable without the sexual dimension. Consider especially his delight in women and his refusal to treat them as second-class citizens. Consider, too, his fondness for touching people and his immediate responsiveness to touch. The beloved apostle lies on his breast at supper and there is something wonderfully humorous about the encounter with Mary Magdalene in the Resurrection garden when Jesus restrains her from embracing him (presumably her normal behaviour towards him) because he is uncertain about the touchability of his new body – an uncertainty which has diminished by the time of the encounter with doubting Thomas. Nowhere in the Gospels, incidentally, does Jesus state that he was a virgin nor do his friends indicate that he was. What is more, Judaism has never been keen on celibacy and it would, therefore, be slightly surprising if Jesus had not married as a young man. Clearly an argument from silence cannot be convincing, but it is perhaps important to point out that it is at least *possible* that Our Lord did marry and that he experienced the genital expression of his sexuality. Certainly if we are really prepared to take his full humanity seriously there can be no question about the *possibility* for him of genital expression and of his desire for it.

In an age when so many people are becoming more and more divorced from their bodies and from the rest of the natural creation and when human sexuality is more and more abused, exploited and dehumanized the Church's task in the field of sexual ethics is urgent. When will the time come when as Christians we can unhesitatingly affirm the goodness of sexual pleasure? When will the time come when as a counsellor I shall no longer have to listen to the misery and the agony of Christians lost in a tangle of inappropriate guilt because they have failed to be angels and don't know how to be human? How much longer must we wait for homosexuals to be recognized by the Church as persons who desire to love and be loved like anyone else? How much longer must we endure the degrading of women which is implicit in the sexist limitations of much in Christian thought and in the life of the Church? The list can be extended and there are times when I am near to despair.

The sexual morality I would have us embrace demands that our sexual behaviour be shaped in accord with the ethics of love. Let me attempt in conclusion to spell that out before someone leaves this Church tonight and spreads it abroad that I have been advocating indiscriminate sexual activity in the name of the Holy Trinity. The ethics of love require commitment, trust, tenderness, a profound respect for the other and a desire for continuing and responsible communion with the other. The ethics of love, always ask too about the meanings and significance of acts in their total context – that is not only in the relationship itself but in society at large and in regard to God's intended direction for human life. And so it is that the sexual ethic which is in accord with the ethics of love can never permit selfish sexual expression, cruelty, impersonal sex, obsession with sex or actions carried out without willingness to take responsibility for the consequences at every level. If that sounds by implication like a full-blooded vote of confidence in the Christian vision of marriage and the loving community of the family then you would be right. It is my profound conviction that once we have learned how to celebrate the God-givenness of our sexuality the more it will be possible for us to proclaim the glory of marriage and the joyful obligation to nurture our defenceless children. In California at the present time children and adolescents are killing themselves in increasing numbers for lack of love. The most sexually liberated collectivity in the world is in danger of spawning a generation of despair because in so many cases the so-called sexual liberation is as far removed from true loving as the worst sexual repressiveness and denial.

Let me give the last word to James Nelson, professor of Christian Ethics and author of a book titled *Embodiment* which explores more eloquently and learnedly than I could ever do many of the issues I have raised tonight. Professor Nelson is not sanguine about the Church's response to its urgent task. He writes:

'The sexual fears are deep-seated. The amount of sexual mis-information is great. And the burden of sexual guilt is heavy. Perhaps in no other area will resistance and avoidance be quite so evident. Nevertheless the promise has been given. The Word became – becomes – flesh. The embodied word dwells among us, full of grace and truth. And we can and do behold that glory.'

(Brian Thorne, 'The Word Became Flesh', *Gay Christian*,
November 1983, pp. 5–7)

(2)

The Bible: friend or foe?

The intention is not a detailed investigation of the biblical texts which are relevant to the question of homosexuality, but to confront the more general question of the place of the Bible in our theological endeavour. This latter question is of high importance to each one of us, since each time that we try to make sense of our lives and experiences in terms of our relationship to God, we are theologizing in the best sense of that word.

Assumptions underlying our title

I begin by reflecting on the title which I have been given. What does that title suggest to me?

1. A concern with the two primary sources for the Christian theologian:

a) The community tradition. For the Christian, the Bible is an important part of that tradition. How does it speak to us? How do we read it?

b) Our present lived experience. In this context, our experience of our own sexuality, of our relationship to other human beings as sexual beings – in particular the experience of those members of our community who experience and live that attraction which we call sexual in respect of another person of the same sex, those who experience the values of community, healing, tenderness and completion in a loving, faithful relationship with a member of their own sex.

2. The phrase 'friend or foe?' suggests to me almost fear, and certainly a reaction to the phobia of society towards those who do not fit into the so-called 'normal' category of male/female attraction (and the reverse).

3. More importantly, I am concerned with the assumptions underlying this title. They are concealed but are nonetheless there. These assumptions concern:

a) The nature and character of that literature which we call The Bible.

b) The nature of the theological task: in particular, the relationship of tradition, the past experience of our community, our heritage, to our present lived experience.

An understanding of the Bible – the 'pennies from heaven' model

Let me try to uncover these assumptions by laying out what I see to be their main consequences in so far as they affect our approach to the theological task.

1. The Bible is conceived as a 'handbook of ethics', and consequently:

• We go seeking ready-made answers. We are approaching the Bible to see if there are any rules which support our position or condemn it.

How can we possibly read off and apply the rules of an ancient community whose historical, economic and sociological context is very different from our own modern situation? If we try that approach, we have problems as to what to do with the difficult text (i.e. difficult to us in this context) of Leviticus 20: 10ff. There, homosexuality is included in a list of vices which merit death.

- We 'proof text'. We go taking texts out of context to try to prove a particular position. The rejection of divorce, for example, seems clear enough in Matt. 19: 3ff, but not in an earlier chapter of the very same gospel (Matt. 5: 22).

  It so easily becomes a game of matching text against text, without taking into account the context and the nature of the text which we are reading. In a discussion of homosexuality, the story in Genesis 19 is often dragged in. While admitting that one element of the story is a suggested homosexual gang rape, we can in no way use that as a proof that the Bible condemns homosexuality.

  We must take into account its nature as a story, and as a story whose main concern is the infringement of hospitality: a stranger has arrived and look at what the yobs are trying to do. If we want to say that is a condemnation of homosexuality in general, we may as well logically say that the conclusion to the story permits gang rape provided that it is heterosexual.

- We treat the Bible as if it were a vast monolithic structure, a coherent system of doctrinal and ethical norms. When asked for his simple 'authoritative' statement about what the Bible says on a particular topic, the Biblical scholar must always interpose a question between the request and his answer: Which book of the Bible do you mean, which author, which tradition?

  Let us accept that our Old Testament, in the form in which we know it, is post exilic, i.e. post 6th century BCE. From then to the composition of the last of our New Testament books we are dealing with a literature which spans a period of five to six hundred years, and whose traditions had a long previous history in the life, and worship of the communities who produced that literature.

  There is then a great diversity of response because the community is interpreting and re-interpreting its tradition in the context of vastly different and changing historical, economic and social conditions.

2. The assumption which I am suggesting is behind all this is that the Bible is God's word, God's revelation, and that it is conceived in one particular fashion or in the light of one particular model.

    This way of looking at the Bible is faithful to the Biblical picture: the Jewish Torah or law was given by God, through Moses, at Sinai. The Decalogue in Exodus 20 and the law material in the following chapters which scholars refer to as the Book of the Covenant are placed at Sinai where we are reminded how God brought Israel out of Egypt and brought them to himself on eagle's wings.

    There we find God taking Israel into a relationship of covenant with himself – Yahweh is Israel's God, Israel is his people. Likewise, the Book of Deuteronomy, which is cast in the form of speeches of Moses, calls for fidelity to this relationship to which we give the name covenant, and presents the 'preached law' of Deuteronomy as the way in which Israel lives out its fidelity. That law was given through Moses at Sinai.

    This is indeed the biblical model and we must see the value of that model. It is a mythical picture – I use the expression in a technical sense – is a story which is concerned to express the authority and significance which Israel attached to Torah as its way of life. She saw it as her way of living out in fidelity the relationship into which her God had taken her and she projected it all back, in story form, to the origins of that relationship.

    That is an important statement, BUT this, what I call the 'pennies from heaven' model, must not lead us to:

- Getting out the scales to weigh texts for and against our position, whatever it is. Which side would the scales come down on in the case of homosexuality?

- Striving with the handful of texts which certainly speak of homosexuality (most are ambiguous), anxiously weighing one interpretation against another, e.g. putting a great deal of weight in one particular interpretation of the Hebrew verb 'yada' (to know) in the story in Genesis 19. The sexual context would suggest to me that it is being used to refer to a genital relationship, but I have already commented on what I think that story is about.

- Kicking out the Old Testament, because we find texts there that are difficult for our position, 'After all, we might say, we are the unity of the New Testament'. On the whole, the New Testament simply assumes and presents the Gospel of Christ in the context of the ethics of the Jewish Scriptures.

A complementary understanding – the dialogue between tradition and experience

We are required to complement that biblical model of revealed Torah and ask about the two sources for the theologian as we see them operating in our texts: tradition and experience. Some elements of modern historic-critical scholarship suggest a picture which complements the biblical model:

1. Much of the contents of our law codes in the Old Testament – about property, slaves, family life, those matters required in the day-to-day organization of a community – are paralleled in the other law codes of the ancient Near East. It is suggested that on the whole, what we are dealing with is the common law of the ancient Near East, of that culture and setting in which Israel grew up.

2. Then, too, if we examine codes or collections of laws in our Bible – the Book of the Covenant, the Holiness Code, the laws of Deuteronomy – scholars point to evidence of their being of different date and showing adaptation to different social, economic and cultural situations.

3. A study of the individual laws shows the different patterns of language in which they are cast and leads us to ask what settings or institutions produced such different patterns. What do I mean by patterns of language? If I am reading a modern novel and come across the taking of oaths, the questioning of witnesses, speeches for defence and prosecution, a summing up, I recognize immediately the language patterns whose setting in our culture is that of a court room.

   A more banal example is how we instantly classify the difference between a letter which begins 'Dear Joe, are you still in the land of the living ...', and one which begins 'Dear Sir, we think you would like to know ...'. We would not be likely to confuse the friend and the bank manager.

A German scholar distinguished two such law patterns, one of which he called apodeictic and the other casuistic. If we take the latter, which conditionally states a situation or case ('If so-and-so happens ...'), and then offers a judgement ('then this is how we decide ...'), we can almost hear the village elders settling the disputes between members of the community and thus building up a tradition of law decision, of the examples in Exodus, chapter 22.

The complementary model which is suggested is that of a community, historically and socially situated, learning to govern itself, building up a tradition of ethical rules and norms, as they apply the experiences and traditions of the past to the experiences, situations and problems which they encounter. The tradition offers them continuity with their past, but it is a past which they must adapt, into which they must breathe life, the life of the present which they are living.

We can give this concrete form in the legend of Moses quoted in Ginsberg, *Legends of the Bible*, p. 395, where we see the great lawgiver unable to understand what later Judaism had made of his law:

> When Moses reached heaven, he found God occupied ornamenting the letters in which the Torah was written, with little crown-like decorations, and he looked on without saying a word ... Then Moses inquired as to the significance of the crowns upon the letters and was answered: 'Hereafter there shall live a man called Akiba, son of Joseph, who will base in interpretation a gigantic mountain of Halakoth upon every dot of these letters.'
>
> Moses said to God: 'Show me the man.' God: 'Go back eighteen ranks.' Moses went where he was bidden and could hear the discussion of the teacher sitting with his disciples in the eighteenth rank, but was not able to follow these discussions, which greatly grieved him. But just then he heard the disciples questioning their master in regard to a certain subject: 'Whence dost thou know this?' And he answered: 'This is a Halakoth given to Moses on Mount Sinai' and now Moses was content.

This is a discussion of the Jewish Oral Law, by which was kept alive and fresh the written code. The Jewish Mishnah of the second century and the later Talmuds, with its atmosphere of the debating chamber, gives us an insight into this never-ending process.

Likewise, the New Testament Gospels offer us little in the way of ethical norm and guidance. They present the gospel of the Kingdom of God, their central principle is agape, or the love commandment. It is only in places that we see the ethical concerns of the community. However, in the epistles we see the authors attempting to relate the theological principles which they have been expounding to the practical decisions required to live a life of fidelity. Above all, we see that their norm is not remembered rules, the faithfully recorded rules of Jesus, but the living spirit of the Risen Lord, as they flexibly adapt their tradition to diverse situations.

Our conclusions:

We do not go to the Bible for answers.

We do not go to the Bible to find support for or against any position.

We go to the Bible as a model of the theological task: there we see a community constantly applying its traditions to new experiences, constantly reshaping that tradition in the light of new experiences.

Our experience today

This leads us to ask what is new in our experience as sexual beings. This is our starting point: Where are men and women today in our society? What fresh questions are being raised?

- By research into the origins and causes of homosexuality.

- By fresh thinking on sexuality in general e.g. the separability of sexual activity from procreation.

- Modern problems of population control and family planning.

Some biblical insights on sexuality

You are certainly more familiar than I am with the range of questions and discussions. However, we cannot simply react to such questioning. Where are the controls, which prevent us slipping into complete relativism? How do we know how to live out in fidelity, Old Testament covenant, New Testament agape?

Our control is the resources of the Christian tradition. Having spent so much time on what I considered to be a more fundamental question, our approach to the Bible, I can do no more than indicate some pointers which might help us in our task.

'Our sexuality is God's ingenious way of calling us into communion with others through our need to reach out and touch and embrace – emotionally, intellectually, physically' (J. Nelson, *Embodiment*, SPCK).

I simply present this as a neat statement from which to start. The Bible knows the darker side of that picture. We see it in story form in the gang rape of Genesis 19 and in the story of the rape of Tamar in Kings. It is also evidenced to in the biblical laws against rape, violence, etc.

The importance of man/woman sexuality is perhaps suggested in Genesis 1, where man and woman are presented as in the image of God, no matter how we interpret that phrase. This is particularly interesting in the biblical context where the subordination of woman is usually the case.

In the biblical view of the human person, body and soul are not separated; rather the person is treated as a psychosomatic unity. On the biblical view there is no way in which we can regard the physical side of our life as evil, degraded, less important. We can compare in post-biblical tradition, the effect of neo-Platonic thought, with its view of soul or spirit entrapped in a body.

A good biblical counterblast to this is the beautiful erotic poetry of the Song of Songs. However much this is seen in the tradition as symbolic of Yahweh and Israel, in origin it celebrates the very physical union of man and woman.

In the Old Testament, especially in the prophet Hosea, the man/woman relationship is used as an image of the relationship between Yahweh and Israel. In the first three chapters of that book however much scholars differ in the interpretation of details, the forgiving attitude and fidelity of the prophet to his faithless wife is that through which he conceives Yahweh's constant fidelity to Israel, no matter how often she has sinned.

The author of Ephesians works in the reverse direction. He has celebrated the reconciliation of Jew and Gentile, and presented God's plan for the reconciliation of all things in the Church which is the Body of which Christ is head. Then he looks at the community and speaks of the relationship of parents and children, master and slave, husband and wife. The relationship of Christ as head to his body, the Church, becomes the model for the relationship of love and caring between husband and wife. True it is, in that cultural epoch, spelled out in terms of the subordinate position of the woman.

The hoped for result

In the Gospels we are given a picture of Jesus – a man who did not apply inherited codes of conduct, but was free, ready to respond to many in society in a way that breaks through rigid institutional norms. At the centre there is agape, the commitment to the realization of the Kingdom. It is this commitment we are called to in all our relationships – from the most intimate to the most casual.

True, all these insights about value, commitment, fidelity, are in the biblical context part of an overriding concern for the building up and preserving of the community. The result is the affirmation of procreation as the purpose of the differentiation of the sexes ('Be fruitful and multiply ...'), the emphasis is on the woman's role as child-bearer. In the context of our society and its needs, fresh questions are being posed.

Basically, I am suggesting that to examine the Bible on the question of homosexuality is too limiting. We are required to take up the above pointers on sexuality in general, and no doubt others not mentioned, examine these biblical insights and bring them to our needs, questions and problems. In this talk I am not offering any answers, but posing a challenge, offering a programme to be carried out.

What is the hoped for result?

- *A help for the individual as he/she seeks to make judgements about how best to live in fidelity to the God relationship.* Are the values and insights on sexuality as part of God's gift being faithfully lived in the manner in which I experience and live out the sexual attraction?

- *At the level of community, a proper understanding of Galatians 3: 23–9.* It is not the doing away with distinctions – there is, for example, no ammunition for an anti-slavery movement or feminist movement here – it is rather the acceptances of differences in unity. Perhaps our modern Christian community may in practice expand Paul's text: ' ... neither Jew nor Greek, slave or freeman, male or female, *heterosexual or homosexual.* All are one in Christ.'

(Joe Mulrooney, *Gay Christian*, February 1986, pp. 23–9)

(3)

What gay Christians seek from the Church

The descriptive terms used to describe gay people tell us much about the treatment they have received from the Church and society. The word 'faggot' reminds us that in the Middle Ages gay men literally provided the fuel for the fires in which witches were burned. The word 'sodomite' characterized gay people as being under the destructive judgement of God, not only for themselves, but more terribly for any community countenancing them. Even today the word 'queer' with its hint of perversion comes easily to those who, like a recent correspondent in the press, classify gay persons with thieves, murderers and adulterers.

It is worth recalling the attitudes implicit in these descriptions, because there is still very little realization among Christians of the appalling cruelty with which gay people have been treated at the instigation of the Church. It is significant that nowhere in the recent report of the Church of England's Board of Social Responsibility, *Homosexual Relationships; a contribution to discussion*, does there appear a hint of repentance or regret for what has been done in the name of the Church and Christian morality. Nor incidentally is there any recognition of the Church's responsibility to those whom it has alienated and driven out through the actions and attitudes of its members.

However the fact that such a report could be commissioned is evidence of a greater awareness of homosexuality in our society. This has come about since the passing of the Sexual Offences Act 1967 made possible a greater openness on the part of homosexual persons by decriminalizing certain homosexual acts and so removing some of the risk of blackmail. This new awareness has led to some changes in attitude. A distinction is now made between the homosexual condition and homosexual acts. Some Christians advocate 'deliverance' from or 'healing' of the condition. Others recognize the condition as irreversible, but insist that the only course open to Christians is abstention from any sexual intercourse. In the Critical Observations contained in Part II of the Board report mentioned above, members of the Board state that 'they believe that people with a homosexual condition do have a moral choice, but consider that the right choice is abstinence rather than the genital expression of love in a homosexual relationship' (A 17).

A more liberal approach, such as that advocated in Part I of the report, allows homosexual practice to those for whom heterosexual marriage, described as the norm of human relationships, is not possible. Such partnerships can only have a 'private and experimental' character and even when displaying the marriage virtues of fidelity and permanence, 'cannot be regarded as the moral or social equivalent of marriage' (para. 168). This 'second best' view of gay partnerships has the effect of creating a double standard for clergy and laity, since the former are called to be 'first class', not 'second best', examples to their flocks.

The dehumanizing process

All these prescriptions take little or no account of what gay people are saying and asserting about their sexuality and their lifestyles. Treating them as 'a difficult but limited problem' (para. 224) or discussing the morality of homosexual practice objectively in terms of concepts and norms established for something else, effectively denies humanity to men and women attracted to or cohabiting with persons of the same sex. This dehumanizing process is as insulting and demeaning as the unpleasant words listed above. If the Church is to understand and respond to gay people, it has to be ready to listen to them much more attentively than heretofore.

What then can they be said to seek from the Church? It might be supposed that they would want *tolerance*. They might hope to be allowed to go about their business without being publicly abused and vilified. But tolerance is a dangerous virtue for a minority that is trying to say something. The British public tolerates an association of White Wizards and a Flat Earth Society. Both are seen as harmless eccentricities that can be accommodated in a culture which takes for granted scientific method and conclusions. Tolerance can silence any protest or threat to the status quo by patronizing the protester and allowing him houseroom within defined limits. Such tolerance denies that the protester has anything of value or importance to say.

It is but a short step from tolerating people on these terms to another attitude gay people might be thought to welcome, that of *acceptance*. Acceptance on the majority's terms can also be a means of rendering ineffective the criticisms of the minority. The emasculation of radical protest by its absorption into established political parties is a case in point. It is just such an acceptance of gay relationships that is proposed in Part I of the Board report, a compassionate acceptance of those 'unfortunates' who cannot manage the heterosexual norm. While for the gay person this is an improvement on being regarded as criminal or sick, it still denies validity and value to anything he or she might have to say, because he or she is accepted as the exception that proves the rule, rather than as an individual with ideas and feelings that in themselves might throw light on the human condition.

If gay people seek neither tolerance nor acceptance on these terms, perhaps they look for *justice*, that is for equal treatment before the law, whether of Church or State. The Sexual Offences Act 1967 decriminalized homosexual acts between consenting males over 21 years of age in England and Wales. Criminal sanctions remain for all those under 21, for any living in Scotland and Northern Ireland and for any serving in the Armed Forces or in the Merchant Navy. Homosexual acts between women are not subject to law. It is clear that the Campaign for Homosexual Equality still has much to do before it achieves equality before the law for gay people, to say nothing of ending the widespread discriminatory practices which they suffer in employment, housing and other areas. But as is clear from the experience of racial minorities, equality before the law is only a framework for a change in public attitudes. As long as difference equals inferiority, injustices will continue to be perpetrated. Minorities need and deserve the protection of the law, but the law of itself cannot bring about changes in attitude.

What gay people do seek is *recognition* and *respect*. They want to be recognized as human beings and, in the case of the Church, as fellow Christians, disciples of the Lord Jesus and members of His Body. They are not prepared to be treated as criminal, sick or unfortunate just because they happen to be (or have chosen to be) different. Gay Christians want to be respected on the grounds that they have an important contribution to make to the Church. There are things that the Church needs to hear, which gay people by virtue of their experience are able to offer. The Church has in its gay members a resource with which to tackle some of the urgent pastoral and missionary tasks facing it, but which, blinded by a long history of prejudice born of fear and ignorance, it has failed to utilize.

Reassessing Christian teaching

First among these tasks is the reassessment of traditional teaching on human sexuality in the light of new insights and knowledge. Homosexuality raises in an acute form questions about the adequacy of teaching that has as yet taken little account of research in recent decades in the areas of psychology, sociology and sexology. We are a generation away from Kinsey's seminal work but have hardly begun to explore its implications in matters of moral concern such as the choosing of sexual preference, change in sexual preference in the course of a lifetime, the degree of social conditioning that is appropriate in allowing a proper choice and all the related questions of the nature of sex education given to young people. At the same time, the Church's norm for human relationships, that is lifelong, exclusive union in marriage, is not standing up well to the new situation produced by the changing role of women in our society, the consequent fluidity of gender roles and the almost complete disappearance of the extended family as a social, moral and financial support system. There may be sound theological reasons for setting up marriage as the ideal of human relationships, but the high expectations with which people enter marriage these days, encouraged by the Church's teaching and the 'happily ever after' aspect of consumer advertising put alongside the divorce rate, suggest that other forms of human relating need to be explored and assessed as ways of witnessing to and expressing the Gospel of sacrificial love.

Second, there needs to be considered the basis of moral judgements, whether this is to be an objective consideration of particular acts, or whether it should be more personalist and consequently give more weight to subjective criteria. Traditional moral theology judges the goodness or badness of an act in accordance with revealed criteria and allows the circumstances and agents as ameliorating factors. Developments in the human sciences and the realization that the rightness and wrongness of particular acts may be the product of cultural conditioning rather than the inherent nature of things, has to some extent undermined the power of authority, whether placed in the Bible or in the teaching office of the Church. Without suggesting complete relativity, it is fair to ask whether the time has not come to give to intentions and personal motivations an equal place in the making of moral judgements to those objective criteria which declare a particular action right or wrong. It is time we moved away from the kind of statement that declares all homosexual acts to be intrinsically disordered but that culpability for them can be graded on a 1–100 scale.

Third, and consequently, there is the question of where moral authority does lie. In the light of personalist ethics and historical criticism what is the proper function of the Bible and the Church's tradition? How is each to be interpreted? What is the place of law and what are the implications of the Gospel in the contemporary understanding of human sexuality?

These are all questions with which gay Christians have to struggle as they seek to relate their faith to their sexuality and try through self-acceptance to live with integrity. They are questions which many in the Church appear not to be asking at all, but which are as critical in the latter part of the twentieth century with the development of the human sciences, as were the questions raised by the natural sciences in the nineteenth century.

The importance of being different

Almost more important for the Church than these questions are the experience and inside knowledge gay Christians have of what it is like to be a deviant and persecuted minority. With this they have something very precious to offer. If it is nothing else, the Church should be the agency that educates the world in the importance of being different. Too often Christian doctrine has been allowed to become an ideology and membership of the Body of Christ an imprisonment in a totalitarian system. Where, as in the West, the Church has become the vehicle of folk religion and the parent and partner of secular culture, it needs help to rediscover the pain and importance of standing over against received truths, standards and norms. As one who is inevitably part of a deviant minority, the gay Christian is well placed to offer this help. In order to live with integrity, he or she has had to 'come out'. This process means coming to terms with one's sexual preference. There are usually three stages. First one has to accept oneself as one is, overcoming the self-hatred and fear which so much 'Christian' teaching is designed to induce in homosexual people. It involves a change from essentially negative learned attitudes to a positive self-acceptance that integrates one's sexuality into one's whole personality. Second one has to test the reality of this self-acceptance by disclosing the fact of one's sexual preference to one's immediate circle of family and friends, that is to those people who might be expected to continue in relationship, even with a 'queer'. The third stage is a readiness to admit one's sexual preference to all and sundry, not necessarily making an issue of it, but being prepared to stand up and be counted and to give reasons for one's stand.

Those who have worked through this process, who have suffered the difficulties and anguish it imposes, yet who have succeeded in 'coming out', can help Christians trying to witness to their faith in an unsympathetic or hostile environment. The call to witness to their faith begins in Christians with a new perspective on their situation. The realization of the love of God in Jesus Christ and the assurance of salvation mirrors the gay person's realization that his or her sexuality is given, is good and is to be celebrated. In each case the new attitude has to be tested, first in a safe context, then in the wider world. In both cases it will involve being different, standing over against many of the accepted truths and values of society, acting as a critical question mark on received opinions. As a Christian does this, so he or she becomes effective light and salt and leaven in the world. So too a gay Christian seeks to be recognized and respected in the Church, not as a deviant to be neutralized for the general convenience but as a sign that points to and helps to answer the questions which others prefer to ignore. The art of being glad and proud to be different is one which gay people have had to cultivate. The Church needs to re-learn it.

(Kennedy Thom, What Gay Christians Seek from the Church
(London: LGCM), 1980)

———— ◆ ————

EIGHT

Towards a new spirituality

Because of the negativity of past ecclesiastical tradition, LGCM members have inherited few signposts to guide them in working out an ethic and spirituality of gay and lesbian relationships. In the first of these extracts Andrew Shackleton of LGCM's Evangelical caucus reflects upon the form that an appropriate sexual ethic might take. In the second the late Simon Bailey explores what are the distinguishing features of a gay spiritual praxis.

(1)

Characteristics of a Christian relationship

What should characterize a gay relationship between two Christians? Because traditional Christian teaching has excluded gay relationships *per se*, we are to a certain extent entering new and uncharted territory. Given that we accept the validity of gay sexuality, it would be all too easy for gay people simply to take the received Christian norm of lifelong monogamy and apply it to our own relationships.

This approach is neither positive nor helpful for several reasons. First, it merely echoes the exclusiveness of the traditional approach, whereby a certain privileged group who achieve this ideal can enjoy the Church's approval to the exclusion of all those who for one reason or another cannot. Second, it is in conflict with reality, for such a norm is not achievable within a society which remains more or less hostile to the idea of gay relationships. We should also note that a large number of heterosexual Christians deviate from the norm in many respects, and that the norm itself is continually, if sometimes reluctantly, being adjusted as attitudes change. Third, and most importantly, it is an attitude which blindly accepts the norm without considering its validity from a Christian point of view.

Gay people are in some ways disadvantaged in the field of sexual relationships, whether through prejudice, false guilt or merely because we are a minority. But we also have a number of advantages. We are in many ways freer of the sexual stereotypes which tend to be imposed on heterosexual unions. For though it is often easier to follow a pre-set norm, this can be stifling where, for one reason or another, it simply does not fit. Looking at the situation from its positive aspect, it is surely good that we, as gay Christians, are forced to reconsider the Christian bases for our relationships, and to work them out afresh in practice.

This is what I shall attempt to do here, though a short article can do little more than scratch the surface. It inevitably poses more questions than it answers in a field which is as wide-ranging as it is relatively unexplored, and which must ultimately embrace all of sexuality.

The Bible itself forms a good starting point, in that it provides a different perspective. What, for example, does the Bible say about sex? Frankly, not very much. The obsession with sex, which is characteristic both (negatively) of 'Victorian' morality and (positively) of the present so-called permissive age (where anyone who *is* anybody *has* to have sex!), is not characteristic of the biblical period.

In the New Testament, Paul is unremarkable in following the conventions of his own society. Christ himself never talked about sex as such. However, he made a point of welcoming those outcast by society for sexual reasons, namely prostitutes. Also, he talked a lot about love, of which more anon. The general tenor of the New Testament writings suggests that Christians should be less concerned about whether or not sex is OK (and if so, when) and more interested in the *quality of the relationships* in which sex may or may not occur.

What then are the essential qualities of a Christian relationship? The essence of the Christian faith as epitomized in Christ is that love is ultimately more important than rules or laws. If we were to love perfectly, then we would always do the right thing by God and each other. We fail in this through our failure to love. None of us is able to love perfectly, but perfect love is a standard in the light of which, with sensitivity and an open mind, we should measure our lives and actions. It would be far easier to follow set rules. These are not necessarily invalid; rather, the love which God has demonstrated in Christ is above and beyond laws. Christian love is a much misunderstood concept. It is neither sexless nor merely sentimental. It should go much deeper than this, and can involve both pain and sacrifice. But it does not involve self-denigration, as so many Christians would have us believe. Indeed, we cannot love others unless we also love ourselves.

Stability and commitment are essential ingredients. The deep affection which forms the basis of a long-term relationship must be given time and space in which to grow. Two people must share more than mutual physical attraction for the relationship to last beyond the troughs through which it must inevitably pass. The need for companionship is as much a gift of God as is the sexual drive. If the two can be combined, this may be for most of us the best way. Where a person is single, other sources of personal stability are needed. Maybe celibacy, or singleness, not necessarily celibate, in which our needs for companionship are sublimated in our service to some other cause, such as a caring profession, can fulfil this role.

Stability in a relationship requires faithfulness, and the mutual trust which this makes possible. Faithfulness is not necessarily synonymous with sexual monogamy. A husband who treats his wife as a housekeeper and exclusive sex-partner, but spends all the rest of his time elsewhere, could hardly be considered faithful in the truest sense of the word. On the other hand, an 'open' relationship, in which other sex-partners are accepted, can also be a faithful one. Indeed, *more* faith and trust may be required to sustain it.

Honesty is if anything even more essential in a relationship which is not rule-based but love-based. Bad feelings such as jealousy and anger must be identified and shared before they can be dealt with and forgiven. More casual relationships can be equally hurtful where dishonesty is present. In a hostile society, we can be dishonest for the best of motives, but we must recognize that this can hurt both ourselves and those we love. However, complete honesty is only possible where there is forgiveness for all the mistakes which must inevitably occur.

It is also important to allow those we love to have a life apart from ourselves. Even monogamous partners must have other friendships which only the most possessive of lovers would interfere with. This is part of the space which every individual needs in order to grow. On the other hand, the more a couple can share, the more their lives will grow together.

The discussion would not be complete without mention of the fact that all relationships come to an end, whether through death or separation. Christians have been too selective in the endings they have accepted as valid candidates for support. Less conventional endings call for *more* rather than less help from Christians. The failure of a relationship must be acknowledged, but this does not invalidate the importance of the relationship, neither should it preclude the possibility of finding another.

The question we should be asking is not 'What is right according to the rules of Christian morality?', but rather 'What is right in the light of the love which God has demonstrated in Christ?' A Christian ethic for relationships should not be *prescriptive*, determining a specific norm. Neither should it be merely *descriptive*, accepting uncritically the way things are. It should be *realistically positive*, accepting what we are given, but seeking the best that we can become.

(Andrew Shackleton, 'Characteristics of a Christian Relationship',
Gay Christian, November 1983, pp. 8–9)

(2)

Gay spirituality

Do gay people pray differently? *Can* they pray differently? *Should* they pray differently? We may like to keep the different parts of our lives, our personalities, as separate as possible but we are part of a generation that has begun to learn – to relearn – that the human being does not divide up easily: all sorts of bits of us affect all sorts of other bits, the compartments are anything but watertight. Moreover we are post-Freudians who know that everything is sex, at least to some extent anyway – even if sex is not everything. We who have allowed ourselves, rightly or wrongly, to be defined by our sexual preferences are clearly acknowledging in some way that this is at least a major factor in our lives and it *does* spread into every other little bit of our personalities. So it does affect the way we pray, the way we turn to God, the way we live in the spirit. This should not upset us but inspire us, excite us, because here somehow we are at a frontier – not many other people are going to join us here: this is a kind of pioneering prayer. We shall return to that.

I first began to think about all this when I was introduced to the work people have begun to do on the spirituality of women; one book especially springs to mind: *Walking on the Water* (ed. Lo Garcia and Sara Maitland, Virago). Women can pray differently, pray outside the straitjacket of conventional spirituality, pray according to themselves:

and it occurred to me to ask, could this apply to gay people too? Could they also be outside the convention, different? There seem to me to be many parallels between the women's movement and the gay one; the main difference being the gay one is a few hundred years behind the women's one. The Church began to break down the race barrier at the Council of Jerusalem recorded in the Acts of the Apostles. This process was carried further by the abolition of slavery rather a long time later. We *are* slowly drawing nearer to the breaking down of the *gender* barrier as women steadily make their way into the Church. As is pointed out in the present issue of the MOW magazine *Chrysalis*, *two* categories of people are now excluded from the priesthood of the Church of England – women and active gays. I believe the women will not be too long before they are accepted – the *sexuality* barrier will be much longer in coming down. In the meantime *we* have the hard task of thinking what cannot be thought and praying what cannot be prayed – not so much because it is thought to be horribly wrong, though it is, but simply because we have none of us ever been allowed to think like this – we are pioneering outside of the very minds – and spirits – our culture has given us. Yet it is here in us waiting for us to find the words. St Bernard of Clairvaux said: 'Everyone has to drink from his own well.' (He had not heard of inclusive language ...) We have to turn to *this* well in us and search its depths: there is not in any case any other way of praying than drinking from your own well – so it is this or no real praying.

This well – I say again – is not simply about 'sex', sex is not everything, we must go on refusing to be defined *merely* by that: we are whole people too; and at the same time we go on refusing to pretend it is not there, will go away, is not important – it *is* important, but it is not all there is: that is all.

What happens is that what *is* important but not everything marks us out devastatingly clearly in a world that is so unbelievably 'normal', 'conventional' and 'straight' in all the worst senses of those words. In the middle of such frantic insecurity we are pushed firmly out of line: what was 'important but not everything' now begins to be our definition. We are on the edge, we experience oppression. This then becomes the first characteristic of gay spirituality, gay prayer: we join the ranks of the oppressed – the Jews, the poor, the handicapped, blacks, women. It is a liberation spirituality. (Even if some of the other oppressed do not actually want us with them – like some of the Jews in Nazi concentration camps who complained there were too many pink triangles in their particular area.) The quotation from St Bernard became the title of a book by Gustavo Gutierrez, *We drink from our own wells* (SCM): a book about liberation spirituality in Latin America, praying people in oppression. Like them we discover in oppression solidarity, a strong sense of common humanity, common prayer. We never pray alone, being pushed out of the world's line leads us into a place together, not so that we can huddle there separately from everyone else, but precisely so that we can discover the solidarity of *all* the oppressed and actually also so that we can discover in this clearer, sharper place what it is by our prayer we have to give back as a distinctive gift to the entire human community – however unwilling it is to receive it at the moment.

One part of that returning gift will be this strong sense of standing together in prayer – you never pray alone: to the individualistic, atomized, nuclear-family-orientated, property-clutching culture of our world we are saying: 'Though we are in this mess with you we are discovering – because you forced us to – that there is no such thing as private prayer, no such thing as personal salvation, we are in this together – we need each other, we pray only together, you never pray alone. We even need you – and worse, you even need us. You cannot pray without us. That is what we and our oppressed brothers and sisters have to give you.'

The other part of the returning gift we might learn in our prayer, if we really do confront that well, is in suffering. To be oppressed is to suffer, to pray out of oppression is to make the suffering positive and that means admitting it. The more you do about it the more you will suffer. Is it *real* suffering? To be rejected *is* to suffer. It is an absolutely classic Christian stance, to make the suffering positive, thus to suffer more but thus to turn the rejection into a gift, a returning gift. That is simply Jesus. If we are going to pray like this we shall have to get our arms and our praying hearts around AIDS, around its huge burden of accompanying fear – we will find ourselves on an unerringly 'correct' Christian route because it will be the way of the cross.

Yet none of this can make us self-righteous because gay people looking into the well of their own spirit will find what all other oppressed people find, that we are part of the mess. It is called 'original sin'. I do not understand people who say they do not believe that people are evil. The *essence* may be good, may even be restorable, but it is unbelievably twisted in all of us. 'The desires of the heart are as crooked as corkscrews' said W. H. Auden. To be human is to hurt – and that means in both senses, we hurt, feel permanently sore, ache inside and we take it out on others, hurt them. We all do it. This too has to inform our prayers. If you know much about gay people and gay relationships you will know how much this is true there. I do not believe it is worse than for straight people – the difference is they have frameworks and patterns and traditions, customs and structures: gay people do not, we are having to make our own.

So there is a proper ambiguity here, informing prayer, about sex itself – we *are* affirming gay sex, glad that it too can be part of gay prayer but like all the rest of sex it is not an unadulterated gift of God. There is something wounded about *all* sexuality, not evil of course and yet not perfect either. Sex is always exploration towards God, not the experience of God: so we go on wounding each other in it, wounding ourselves, longing to heal. And so we also sometimes glimpse the glory.

The sense of 'being out of line' leads directly to what is perhaps the second major characteristic of any gay spirituality there might be. That is self-awareness and self-knowledge. Of course it is entirely possible to be gay and resist all self-knowledge: people stay on the surface, do not want to know about gay rights and Section 28 and General Synod or about themselves, but coming to terms with being different must include some degree of self-awareness, some potential at least for self-knowledge and reflection. This may be merely the narcissism that homosexuality is frequently accused of: it was said of nineteenth century German theologians searching for the historical Jesus that they gazed deep into the well of truth and saw there the reflection of their own faces. But it *is* possible to gaze below the surface of this inner well and search for the bottom, the depths.

One thing this self-awareness seems to mean for many gay people is a deeper, stronger consciousness of the body (and indeed sex as part of the body). Women too in their prayer are bringing back the earth and the rootedness of our bodies in it, in matter, in the physical, the touchable. Our bodies pray too, not just our 'souls' so-called, God made it all after all. This sense of self-aware body leads also to a sense of solidarity with all creation. I am part of the continuity of the universe, just a little bit and yet with a bit to do as well – part of the whole and not alone; a body and a range of feelings, a set of emotions, a hurt and a happy thing, something like a unity – but also capable of being fragments that I need to admit to in prayer as well. Admitting the earth, the body, the bits seems to be part of an honesty that such earthiness invites. It's an earthiness the rest of the earth is crying out for in its limitedness to the 'soul alone'. So here is another gift, with others, we can return to the prayers of the earth.

But beyond the body, with it and on it, is the whole sense in this stronger potential for self-awareness of 'being different'. To accept that you are different from what most are or want to be is to set out as a pilgrim pioneer. The territory has not been explored, there are no landmarks, milestones, not even any oases – not marked anyway, only unexpected ones: you are to be a pioneer on a lonely journey. The journey inwards. Here we become in Jim Cotter's phrase 'God's spies' – discovering new territory, but discovering it once again in order to make a returning gift. There's a time for going back on this journey bearing presents – perhaps the pearl of great price – for those who have not yet left, did not know there was a journey to be made.

It is a lonely journey but again not individualistic. You are still never alone. And again the result of the journey is to discover not only what you share within with all gay people, deep in the heart, but also what you share with all people everywhere of every kind. Another gift to come back with.

And here again we come to the last and maybe the great character-istic of gay spirituality. The other two are not the *direct* result of being gay but more of being oppressed: a sense of being out of line but in solidarity is part of the liberation spirit of the downtrodden and marginalized; and a sense of greater self-awareness and knowledge is the result of that or of other factors not specifically related to homo-sexuality. But one specific consequence of being gay that changes the way we pray is that we threaten the institution of the family, and thank God for that! Why else do they get so worried about 'pretended family relations'? To be gay and to make relationships has to mean doing something other than the traditional family: it is properly subversive. It has to be shown that there *are* other ways of living than in family, there are other equal, possibly greater, relationships. We are pioneering again and so we will stumble where there are no paths, but the world needs to be given back the gift of human relationships wider and richer and more infinitely varied than 'the family' is able to be. One (straight, married, father) expert I heard speak recently on homosexuality said that gay relationships could not achieve the top notch of human relationships because they could not be procreative, they did not have that 'commitment to the future'. There lurks the demon of indi-vidualism again, the enemy of the sense of the *Body* of Christ. Do the children who are created 'belong' to their parents? – surely under God children belong to all of us: those of us who will not actually assist in the conception of children are still committed to the future through children – all children. Who can own a child? Jesus said 'You have one father and he is in heaven.' If we could escape from the nuclear family, shake up these tired institutions we could give so much to each other in a mutuality of sexualities – and straight people might actually rejoice at what gay people can give to their children.

But in our prayer there is something even more distinctive gay people are bringing. It is in the possibility of friendship. Here we can, it seems to me, more easily than the rest of the world inherit the great tradition of the Celtic *anam-chara* or Soul Friend, the Spiritual Friendship of St Aelred, the friendship that Jesus speaks of in St John's gospel.

This is the way of discovering in the variety and richness of different un-institutionalized friendships a complex of ways into God. To affirm the difference and the attractive otherness of someone else is another way of praying, celebrating the gifts of God: to affirm someone else is itself an act of prayer. Gay prayer could stretch here – freed from the rigid structures of the family – from the intimate prayer of making love to a partner to the freedom of friendships with the opposite sex and to the possibilities of the relaxed intimate affection of friendship without a partnership. And it can all be ways of praying – exploration, unbeaten tracks, unapproached horizons.

St Aelred glories in this in the rich, gentle and loving celebration of such relationships in his book *Spiritual Friendship* (Cistercian Publications). Listen to Aelred writing at about 1150:

Speaking of a friend: 'Was it not a foretaste of blessedness thus to be loved and to love; thus to help and thus to be helped; and in this way from the sweetness of fraternal charity to wing one's flight aloft to that more sublime splendour of divine love, and by the ladder of charity now to mount to the embrace of Christ himself; and again to descend to the love of neighbour, there pleasantly to rest?' (p. 129, sec. 127). 'Added to all this there is prayer for one another, which, coming from a friend, is the more efficacious in proportion as it is more lovingly sent to God, with tears which either fear excites or affection awakens or sorrow evokes' (p. 131, sec. 133).

'What does all this add up to? Shall I say of friendship what John, the friend of Jesus, says of charity: "God is friendship"?' (p. 65, sec. 69).

'Friendship is a stage bordering upon that perfection which consists in the love and knowledge of God, so that a man from being a friend of his fellow man [sic] becomes the friend of God, according to the words of the Saviour in the gospel: "I will not now call you servants, but my friends"' (p. 73, sec. 14).

And that brings us securely back to Jesus and the gospel and the heart of our spirituality and our prayer – and there it is: friends, I call you. Your prayer is to be the prayer of my friends, your spirit is to be the spirit of strong and deep and trusting friendship – free from the constraints of flesh and blood, of power and dominion, just friends: freely given and received relationships of every kind, with everyone, in every place. There, there is the real possibility of real freedoms, relaxed spirits with deep connections springing from wells of our own that we have carefully, honestly and generously begun to fathom.

(Simon Bailey, 'Gay Spirituality', address to
Leeds LGCM meeting, 1988)

PART III

Essays

———— ◆ ————

Flies in the elephant's nose: a lesbian theologian reflects on the future of LGCM

Elizabeth Stuart

Dr Elizabeth Stuart is Professor of Christian Theology at King Alfred University College, Winchester, UK. Her recent publications include *Just Good Friends: Towards a Lesbian and Gay Theology of Relationships* (London: Mowbray, 1995) and the co-authored volume *People of Passion: What the Churches Teach about Sex* (London: Mowbray, 1997).

Claiming an equal voice

I stand within LGCM as a resident alien. Of all the many lesbian and gay organizations I support and have some involvement with, LGCM is the one in which I feel most at home. Its uncompromising affirmation of the goodness of sexuality, its ecumenical breadth, its support for the ordination of women and its awareness of the need to combine the pastoral and the political as two sides of the same coin of liberation, are unique within the context of lesbian and gay mixed-gender Christian groups in Britain, and all connect with different parts and concerns of myself. Being white and middle-class also places me within the majority of LGCM members. Yet being a lesbian, feminist and Roman Catholic from a non-metropolitan area simultaneously yanks me away from the centre of the movement. Just like a resident alien I choose to be in LGCM because it is there that I feel most at home, but I often experience cultural dissonance – language, action, assumptions remind me that LGCM is still predominantly Anglican, gay and male.

It is from the perspective of a resident alien that I want to reflect theologically upon the future of LGCM by taking up some of the issues from LGCM's past. In so doing I do not wish to claim a privileged voice within the movement, but as a lesbian, woman and a Roman Catholic

I claim an equal voice. I want to make this distinction clear because I think it is relevant not just to the internal politics of this particular movement but also to the interaction between self-affirming lesbian, gay and bisexual persons and the rock face of the Churches. The rhetoric of equality and inclusiveness is often used within liberation movements of all types and within the Churches unconsciously to retain the *status quo*. There is within the governing structures of LGCM a genuine desire I am sure to empower women and members of non-Anglican Churches but by organizing these groups into a cluster of caucuses the exact opposite happens, for the centre where the power, wealth and primary access to the movement remains is identified with white Anglican London-based men. The rhetoric of giving caucuses and local groups autonomy actually allows those at the centre of the movement to ignore the concerns of these groupings. A different strategy on a similar theme is one now adopted by almost every mainstream Christian denomination in Britain and the USA. This is the strategy of 'listening to lesbian and gay people'. One of LGCM's greatest triumphs in the last 20 years has been its success in injecting the voice of lesbian and gay people into the Christian debates on sexuality. Sometimes it can seem that Church leaders of all hues and members of report committees are falling over one another to meet lesbian and gay people and listen to their stories. At one level it can do nothing but good to confront these people with the reality of our lives, but at another level it is a system of exclusion. As Gary David Comstock and Mary Hunt have both noted with reference to gay and lesbian theologians in the academy, we are tolerated only as houseguests or houseservants brought in on a temporary basis to provide information or do a job, where we might be treated very well (or not well at all) but are then very politely shown the door whilst the residents get on with the job of deciding what weight to put on our experience.[1]

We are not treated as part of 'the family' even whilst the rhetoric assures us that we are. We are not given a voice, we are given a sound bite. Or to borrow some imagery from the black lesbian socialist Linda Bellos, they 'privilege our experience' by putting us on a pedestal, taking a brief look and then get stiff necks and give up, leaving us there.[2] To claim an equal voice is not to claim a privileged voice but to claim a place at the centre, to claim what is ours by virtue of our baptism, a central place and voice in the Kingdom of God.[3] Other voices are no less or more valid than our own. The problem is that in the past certain voices have claimed to be and structures have emerged to guard that claim. It could well be that the first step to realizing equality of voice is for those who up to now have been privileged to choose temporary voluntary silence in order that the voices of the silenced might have space to grow, expand and be heard. We need what Nancy L. Eiesland in her ground-breaking liberatory theology of disability has called a 'theology of access'.[4] Those at the centre need access to the 'social-symbolic' lives of those at the edge and those at the edge need to gain access to the social-symbolic life of the centre if the Church is to be the inclusive community it claims to be. Silence has a venerable history in the Christian tradition as a mode of revelation. But it has to be open, willing, attentive, warm silence. In the silence of resentment you can only hear your own resentment. The willingness to go silent is perhaps the greatest sign and sacrament that those in privileged positions of power can give to those whom they claim they want to include. This is, of course, a very different kind of silence from the one many Church leaders are now trying to impose on this issue for being 'divisive' and causing too much pain. Although this is often said to be in the best interests of lesbians and gay men, they are never actually consulted. It is only when the stage of attentive silence has been reached and occupied for sufficient time that true dialogue between equal partners can begin. None of us at this stage can predict what the outcome of that dialogue might be. So in this essay I speak with a distinctive voice, making no claims for it except the claim of equality within LGCM and within the Church.

'I want to walk like you, talk like you ... ?'

For the past 20 years LGCM has nobly campaigned for the voice of lesbian and gay people to be heard in the Christian communities and within the past five years we have seen that campaign bear fruit in dialogue with bishops and high-ranking officials of a number of denominations. Leaving aside for a moment the issue of the latter's motive and the much more thorny problem which arises out of the fact that in large part LGCM has attained 'respectable' status as a result of the activities of the direct-action group OutRage!, in contrast to which it has been labelled a 'good gay' group, LGCM will obviously have to reflect very hard in the next few years on what it wants to say with its voice. What is it that we want? At the present moment there is no consensus in the lesbian and gay Christian community. A substantial number of lesbian and gay Christians seek a place at the Church table. They want to be able to be open about their sexuality without negative consequences, they want their relationships to be blessed by the

Church, perhaps even recognized as marriages, they want equality of opportunity within the Church including ordination. This is a radical enough agenda, as the strength of resistance to it demonstrates, but from a lesbian feminist perspective it is problematic. First such an approach concedes virtually all power to what we might call hetero-Church, those who equate heterosexuality with Christian normativity, and place us in the position of beggars. Even though she is these days hailed as a great feminist heroine there is something deeply disturbing about the way in which the Syrophoenician woman in Mark 7 accepts Jesus' designation of the Gentiles as dogs and uses it to argue against his refusal to heal her daughter. Of course it is possible to interpret her words as ironic and subversive (after all, her wish is granted) but the argument is still won on the basis of Israelite normativity. This is a far cry from the glorious liberty of the children of God envisaged by Paul, in which no one's experience is normative (Galatians 3: 28) but all is taken up into the Christ-event.

Those who seek a place at the table often do so on the basis that homosexual people are really just like heterosexual people with one minor difference. The gay Roman Catholic theologian Richard Cleaver regards this line of argument as a short cut to liberation, and reminds us that according to the biblical narrative when the Israelites left slavery in Egypt they were not guided along the quickest route to the promised land, on the contrary they were taken the longest route possible.[5] He, like most openly gay male theologians these days, and all lesbian feminist theologians, believes that such short cuts to liberation do not in fact lead to liberation at all but to 'places of safety in Egypt'. Cleaver illustrates this with reference to the tendency to collapse gay and lesbian liberation into commerce. We equate freedom with gay bars, lesbian restaurants, lesbian and gay neighbourhoods, because this is what capitalism tells us is freedom. We thus try to bribe ourselves into a system which was not only built upon our backs and exclusion but which perpetuates oppression by dividing rich (usually male and white) gay against poor (usually black and female) gay and indeed all who are poor, therefore scuppering any chance of solidarity among marginalized peoples. It also ultimately offers no safety at all. As Cleaver notes, ghettos are easy to locate and destroy when a sacrifice is needed. Similarly I would argue it is ultimately futile to simply seek a place at the table of hetero-Church, since very little that rests upon it can be nourishing for us.

The embracing of the ideal of marriage is a clear case in point. The theology and structures of Christian marriage, from its Pauline contextualization in the institution of slavery to the modern attempts

to construct it within the Jungian concept of male/female complementarity, have been built upon gender inequality and caused untold
suffering to men and more particularly women by locking them into
hierarchical roles. This is not to say, of course, that couples cannot resist
and transcend these roles but no one should underestimate the
difficulty of doing so. Indeed as someone who has been in a lesbian
partnership for 15 years I can testify to the difficulty of resisting falling
into these roles even outside of marriage and heterosexuality. Since a
large part of the threat that lesbian and gay people pose to Church and
society is their subversion of 'natural' gender roles, it seems odd that
we should desire to be part of an institution which still enshrines those
roles and it is even odder when one considers the fact that heterosexual
people, particularly women, are abandoning the institution in droves.
It has often been said that the only people who hold marriage in any
esteem now are gay people who desperately want to be incorporated
into it. I think this is a somewhat skewed observation – what we
primarily want is legal recognition and protection of our relationships,
which is not quite the same as wanting to buy into the whole marriage
package and/or theology, although some do. It would be oversimplistic
to state that opinion on this issue is divided by gender – gay men being
happier to see lesbian and gay relationships incorporated into the
institution of marriage than lesbians – although there is some truth in
that generalization. Much more significant to my mind is the fact that
the most outspoken advocates of incorporation are heterosexual men.[6]
Although their concern springs from the best possible of motives, what
these men cannot even begin to contemplate is that marriage as it has
evolved may have little or nothing to do with the gospel and may
indeed be anti-gospel. They have swallowed the identification of
Christianity with heteropatriarchy. It is extremely difficult for heterosexual men to see the forces of heteropatriarchy at work because those
forces give them power and privilege, just as it is virtually impossible
for me as a white woman to be fully aware of the forces of racism which
operate around me. I need black people to point them out to me.

It is not always easy for those who are marginalized themselves to
detect forces of oppression. Our eyes have been trained to focus on
Christianity in such a way as gospel, patriarchy, heterosexism, sexism
and racism merge into one package. We are led to believe that we
cannot remove one element without destroying the whole picture.
Perhaps the further away from the centre of the picture that you are
the clearer the picture becomes. Heterosexual men have the best seats
at the table of the Church, they are closest to the picture; gay men

simply by virtue of being men (albeit subversive men) are also often quite close to the table, often literally in the role of servant. As Cleaver points out, if all the gay men bailed out of the Churches tomorrow the Churches would lose innumerable liturgical specialists – readers, altar servers, choir members, organists and of course priests would be gone.[7] Lesbians on the other hand are generally much further away from the table and therefore have a different view of what constitutes the picture that is presented as Christianity. We notice in a particular way the clash between forms and colours, the basic discordance between an increasing identification of Christianity with marriage and family life and the radical subversion of family life.[8]

One of LGCM's most urgent tasks as it moves into its third decade is to be prepared to be a great deal more suspicious of the dominant constructions of Christianity than it has been up to now. Christian feminism has embarked upon the mammoth task of exposing the patriarchal construction of Christian doctrine and redeeming and reworking it to reflect women's experience. Similarly gay and lesbian people must become conscious of the *hetero*patriarchal assumptions at the root of so much Christian thinking and practice and remould it. To do this, heteropatriarchy and heterosexism must be named as sin. This is a much bigger and bolder step than naming homophobia as sinful. Homophobia is the irrational fear and demonization of gay and lesbian persons. Church leaders fall over one another these days to condemn homophobia, but the fact that these condemnations do not result in demonstrations of solidarity with lesbian and gay people against attacks upon their persons or liberty should alert us to the fact that homophobia is just a symptom. The key problem is the assumption of heterosexual normativity and its equation with the essence of Christianity. It is reasonably safe, even respectable in some Church circles these days, to take the line that 'homosexuals' are 'just like' heterosexuals really and therefore do not constitute any real threat to the Christian faith or society or the family. I believe that the greatest temptation lesbian and gay Christians face is to try to bribe our way into a short-cut liberation by accepting heterosexual normativity and endeavouring to conform ourselves to it. There are several reasons for this: first, such a tactic necessarily involves disassociating ourselves from the 'non-respectable' gays and lesbians, those who cannot or will not conform – the camp, the butch, the 'promiscuous', the transsexual. Not only does this approach grate against the gospel witness, that it is amongst the least respectable that Christ and the Kingdom are to be found, but it also flies in the face of our own pain.

LGCM supported the ordination of women in the Church of England because it came to see that the issue of the construction of gender lay beneath both struggles, but the compliment was not returned. Although some individual supporters of women's ordination were also outspoken in their support of lesbian and gay people, the movement as a whole would not make common cause. As a tactic to achieve the immediate aim of the ordination of women it undoubtedly worked but whether the cost in terms of a radical analysis of the interaction of gender and sexuality and Christianity was worth it has yet to be established. I am still haunted by a story I heard as a child of a woman languishing in hell, an angel reviewing her life finds that she committed one kindly act in her life, offering a leek to a starving person. So the angel takes the leek and reaches down into the depth of hell, calling upon the woman to grab hold of it. She does so and is being pulled out of hell when others in hell notice and grab on to her legs in order to be lifted out too. Fearing that the leek will not stand the weight the woman kicks the others away but as she does so the leek breaks and she falls back into hell. Kicking others away in order to gain respectability will not ultimately save us. As both the Hebrew and Christian Scriptures testify, salvation is primarily a communal event, a choosing to be part of a community, which in essence involves identification and solidarity with the non-respectable for the community is built upon a disillusionment with worldly notions and structures of power and the recognition of ultimate and complete dependence upon God.

The second danger of getting trapped into the 'just like you' line of argument is that we get drawn into essentialist understandings of sexuality, in which homosexuality is regarded as a 'natural', perhaps even genetic, variation to the heterosexual 'natural' norm. If we adopt this line then not only do we concede normativity to heterosexuality, forever placing ourselves at the mercy of the tolerance of heterosexuals, but a mockery is made of the gospel notion of redemption and rebirth. If we are naturally and innately consigned to certain roles then there is simply no hope for the Christian vision of equality, mutuality and community. Men and women, gay and straight, white and black will never be able to escape structured inequality.

Third, to buy into heterosexual normativity may be to betray a prophetic vocation to expose the construction of heterosexuality. As Michael Vasey has demonstrated, the emergence of the gay identity from the eighteenth century onwards is in reaction to the construction of heterosexuality, particularly male heterosexuality, characterized as it is by almost paranoid individualism, competition and aggression, which collides with the gospel ethic of friendship, mutuality, strength in love and community.[9] Lesbian and gay people have a prophetic role to proclaim liberty to millions of captives, in the good news that there is something better than heterosexuality (and the homosexuality that is constructed in reaction to it) over the rainbow. We are a people of process, of clay which can be moulded differently when soaked with life-giving water. With Jesus we can proclaim that there is no marriage or family life in heaven (as it was structured in his day and in ours) and therefore it is possible to begin building something different now.

The one thing that most heterosexuals have difficulty in grasping is that heterosexuality is constructed and therefore changeable. The Temple staff at Jerusalem could not have begun to comprehend that the Temple system was humanly constructed and served actually to hamper rather than promote God's purpose, and it took a movement from the edges of Judaism, involving Galileans whose mixed racial background made them outsiders within their own faith, to expose this fact and to pose an alternative. So lesbian and gay Christians need to consider the possibility, that however uncomfortable it might be, the place where they find themselves may be a prophetic place from which to observe the destructiveness and sinfulness of so many of the structures that have become identified with Christian life. If we are perceived by our most vicious opponents as potential destroyers of 'the family' then perhaps this is an accusation we should accept and embrace as a gospel imperative.

Lesbian and gay theologians are only just beginning to question the Christian normativity of monogamy in sexual relations. This is a question that causes even deeper division within lesbian and gay Christian communities than that of marriage. Considering the hetero-patriarchal origins of monogamy and the privatized, inward-looking units it tends to create, is monogamy in sexual relations the only way of being faithful in Christian terms? Kathy Rudy has dared to suggest that gay male communal sex sometimes functions to create communities that Christians these days only dream of.[10] Such bold reflection on our own experience is necessary to help us redeem the Christian tradition from heteropatriarchy. We may end up with the conclusion that monogamy is identifiable with the Christian vision, but we have to deconstruct before we can rebuild.

Another company which we seem to want to join just as every one else is leaving is the clergy. In the 1990s the 'homosexuality' debate within the Reformed traditions seems to have focused on the question of the ordination of lesbians and gay men, thereby giving the erroneous impression that lesbian and gay 'laity' are fully accepted and affirmed in the Churches. By collapsing the struggle of lesbian and gay Christians into the ordination issue the Churches effectively guard themselves against a dangerous heteropatriarchal decoding. For once ordination is granted, as has become transparently clear in the aftermath of the ordination of women in the Church of England, the Church feels its duty is done, the mavericks have been incorporated into the system, 'equality' has been achieved and there is nothing more to be said. In addition, just as the structures of marriage can conspire to consign couples to certain roles, often against their initial will, so the structures of ordination operate to keep people quiet and obedient, although as with marriage some manage to resist this force. Lesbian and gay people need to reflect on whether the institution of priesthood as presently constructed in theology and practice may in fact be another brick or indeed pinnacle of the wall of heteropatriarchy reflecting and embodying the power relations of the patriarchal household rather than the radical kinship based upon friendship that the early Christian community advocated. Adding 'out' lesbians and gay men to the priesthood would undoubtedly make our time in Egypt a little sweeter, as the addition of women and gay people who get under the wire does. We do need such consolation and places of relative safety now and this is why I would want to act in solidarity with those who work towards this or any other goal like it. I just want to suggest that the danger is that we will persuade ourselves that when it happens we have reached the promised land.

The truth is out there

LGCM's mission statement is to 'offer gay liberation to the churches and Christ to the gay community'. In its first 20 years of existence it has tended to focus on the first part of that statement, effectively challenging the churches and offering excellent pastoral support to lesbian and gay Christians. Perhaps the time has come to ask what it means to bring Christ to the gay community? There is understandably enormous hostility to Christianity in the gay and lesbian community but there is also a great deal of spirituality, the spirituality that is born of hardship and marginalization. I want to suggest that the most effective and gospel-like way to bring Christ to those communities (and gay liberation to the churches) is to recognize that s/he is already there. In other words, that there are events, experiences, hopes and ideas within these communities that reflect and embody the Christ-event.

In the Stonewall Riots of 1969, which have assumed the status and form of the creation myth of the modern lesbian and gay community, we know something of the spirit active in the Passover and resurrection that unexpectedly and inexplicably lifts and turns the most unlikely ragbag of misfits into a self-affirming community. In the experience of 'coming out', of moving from an unsatisfactory, shadowy identity into an identity that sets a person right with themselves and with reality despite opposition, lack of understanding and violence from others, lesbian and gay people know something of what it is to be born again, to be in the world but not of it, to exist in an eschatological dimension between time.

Julia Brosnan in her book *Lesbians Talk Detonating the Nuclear Family*[11] brings together the voices of many women who long for the end of the modern nuclear family in which so many of them have felt unprotected, vulnerable and lonely, emotions they recognize in other women and the elderly, and its replacement by a broader, more open and outward-looking family of choice. This vision, as I have already argued, is extremely close to the gospel subversion of the family. In the experience of an obviously imperfect community in which there is a celebration of diversity and a sense of solidarity, lesbian and gay people know something of what it is to be *ekklesia*, to be called out of society's structures into a different pattern of relating based upon different values which still exist at the heart of that society and pressurize its boundaries. Lesbian and gay people have done more eschatological reflection in recent years than most of their Western Christian friends. A considerable body of lesbian science-fiction literature reflects on life after death and through such imaginative vision offers an incisive critique of the present. The AIDS pandemic has also forced lesbians and gay men into the kind of reflection upon death, embodiment and mutual connectedness that seems to have faded out of modern Christianity. One of the most powerful resurrection scenes I have ever witnessed occurs in the final moments of one of the first films made about AIDS, *Long-time Companion*.

In a paper on Christian/lesbian identity the lesbian theologian Alison Webster draws upon the point made by the queer theorist Judith Butler that oppression does not just take the form of active prohibition but also results in the creation of 'unviable subjects'.[12] The lesbian Christian (and to some extent the gay Christian) has been made into an unviable subject, an oxymoron, both by heteropatriarchal Christians and by sections of the gay community who accept the essentialist notion of Christianity that is peddled to them. Webster points out that the idea that there is an essential core to Christianity to which one assents in order to become a Christian is extremely problematic, as the ecumenical movement has proved. Again drawing upon Butler's understanding of gender, she suggests that faith is performance, something which one creates through action, not assent to a body of teaching, and this leaves open the possibility of constructing a better form of Christianity in the future. This resonates with liberation theology's privileging of orthopraxis over orthodoxy. Lesbian and gay Christians 'queer' or destabilize notions of what constitute a Christian and offer a radically different model of what being a Christian is about. This understanding may resonate with a queer community in a way that an essentialist notion of Christianity does not, and also provides the lens through which we can observe and make sense of the Christ-event being acted out in the lesbian and gay communities. Of course the tradition is still valuable as a resource through which our ideas and actions are challenged and questioned, but it is no longer constitutive of Christianity. If lesbian and gay people can be shown that Christianity is not something outside and alien which others seek to impose upon them but something which, to a large extent, they perform already and which they can have an equal voice in shaping, then something will have been done to redeem Christianity from its homophobic, heterosexist prison.

Speaking with many voices

Undoubtedly one of the greatest challenges LGCM faces in the near future is how to stand in solidarity with and listen to the concerns of black and working-class lesbians and gay men and bisexuals who are grossly under-represented in the movement. This will be an uncomfortable process. Those of us who are white and middle-class have yet to begin to theologize around the reality of being oppressed and privileged at the same time. Bisexuals challenge our constructions of sexuality to such a degree that they are often despised by gay and straight alike, and yet their ability to love intimately and passionately people of both sexes might provide some rich material for theological reflection upon an all-loving God in whose image we are all made. Perhaps the biggest challenge facing the movement is how it can with integrity and honesty represent the diversity of voices within it. Here I would suggest that the movement slip out of the very Anglican notion (observable in practice rather than in theology) that the 'Church' is constituted primarily by bishops and clergy and move towards a more Catholic notion of the Church as a whole as the pilgrim people of God.

LGCM needs to learn to understand itself as Church, not as a Church – the last thing the world needs is another Church – but a base community that subsists in other forms of Church as well. In many respects it represents what the ecumenical movement has been working towards for a century – unity in diversity, based not upon a belief system but a practice of mutual support and solidarity and a vision of inclusivity and mutuality. It would therefore cease to be an organization negotiating terms of acceptance in 'the Church' and become what it claims to be, a glorious rainbow people which invites all denominations to join in the process of listening, dialogue, love and celebration that it lives out within its own structures. We can cease to be beggars at the table and become instead the bread and wine – the sacrament of inclusive diversity and mutuality which all churches so desperately need to receive. We must also become sacraments within the gay and lesbian communities, condemning in the name of Christ what the churches will not condemn and being where the Church should be but is not. If Christianity is about performance then LGCM needs to perform within the lesbian and gay community to a much greater degree. Our voice needs to be heard not only condemning that which the Christian leaders will not but also condemning what lesbian and gay people will not – whatever is not Christ-like among our own people.

The elephant's nose

The lesbian poet Judy Grahn in her work 'Elephant Poem' envisions heteropatriarchy as an elephant which can resist all forms of attack except a fly up his trunk. She urges us to become flies in the elephant's nose and then goes on to ponder all the types of flies there are in the world which together and alone can turn the elephant upside down.[13] It has often been a criticism of LGCM that it 'gets up the nose' of bishops and so on by its uncompromising and outspoken advocacy of the dignity of lesbian and gay people. Getting up the nose of the heteropatriarchal elephant is a noble, gospel-based activity which has barely begun. Grahn is surely right that the elephant will only be felled by a coalition of flies. As I celebrate the twentieth birthday of LGCM with deep joy and thanks, I will also be praying that LGCM has the vision to realize that its prophetic vocation lies in coalition and solidarity with those also flicked away by the tail of the elephant as inconsequential irritants or dangerous threats. May it never yield to the temptation to be respectable.

Notes

1 Gary David Comstock (1994) 'One of the family? Gay scholars and the politics of the academy', *Theology and Sexuality*, 1 (September), pp. 89–95. Mary Hunt (1995) 'Lesbian innovators reshape the academy', *Theology and Sexuality*, 3 (September), pp. 98–103.
2 Linda Bellos (1996) 'Dealing with diversity: What an inclusive feminism might look like', paper given at the 9th Women's Studies Network (UK) Conference, July.
3 This term is used by some feminist theologians to avoid the male monarchical tones of 'kingdom' whilst still capturing the essence of Jesus' use of the Greek term 'basilea' in the gospels as a radical alternative to the family structures of his day.
4 Nancy L. Eiesland (1994) *The Disabled God: Towards a Liberatory Theology of Disability* (Nashville: Abingdon Press), p. 20.
5 Richard Cleaver (1995) *Know My Name: A Gay Liberation Theology* (Louisville: Westminster/John Knox Press), pp. 34–7.
6 I think in particular of J. S. Spong (1988) *Living in Sin? A Bishop Rethinks Human Sexuality* (San Francisco: Harper and Row); and Adrian Thatcher (1993) *Liberating Sex: A Christian Sexual Theology* (London: SPCK).
7 Cleaver (1995), pp. 133–4.
8 For a deeper exploration of friendship as the replacement of marriage as the primary paradigm for relationships see Elizabeth Stuart (1995) *Just Good Friends: Towards a Lesbian and Gay Theology of Relationships* (London: Mowbray) and Mary Hunt (1991) *Fierce Tenderness: A Feminist Theology of Friendship* (New York: Crossroad).
9 Michael Vasey (1995) *Strangers and Friends: A New Exploration of Homosexuality and the Bible* (London: Hodder and Stoughton), pp. 69–162.
10 Kathy Rudy (1996) '"Where two or more are gathered": Using gay communities as a model for Christian sexual ethics', *Theology and Sexuality*, 4 (March), pp. 81–99.
11 Julia Brosnan (1996) *Lesbians Talk Detonating the Nuclear Family* (London: Scarlet Press).
12 Alison Webster (1996) 'Queer to be religious: Lesbian adventures beyond the Christian/post-Christian dichotomy', unpublished paper given at Lancaster University, 13 March.
13 Judy Grahn (1985) 'Elephant Poem' in *The Work of a Common Woman* (London: Onlywomen Press), p. 335.

TEN

Doing your own thing: lesbian and gay theology in a postmodern context

Sean Gill

Dr Sean Gill is Senior Lecturer and Head of the Department of Theology and Religious Studies in the University of Bristol, UK. His publications include *A History of Women and the Church of England from the Eighteenth Century to the Present* (London: SPCK, 1994) and the co-edited volume *Religion in Europe: Contemporary Perspectives* (Kampen: Kok Pharos, 1994).

Postmodernism and sexual liberation: transformation or regression?

That we live in a postmodern culture has become a commonplace, though just what we mean by this has been endlessly debated.[1] One way the term has frequently been used is as a descriptive label which draws attention to the way in which economic and social change, and the impact of global communications, have combined to bring about a juxtaposition of lifestyles and a relativization of moral values in Western societies. Viewed as a cultural process, the impact of postmodern culture upon gay and lesbian lifestyles is highly ambivalent. The free exchange of information and the ability to travel worldwide have, it could be argued, been powerful solvents of traditional sexual taboos and moralities – a process which has greatly benefited previously marginalized sexual minorities. On the other hand, there is also a strong case for regarding much of this freedom as illusory and fraught with ethically dubious consequences. Globalization and the communications revolution are, after all, products of late Western capitalism, and have promoted the growth of pink pound consumerism, sexual tourism and ecological degradation. It is not suprising that gay and lesbian theologians, whilst welcoming the enticing freedoms offered by postmodernity, have criticized many of its less desirable results.[2] It is also the case that postmodern cultural change is not as simple or undifferentiated a process as many globe-trotting Western academics seem to suppose. It has already spawned fundamentalist religious and social backlashes whose consequences for sexual minorites have been far from beneficial.

I want, however, to concentrate on another usage of postmodernism, that which draws attention to the epistemological scepticism of late twentieth-century thought, and which as an intellectual credo calls into question the existence of universal and trans-historical standards of truth and morality. In Jean-François Lyotard's formulation, the postmodern condition is one characterized by incredulity towards meta-narratives, be they of a religious or post-Enlightenment variety.[3] The problematizing of tradition in this way has great potential benefits for sexual minorities which have suffered discrimination and persecution as a result of the kinds of hegemonic sexual discourses which post-modernism has called into question. The undermining of rigid and polarized conceptual hierarchies of gender and sexual orientation is also vital for any true form of liberation for gay and lesbian people, for without such a reconfiguration of traditional theologies of sex and gender we can never go beyond the status of tolerated outsiders at the heteropatriarchal banquet. Indeed the dazzling efflorescence of sexualities and of sexual theologies which characterizes queer theory and praxis, might be said to be one of the most typical and exciting products of the postmodern perspective and sensibility. Yet, I would suggest, not all aspects of these changes are unproblematic and two in particular have been particularly troubling. As has frequently been pointed out, the celebration of difference and diversity may threaten the cohesion and therefore the political effectiveness of sexual liberation movements – a problem which LGCM has not been alone in having to negotiate. Perhaps more seriously, the advent of queer theory and praxis, which seeks to dissolve all received conceptualizations of gender and sexuality, may also undermine any appeal to a common set of moral values on which claims for legal, social and theological change could be grounded. If neither the Judaeo-Christian moral tradition nor some version of neo-Kantian universalism are normative – and it is now hard to see how they could be – do we have a sufficiently coherent notion of sexual ethics and of human rights on which to sustain projects of sexual liberation? At the risk of oversimplification, between the Christian homophobe and the sexual visionary, who is to judge? This is far from being merely an academic question since it is one which immediately translates into questions of political and legislative equality. For the rest of this essay I want to consider both the positive and potentially more problematic implications of the postmodern condition in more detail.

The demise of the sexual meta-narrative

Two traditions, or to adapt Lyotard's term, two meta-narratives have traditionally dominated discourse concerning same-sex relationships. These might be described as the Judaeo-Christian tradition of sexual ethics, and the post-Enlightenment tradition of sexual science – traditions whose founding fathers include St Paul, St Augustine and St Aquinas on the one hand, and Krafft-Ebing, Havelock Ellis and Freud on the other. In concentrating upon their impact upon the lives of gay men I do not want to suggest that they were any less oppressive for lesbians. In so far as there was an erasure of lesbianism from hegemonic heteropatriarchal discourse, this was a reflection of the way in which a patriarchal social order viewed the undermining of traditional concepts of masculinity as a far more serious matter.

Christianity inherited from Judaism a sexual ethic strongly committed to the defence of procreation and family life, and as a result all other forms of sexual activity were viewed as illicit. Few references to such behaviour are found in the Gospels, of which the most important are in the Epistle to the Romans, where Paul denounces such conduct as a feature of pagan society,[4] and the First Epistle to the Corinthians where he warns that such activity – listed along with adultery, theft and drunkenness – is a bar to entering the Kingdom of God.[5] In recent years much discussion of these passages has centred upon the question of their relevance for contemporary ethics, given that the New Testament world knew nothing of the modern understanding of sexual orientation.[6] Nevertheless Paul's repudiation of homosexual behaviour is in keeping with his Jewish inheritance and with his insistence that sexual activity be limited to monogamous, permanent marriage. Augustine's few references to homosexuality are strongly influenced by the traditional but false exegesis of the story of Sodom as evidence of God's divine punishment of behaviour which he regards as a form of perverted lust.[7] As with the writings of St Paul, John Boswell has argued against seeing in Augustine's use of the word 'unnatural' in this context a blanket condemnation of homosexuality *per se*, but rather of those heterosexuals who indulged in activity which went against their natural sexual inclination.[8] However, given the strong emphasis found elsewhere in Augustine's writings upon procreation within marriage as the sole permissible locus for sexual activity this seems unconvincing. Whilst it may be true, as Boswell argues, that Aquinas's condemnation of homosexual acts as contrary to natural law may represent a very different and more sophisticated understanding of the concept of the natural than any known to Paul or Augustine, it represents a development and not a new departure in a tradition consistently hostile to any expression of homosexual genital activity. The force of this prohibition is lost by treating Christian attitudes to homosexuality in isolation from the wider sexual ethic of marriage and procreation which the early and medieval Church espoused and which Protestantism, with its hostile re-evaluation of celibacy, did little to alter.

It is the authority of this tradition as a whole which postmodernism now calls into question. Divinely ordained sexual norms apprehended by the use of human reason properly deployed have been transmuted into Foucaultian discourses of power, whose appeal to notions of the natural disguises their all too human origins and their attempts to marginalize dissident voices. Exercises in what Foucault has aptly called the archaeology of knowledge have undermined the authority of the dominant Judaeo-Christian sexual ethic in a number of significant respects.[9] For example, before we accept Augustine's rejection of homosexual behaviour as a form of perverted lust, we ought to consider how alien his understanding of human sexuality as a whole is from our own, based as it is upon a dualistic philosophy deeply suspicious of human sexual activity as a threat to the higher faculties of mind and will. For Augustine, all forms of sexual intercourse – including those within marriage – are to be regarded as a consequence of the fall, as occasions for the transmission of original sin, and therefore in a very real sense as lustful.[10] Similarly in appraising Aquinas's arguments we ought to be aware of the extent to which he relies upon a now discredited Aristotelian biology in which only the father is the active generative force in conception.[11] Protestant theologians, who are more likely to appeal to the Bible alone as the source of authoritative teaching in the realm of sexual relations, have also been made aware of the extent to which the ethics of the New Testament are coloured by what to us are unacceptable notions of ritual purity and of women as a form of sexual property within a patriarchal society.[12] More generally, it has been the growth of a powerful feminist critique of Christian teaching about sex as instrumental in the subordination of women and in the maintenance of gender hierarchies which has done most to undermine the authority of the tradition.[13] The feminist deconstruction of gender hierarchies as socially constructed rather than immutable truths fallen from heaven, has also had a direct bearing upon arguments about male homosexuality. As has been recognized, one powerful impulse behind the high levels of homophobia within Western society has been the fear of homosexual behaviour as in some senses inappropriately passive and therefore feminine – a revealing insight into the sexism which lies at the heart of our culturally constructed discourse of polarized gender identities.[14]

In trying to assess the impact of this tradition on the lives of gay men we must proceed with some caution. For much of the history of Western society the concept of homosexuality as a distinct identity was unknown, and the Church condemned particular sexual acts, most notably sodomy. There was also a wide gap between what the Church proscribed and people's actual behaviour. Nor was the severity of ecclesiastical and secular punishment constant. European society in the eleventh and twelfth centuries became harsher in its attitude towards homosexuality than it had been previously, as part of the development of what R. I. Moore has called a persecuting society in which the fear of minority groups such as religious heretics, Jews and lepers tells us more about the insecurities of the majority in a period of economic and social change than it does about any actual threat which such groups posed to the dominant social order.[15] Perhaps as a result of concerns over the population crisis occasioned by the Black Death after 1348, denunciations of sexual deviancy as a grave threat to society became shriller and legal penalties harsher – often including burning alive, though this was usually reserved for cases involving rape. Even so, most men convicted of sodomy faced fines, public whipping, exile, the confiscation of their property and the denial of their right to make a will.[16] Even more than the Jews, they also lived in a society in which demonization by the Church made the threat of violence an ever present one, and the possibility of developing any kind of cultural identity non-existent. As the popular Franciscan preacher St Bernadino of Siena put it, homosexuals were the Devil's creatures and 'as refuse is taken out of the houses … so wicked men should be removed from human commerce by prison and death'.[17] Notwithstanding the development of more liberal Christian attitudes, homophobia of this kind still characterizes the tradition, as is evident in right-wing Protestant fundamentalist attempts to recriminalize homosexual activity in Britain,[18] and in the Vatican's opposition to the granting of equal rights to gay and lesbian people in employment and in military recruitment in America.[19] Both of these campaigns continue to employ the language of demonization and contagion which has characterized the tradition from its outset. For gay men, the postmodern rejection of the authority of traditional Christian moral discourse spells not anomie and moral chaos, but the first real possibility of a life of dignity and self-affirmation.

This is not, however, to imply that the incredulity towards the possibility of meta-narratives, which Lyotard claims lies at the heart of the crisis of legitimation in modern society, is any less serious for the tradition of post-Enlightenment reason and empirical science than for the metaphysical world view which it set out to replace. If the Judaeo-Christian tradition of theorizing about sexuality is in disarray in a postmodern age, then the same can be said of its putative successor, the tradition of scientific discourse which dominated the nineteenth and much of the twentieth centuries. In many ways this was almost the archetypal Enlightenment project seeking to replace outworn religious prejudice and custom through the application of reason to human sexuality as to all other areas of existence. Taboo, secrecy and sin were to be replaced by openness, objective classification and understanding. One of the key texts in the creation of the new science was Richard von Krafft-Ebing's *Psychopathia Sexualis* which appeared in 1886. According to its author, who was Professor of Psychiatry and Neurology at the University of Vienna, scientific study alone could disperse the miasma of erroneous opinions upon which unjust legal sentences had been promulgated in this area.[20] The English pioneer Havelock Ellis, who began his six-volume *Studies in the Psychology of Sex* in 1896 was similarly confident in the power of science to transcend the traditional approach of the theologians whose competency in this area Ellis now regarded as altogether superseded.[21]

Yet though the preconceptions of the founders of sexology were very different from those of the Judaeo-Christian tradition, they now seem no less questionable. Thus in his discussion of the differences between men and women Krafft-Ebing could claim that:

> Undoubtedly man has a much more intense sexual appetite than woman. As a result of a powerful natural instinct, at a certain age, a man is drawn toward a woman. ... With a woman it is quite otherwise. If she is normally developed mentally, and well bred, her sexual desire is small. If this were not so the whole world would become a brothel and marriage and a family impossible. It is certain that the man that avoids women and the woman that seeks men are abnormal.[22]

The androcentrism of the first generation of male sexual researchers has, not surprisingly, attracted feminist criticism,[23] whilst its implications for homosexuals are equally clear: a traditional model of the sinfulness of sexual acts has given way to an 'objective' classification of abnormality in which biologically determined male initiated heterosexual coitus is the norm.[24] In Ellis's initial formulation, 'Sexual inversion is caused by inborn constitutional abnormality towards persons of the same sex.'[25] His conclusion was that it was 'an aberration from the usual course of nature' and one which, whilst it was not the province of the criminal law to punish, 'bears for the most part its penalty in the structure of its own organism'.[26]

Freud's most significant contribution in this area lay in the distinction which he drew between the sexual instinct and its object, and in what he saw as the 'polymorphously perverse' nature of infantile sexuality. This had the effect of problematizing all forms of sexual orientation including heterosexuality:

> Psycho-analytic research is most decidedly opposed to any attempt at separating off homosexuals from the rest of mankind as a group of a special character. ... On the contrary, psycho-analysis considers that a choice of an object independently of its sex – freedom to range equally over male and female objects – as it is found in childhood, in primitive states of society and early periods of history, is the original basis from which, as a result of restriction in one direction or the other, both the normal and the inverted types develop. Thus from the point of view of psycho-analysis the exclusive sexual interest felt by men for women is also a problem that needs elucidating and is not a self-evident fact based upon an attraction that is ultimately of a chemical nature.[27]

But although Freud was strongly opposed to the imposition of criminal sanctions upon homosexuals, his stance was nevertheless ambiguous in terms of the development of any widespread acceptance of gay men in society. The radicalness of his insights into the fluidity of sexual orientation was still tempered by his belief that although less natural and more difficult to attain than had previously been assumed, heterosexuality remained the normative ideal towards which socialization should endeavour to lead the individual. This meant that what Freud called 'any established aberration from normal sexuality' could be seen as 'an instance of developmental inhibition and infantilism'.[28] It was the complexity of Freud's views which allowed his successors to argue that a homosexual orientation should be regarded as a psychiatric illness amenable in varying degrees to treatment – a view that was not to be repudiated by the American Psychiatric Association until 1973, and only then by a small majority.[29]

Viewed from our own day, the tradition of objective scientific study of homosexuality was part of a much wider concern with the classification and regulation of sexuality which was in many respects a secularized version of the theological view which had preceded it. Like its predecessor it was formed upon presuppositions which were anything but objective. What purported to be a tradition of detached scientific enquiry was deeply influenced by the cultural assumptions and social anxieties of the age. The androcentrism so evident in Freud's theory of sexual differentiation, which problematizes female rather than male development, was part of a much wider late nineteenth-century white middle-class crisis of identity. For example many of the pioneers of sexual research were also fearful of the effects of unrestrained breeding by the lower classes and espoused eugenic programmes as a remedy for what they saw as the potential eclipse of the productive middle classes by the offspring of the undeserving poor.[30] Nor do their scientific strictures against the evils of masturbation as a source of both physical and mental decay seem so great an advance upon Aquinas's condemnation of the practice for its waste of potentially procreative semen. The medicalization of homosexuality was ultimately no more emancipatory for gay men than the tradition it sought to replace.

The challenge of postmodern Christian political action and sexual ethics

The demise of hegemonic sexual discourses of these kinds is then to be welcomed, but will their replacement by the celebration of pluralism and difference weaken political movements which derive their effectiveness from a shared identity forged out of a common sense of oppression and discrimination? As Joan Hoff has warned with regard to the women's movement, is there not a risk that the very awareness of cultural difference which seeks to overcome the undoubted ethnocentrism and racism of much Western feminist writing will become 'a potentially politically paralyzing and intellectually irrelevant exercise for endlessly analyzing myriad representations of cultural forms and discourses'?[31] Undoubtedly this may be the case unless sexual liberation movements are earthed not in theology as an abstract discipline but in a form of social praxis which contests oppression and injustice in the real world. So long as this occurs, then the recognition of difference is not a distraction but a precondition of effective political action. This is so since queer theory and praxis are crucial for our awareness that conceptual and social exclusions and closures are not external to movements of sexual liberation, but need to be acknowledged and overcome from within as an integral part of any genuinely liberative action. As Robert Goss has argued, gay and lesbian Christians cannot exclude other oppressed groups from their own practices of liberation, otherwise 'their resistance from the margins is doomed to replicate the social strategies, structures, and value systems of their oppressors'.[32]

But finally, is the celebration of difference and diversity compatible with overcoming the ethical relativism and ultimately the nihilism which some forms of postmodernism threaten? This question has been acutely discussed by the feminist theologian Lisa Cahill, who has observed of women's liberation movements that 'many feminist deconstructions of moral foundations create a normative vacuum which cripples their political critique' whilst 'they allow values like autonomy and freedom, traced to Enlightenment roots, to slide in as tacit universals, operative without intercultural nuancing or explicit defense'.[33] If we accept the force of the postmodern claim that we have no God-given or humanly constructed vantage point beyond history and culture which we can access, does it not follow that the provisionality and relativism of our moral judgements seriously weaken their force as instruments of transformation and liberation? Gay and lesbian liberation movements have faced similar dilemmas, quite rightly rejecting not only traditional Christian sexual ethics, but also liberal appeals to universal frameworks of human rights, on the grounds that the latter grant toleration to lesbian and gay minorities without challenging the notions of polarized and immutable gender and sexual hierarchies which have helped to create discrimination and exclusion in the first place, and which downplay crucial differences of class, race and culture in the creation of injustice.[34]

One possible answer to this question is suggested by Laurie Shrage who has argued that the cultural pluralism and relativism implied by a postmodern perspective need not, as its critics have claimed, result in a kind of subjectivism which argues simply on the basis of what is right for one's own particular group or subculture. Thoroughgoing pluralism, she claims, provides greater familiarity with the great arc of human possibilities in order to educate our perceptions. But this process of ethical growth can only occur if we are prepared to genuinely confront the challenge posed by the other on its own terms, and thereby to become more aware and more self-critical of our own presuppositions and their limitations.[35] Such a process might lead me, for example, as a white middle-class gay man to consider more closely why it is that I have difficulty in forging a sense of solidarity with bisexual men. Might it be that they interrogate my assured and hierarchical understanding of a gay sexual orientation? Or again, why am I not always comfortable with the lesbian critique of a hetero-patriarchal social order? Surely because it positions me within that society as oppressor as much as victim.

Another possible response to the ethical and theological relativism of the postmodern turn might of course be to deny its force completely. It can after all be argued that the postmodern rejection of the meta-narrative falls into contradiction, since it in turn implies a vantage point beyond culture and history and is itself a negative meta-narrative. Yet even if this point is accepted, it does not undermine the force of postmodernism as a persuasive analysis of the unique and unprecedented degree of cultural and social pluralism which characterizes late twentieth-century society, and from which sexual minorities have derived great benefit. The normativity of any distinctively Christian lesbian and gay theology in this situation must be one that can appeal to an ideal of human flourishing and well-being which is ethically stringent, such that the exploitation and dehumanization of others is always to be condemned. But it must also be far more capable than the sclerotic and hermetically sealed theology of the mainstream churches of recognizing that human well-being can take a wide variety of cultural forms. Augustine's much used and abused injunction that we should love and do what we will has not just a modern but a very postmodern resonance.

Notes

1 A particularly helpful introduction which takes religion and theology seriously is D. Lyon (1994) *Postmodernity* (Buckingham: Open University Press).
2 See for example J. M. Clark (1993) *Beyond our Ghettos: Gay Theology in Ecological Perspective* (Cleveland: The Pilgrim Press).
3 J. Lyotard (1984) *The Postmodern Condition: A Report on Knowledge* (Manchester: Manchester University Press) p. xxiv.
4 Romans 1: 26–7.
5 I Corinthians 6: 9–10.
6 See for example J. Boswell (1980) *Christianity, Social Tolerance, and Homosexuality* (Chicago: Chicago University Press), p. 109; G. Coleman

(1995) *Homosexuality: Catholic Teaching and Pastoral Practice* (New York: Paulist Press), pp. 56–72; J. Siker (ed.) (1994) *Homosexuality in the Church: Both Sides of the Debate* (Louisville: Westminster John Knox Press), pp. 3–35; M. Vasey (1995) *Strangers and Friends: A New Exploration of Homosexuality and the Bible* (London: Hodder & Stoughton), pp. 113–40.

7 A. Oulter (ed.) (1955) *Augustine: Confessions and Enchiridion* (London: SCM Press), pp. 70–1. See too *City of God*, XVI, 30 for the same point.

8 Boswell (1980), pp. 150–1.

9 M. Foucault (1972) *The Archaeology of Knowledge* (London: Tavistock Publications).

10 Augustine, 'On Marriage and Concupiscence', in P. Schaff (ed.) (1978) *A Select Library of the Nicene and Post-Nicene Fathers of the Christian Church*, 5, pp. 266–7.

11 For a detailed discussion of this topic see K. Borrensen (1995) *Subordination and Equivalence: The Nature and Role of Woman in Augustine and Thomas Aquinas* (Kampen: Kok Pharos).

12 W. Countryman (1989) *Dirt, Greed and Sex: Sexual Ethics in the New Testament and their Implications for Today* (London: SCM Press), p. 237.

13 For this subject in general see C. Mackinnon (1987) *Feminism Unmodified: Discourses on Life and Law* (Cambridge, Mass.: Harvard University Press), pp. 1–17; and from a specifically Christian theological perspective, B. Harrison and C. Heyward 'Pain and Pleasure: Avoiding the Confusions of Christian Tradition in Feminist Theory', in J. Nelson and S. Longfellow (1994) *Sexuality and the Sacred: Sources for Theological Reflection* (London: Mowbray), pp. 131–48; and R. Ruether (ed.) (1974) *Religion and Sexism: Images of Women in the Jewish and Christian Tradition* (New York: Simon & Schuster).

14 For a more extended treatment of this theme see S. Bem (1993) *The Lenses of Gender* (New Haven: Yale Univeristy Press), pp. 165–7. As Grace Janzen has observed of Hildegard of Bingen's typical abhorrence of homosexual acts in the medieval period, its basis lay in a rejection of the possibility that men might adopt the role of women and as a consequence 'change their virile strength into perverse weakness'. Quoted in G. Jantzen (1995) *Power, Gender and Christian Mysticism* (Cambridge: Cambridge University Press), p. 234.

15 R. Moore (1987) *The Formation of a Persecuting Society* (Oxford: Blackwell).

16 J. Brundage (1987) *Law, Sex and Christian Society in Medieval Europe* (Chicago: Chicago University Press), pp. 533–5.

17 J. Richards (1991) *Sex Dissidence and Damnation: Minority Groups in the Middle Ages* (London: Routledge), pp. 146–7.

18 M. Durham (1991) *Sex and Politics: The Family and Morality in the Thatcher Years* (London: Macmillan), pp. 124–6.

19 R. Peddicord (1996) *Gay and Lesbian Rights. A Question: Sexual Ethics or Social Justice?* (Kansas City: Sheed & Ward), pp. 123–9.

20 R. Krafft–Ebing (1894) *Psychopathia Sexualis, with Special Reference to Contrary Sexual Instinct: A Medico-Legal Study* (London: F. J. Rebman), p. iv. This was an English translation of the enlarged and revised German seventh edition.

21 H. Ellis (1936) *Studies in the Psychology of Sex* (New York: Random House), 1, p. xxix.
22 Krafft–Ebing (1894), p. 13.
23 M. Jackson (1994) *The Real Facts of Life: Feminism and the Politics of Sexuality c.1850–1940* (London: Taylor and Francis).
24 For the development of a scientific model of homosexuality and its implications see G. Hawkes (1996) *A Sociology of Sex and Sexuality* (Buckingham: Open University Press), pp. 56–71; J. Weeks (1985) *Sexuality and Its Discontents: Meanings, Myths and Modern Sexualities* (London: Routledge), pp. 64–79.
25 Ellis (1936), p. 1.
26 *Ibid.*, p. 356. Like Krafft–Ebing, Ellis distinguishes between what he regarded as congenital and acquired inversion, or 'pseudohomosexuality', the latter the result of individual weakness or faulty social institutions such as single-sex schools and capable of treatment by 'sound social hygiene'.
27 S. Freud (1949) *Three Essays on the Theory of Sexuality* (London: Imago Publishing Company), pp. 23–4.
28 *Ibid.*, p. 108.
29 For Freud's views and their impact in this area see H. Abelove 'Freud, Male Homosexuality, and the Americans', in H. Abelove, M. Barale, and D. Halperin (eds) (1993) *The Lesbian and Gay Studies Reader* (London: Routledge), pp. 381–93.
30 J. Weeks (1989) *Sex, Politics and Society: The Regulation of Sexuality since 1800* (London: Longman), pp. 128–38.
31 J. Hoff in C. Farnham and G. Fischer (1992) *Journal of Women's History Guide to Periodical Literature* (Bloomington: Indiana University Press), p. 26.
32 R. Goss (1993) *Jesus ACTED UP: A Gay and Lesbian Manifesto* (San Francisco: HarperSanFrancisco), p. 174.
33 L. Cahill (1996) *Sex, Gender and Christian Ethics* (Cambridge: Cambridge University Press), p. 2.
34 I have discussed this point and its implications for a Christian sexual theology in S. Gill (1995) 'Odd but not Queer: English Liberal Protestant Theologies and the Gay Paradigm', *Theology and Sexuality*, 3 (September), pp. 48–57.
35 L. Shrage (1994) *Moral Dilemmas of Feminism* (London: Routledge).

———— ◆ ————

ELEVEN

Sexual visionaries and freedom fighters for a sexual reformation: from gay theology to queer sexual theologies

Robert E. Goss

Dr Robert Goss is Professor in the Religion Department, Webster University, St Louis, USA. His numerous contributions to gay and queer theology include *Jesus ACTED UP: A Gay and Lesbian Manifesto* (San Francisco: HarperSanFrancisco, 1993).

I have the task of envisioning what direction gay Christian liberating praxis and theology will take in the next century. I have no particular clairvoyant gifts to offer but can make some reasonable speculations by examining how the translesbigay Christian movement came into existence, its organizational developments, and directions for theological growth and practice. The lesbian/gay Christian movement developed during the radical 1960s and the revolutionary 1970s to solidify theological growth. Theological growth has accompanied the organizational advance and development of the gay/lesbian movement.

Ground-breaking for the emergence of gay theology was Derrick Sherwin Bailey's *Homosexuality and the Western Christian Tradition* in the mid 1950s.[1] Bailey, a heterosexual scholar, traced the development of homohatred from the biblical texts through the formation of Christian practice and theology in the early and late medieval ages. Homosexual theology started in the late 1950s with Robert Wood's *Christ and the Homosexual* and the 1970s saw the blossoming of homosexual theology with such works as Tom Horner's *Jonathan Loved David*, John McNeill's *The Church and the Homosexual* and Virginia Ramey Mollenkott's and Letha Scanzoni's *Is the Homosexual My Neighbor?*[2] These were apologetic works that attempted to reconcile the opposition of the churches to homosexuality and offer a theological interpretation of homosexuality. They strengthened the nascent formation of denominational groups.

John Boswell's *Christianity, Social Tolerance, and Homosexuality* marked a development from a theology of homosexuality to the historical reclamation of gay voices within Christian traditions.[3] Boswell's work met with general academic acclaim but also empowered denominational gay/lesbian groups in their loyal opposition. Boswell initiated serious discussion of the social context of the biblical texts of terror but was generally ignored by Church leaders. In the 1980s, debate shifted to apologetic battle for the interpretative control of the biblical text. Such heterosexual bibical scholars as Robin Scroggs and George Edwards and openly gay biblical scholar L. William Countryman contextualized the texts of terror and elaborated on the general lines of biblical interpretation initiated by Boswell.[4] The debate still fiercely rages over interpretative control of the biblical texts.[5]

Gay theology in the 1980s centred on two issues: the reinterpretation of biblical texts that had been used to justify the idea that homosexuality was sinful; and support for psychological interpretations of sexual orientation which could be used to deconstruct moral theologies based on natural law. Gay theology found itself in an apologetic mode attempting to make cosmetic changes within the churches to justify acceptance of gays/lesbians. Gay theology did not address the issues of sexism; it was unable to make connections between misogyny and homophobia or connect homophobia to other forms of oppression. The writings of Maury Johnston, Chris Glazer, John McNeill, and John Fortunato among others hardly joined in dialogue with the lesbian theologies of Carter Heyward, Mary Hunt, or Virginia Mollenkott.[6] Gay theology focused on the expulsion of openly gay male and sometimes lesbian clergy, the denial of ordination to gays/lesbians, and the refusal to bless same-sex unions. Theological anthologies – with gay, closeted gay, and straight contributors – responded apologetically for or against Church statements on the issue of homosexuality.[7]

Gay theology inevitably became problematic in its singular focus on gay male issues, excluding lesbian voices. The theological split along gender lines between gays and lesbians started in the late 1970s with the feminist movement, slowed in the early years of the AIDS pandemic, but resurfaced in the late 1980s and early 1990s. While John Boswell's earlier work was important to the gay/lesbian Christian movement in the 1980s, it had major shortcomings. Almost all the material that Boswell covered was male homoeroticism. The history of female homoerotic relations and desires within Christianity was conspicuously absent. Recently, Bernardette Brooten's *Love Between Women: Early Christian Responses to Female Homoeroticism* provides a correction to the absence of female voices in Boswell's work.[8] A second factor that problematized gay theology was the failure to include bisexual and transgendered voices and the voices from persons of colour. The push for inclusion of lesbian, bisexual, and transgendered voices impacted upon gay theology, expanding beyond its white, middle-class male parameters and addressing issues of gender, class, and race.

The final context which problematized gay theology was the ravages of AIDS and the escalating social hatred of churches. Both AIDS and cultural homohatred forced gays into coalition with other groups. Translesbigays had responded to the AIDS pandemic as it affected gays. Many infected by HIV and those affected by HIV have found themselves defensive in affirming that sexuality is a gift from God despite the condemnation of churches. Coalitions expanded gay concerns from a single issue focus. Gays became concerned with women's issues such as reproductive freedom, sexism, and health issues because lesbians were there for their HIV gay brothers. AIDS activism and queer activism developed from social violence, apathy, and exclusions. The explosion of activism in the late 1980s and early 1990s transformed gay theology into queer theologies and widened their dialogue partners.

The transformation of gay theology into postmodern queer theologies continues, currently revolving around four inclusionary challenges: 1) changing churches or create a post-denominational church; 2) the challenge of post-Christianity, feminism, and other spiritual paths; 3) queer sexual theology, and 4) justice perspectives of other cultural contexts. These challenges will determine the success of new inclusive liberating theologies of the translesbigay Christian movement in the next century.

Change churches or create a post-denominational church?

The erotophobia and homophobia of churches force the question of how much progress gay/lesbian Christians have made in churches in the last three decades. Is Church any longer a relevant category for gays/lesbians? Churches have been, at best, an inhospitable social community to gays/lesbians, refusing to bless their unions and ordain open 'practising' homosexuals. At its worst, the Church is as hostile a community as the rapists of Sodom in Genesis 19, commiting overt violence against gays/lesbians. What binds gays/lesbians to their churches is no longer cultural denominational loyalties in the face of ecclesial violence and exclusion. The continual broadsides of denominational homophobia have forced a number of assimilationist and separatist strategies vis-à-vis the churches. The divisions within American churches, for example, have not raged so intensely since the abolitionist movement against slavery.

One of the earliest strategies was the the formation of denominational groups such as Dignity, Integrity, Affirmation, Lutherans Concerned, and others as points of loyal resistance to ecclesial homophobia. In existence for nearly a quarter of a century, these mainline denominational groups have been generally gay male dominated and resistant to women's issues. Many gay/lesbian Christians hoped that these denominational groups would not merely resist the violence and exclusion from their own churches but would eventually overcome denominational opposition to themselves.

How much success have they had in moving their denominations to recognize gay/lesbian ordinations and bless same-sex unions? Some have had more impact than others on their churches. But for the most part, denominational groups have experienced a period of decline because of the various church strategies to render them ineffective, the public anti-gay/lesbian campaigns of religious extremists, the failure of gay men to engage lesbian feminist concerns, and the failure to articulate a coherent vision of the interrelationship of homophobia to other forms of oppression. The challenge before mainline denominational groups is whether they can overcome their impasses and articulate an inclusive vision for the next century.

The formal Church groups, More Light, Reconciling Congregation Program, and Open and Affirming Churches have made efforts to draw gays and lesbians back into their churches. Some translesbigay Christians have not given up hope of effecting change. Many are happy that individual churches are finally facing their own homophobia. Catholic outreach groups have set up parishes to welcome gay/lesbian Catholics with a 'Don't Ask, Don't Tell' policy. Welcoming back lesbian/gay Christians, however, means full inclusion: the blessing of our unions and ordaining us. These welcoming churches are not yet prepared for full inclusion, but only token assimilation.

When should translesbigays say 'enough is enough' and get out? How much pain is necessary before it is time to shake the dust from our feet and move into exile and create a space that is more welcoming? For many translesbigay Christians, their churches have betrayed God's gift of sexuality and continue to pursue an erotophobic agenda. Many queer Christians see moving out of their denominational churches as the only way to experience God's liberating grace. To leave and embrace exile takes a commitment of faith. Dan Spencer uses the image of the diaspora church in his discussion of the ecclesia of lesbians and gays.[9] I have used the liberation model of a 'base community' from Latin American liberation theology or the queer ecclesia to image our creating church and struggling with ecclesial homophobia.[10] Both diaspora and base community are contained in the image of the queer post-denominational church.

In the last two decades, there has been a proliferation of independent churches, imitating their denominational churches: independent orthodox and ecumenical Catholic churches; evangelical, non-denominational and fundamentalist churches. These churches attempt to duplicate their churches of origin with the one exception of including gays/lesbians.

The lesbian/gay Christian movement has witnessed the emergence of post-denominational religious organizations and churches. In the US and Europe, Other Sheep, a non-profit, ecumenical organization, has developed a ministry to sexual minorites in Latin America. It has fostered and developed lesbigay Christian networks in Latin and South America, even fostering connections with gay/lesbian Christians in Cuba, Africa, and India. In America, Evangelicals Concerned have created a cross-denominational movement of translesbigay evangelical Christians. In Europe, Protestant and Catholic gays/lesbians have come together in Jonathan and David communities while in the UK the Lesbian and Gay Christian Movement was formed to support individual gay/lesbian Christians across denominational lines and to help the churches re-examine their narrow position on human sexuality. Such global groups have crossed ecumenical, national, and cultural lines to build faith coalitions and justice networks. They have become visible in pre-sessions to International Lesbian and Gay Association (ILGA) conferences.

In 1968, Troy Perry founded the Universal Fellowship of Metropolitan Community Churches (UFMCC) as an alternative to the churches.[11] UFMCC is unlike the mainline denominational groups or independent churches in that it is a post-denominational church, representing and blending the diverse traditions of a number of Christian denominations. Mainline denominational groups place doctrinal adherence at the centre of their churches. They differ with their denominations in the area of sexual orientation. UFMCC is post-denominational in that it does not start with the principle of doctrinal adherence but doctrinal diversity, allowing for a wide range of ecumenical interpretations of doctrine and a blending of a variety of liturgical practices.

UFMCC has churches in 14 countries. It has founded the first openly queer seminary, the Samaritan Institute for Religious Studies. Nancy Wilson, an elder involved in ecumenical relations, narrates how the UFMCC met the National Council of Churches' (NCC) requirements of membership and the NCC's continual denial of admission because of ecclesial homophobia. Though the UFMCC met all the membership requirements of the NCC, there was strong pressure for the queer church to withdraw its application to that body. The NCC refused to acknowledge the genuine spiritual awakening in the translesbigay Christian community.[12] One challenge to such a queer post-denominational church as UFMCC is the inclusion of heterosexuals. In Nigeria, the 22 UFMCC churches are principally heterosexual.

Dismantling barriers of ecclesial homophobia in the next century will only take place as a result of pressures from within the churches over the continual scandal of exclusion and violence and from the challenges of inclusive love by translesbigay Christians within mainline denominations and post-denominational churches. Alexander and Preston argue for a combination of insider and outsider 'ACT UP' strategies, building networks inside and outside denominations to change the homophobic exclusion and violence of the churches.[13] The building of interdenominational networks will only increase in the future, crossing national and cultural boundaries. These ecumenical networks will give rise to new post-denominational churches where inclusion of all peoples at the table will be a common mission.

The challenge of post-Christianity, feminism, and other spiritual paths

As the spirituality of gays/lesbians has increasingly become postmodern, it also has become post-Christian. Some post-Christians perceive gay/lesbian denominational groups and post-denominational churches as rearranging deck chairs on the Titanic.[14] Many queers find Christianity irrelevant at best and too often violent and oppressive. Can we create a Christianity that escapes from its heritage of violence and from its irrelevancy in addressing the spiritual needs of gays/lesbians? There is much value in the gay/lesbian Christian movement and its theologians wrestling with post-Christian theologies, feminist theologies, and other non-Christian spiritualities that have arisen within the translesbigay community.

A number of gay/lesbian theologians have moved from the stagnant doctrines and violent practices of the Christian churches into a post-Christian theology. New post-Christian theologies have no place for Christological claims.[15] Post-Christian theologies reflect some currents in the queer community, but there is no defined constituency as particular churches. Thus there is little connection between theological and communal practice. But this does not mean post-Christian lesbian/gay theologies are irrelevant to Christian gay/lesbian liberation theologies.

Ron Long's gay indigenous theology, for example, attempts to make a link between gay sex and religious experience.[16] Long disengages gay sex from a question of legitimate, intimate relations and focuses on the religious dimensions of gay sex. He maintains that sex constitutes for gay men a religious experience. His phenomenology of gay sexual experience, while questioning Christian constructions and restrictions, provides a dialogue partner for gay/lesbian Christians. J. Michael Clark, on the other hand, builds on feminist theologies and pushes gay theology into environmental issues.[17] Clark reminds us that Christian complicity in abdicating earthly responsibilites has led to a rampant view of disposability. There is much in the works of Clark, Long, and many others to which Christian gay/lesbian theologians need to give serious consideration to develop their theologies.

A second challenge to gay theology is listening to feminist, lesbian-feminist, and womanist concerns. Gay misogyny is as destructive as heterosexual misogyny or lesbian separatism. It has often rendered lesbians invisible or submerged lesbian voices within gay concerns. Gay theology and spirituality have recently undergone revision and become more aware of women's issues. For instance, Comstock and Cleaver have articulated a gay theology that is feminist-identified, liberation-oriented, and unapologetic.[18] Their theology is widening its male perspective to engage feminist, lesbian-feminist, and womanist theologies but is certainly not identifiably queer in its tonalities and its political strategies.

Finally, the Christian lesbian/gay movement needs to also engage in dialogue with other spiritualities. Mark Thompson's *Gay Soul* has made a significant contribution to the discussion of gay spiritualities in the 1990s.[19] Thompson sought 16 diverse elders who have pioneered the development of gay spiritualities, covering such topics as transvestism, S/M, the gay wounded soul, androgynes, embodied and erotic spirituality, AIDS, homophobia, astrology, and gay archetypes. These indigenous gay spiritualities and practices form the matrix for the new queer theologies.

Post-Christian gay/lesbian theologies, feminist theologies, and diverse gay/lesbian spiritualities will not be easily dismissed. Rather, they will become foundational for reformulating and re-envisioning new Christian queer theologies.

Queer sexual theologies: inclusive challenges

The queer revision of gay theology is grounded in strength, no longer in self-hatred, nor in accommodation or apology. Queer theologies respond to the peril of political violence. Political and social violence made the queer movement 'queer'. While conservative gays argued that we are just like straight people, such arguments for assimilation into straight society rang hollow as social violence escalated. There are still strong gay currents for assimilating into heterosexual society.[20] Emerging with AIDS and queer activism, queer liberation theologies have refused to be coopted into non-critical assimilationism and have taken critical, even transgressive, stances to the dominant culture. ACT UP, Queer Nation, OutRage!, and other AIDS and queer activists have reclaimed the epithet 'queer' from cultural homophobic practice to brand our sexual desires and transformed it into a postmodern label of political dissidence. It has evolved as a coalitional term for translesbigay people and is inclusive of heterosexual activists who identify with queer sexual dissidence. Queer designates transgression, political dissidence, differences, and coalitional diversity. Queer as a verb means 'to spoil the effect of, to interfere with, to disrupt, harm, or put in bad light'.[21] Queering is a deconstructive critique of the homophobic and heterosexist political theology that already excludes us. It inverts cultural symbols, perverts and disrupts valued theologies and church practices that are already spoiled for us. Queering imaginatively reconstructs theology, spirituality and church practices in new, inclusive configurations.[22]

Robert Williams, Nancy Wilson, Elias Farajaje-Jones, and myself among others identify our theologies as queer.[23] Queer theologies represent a liberation discourse of sexual dissidence, deconstructing Christian theology and reconstructing Christianity from a genuine perspective of marginality, difference, and dissidence. Each author speaks from a particular intersection of political struggle and oppression. Williams speaks as a gay queer, Wilson as a lesbian queer, and

Farajaje-Jones as a bisexual queer. None of the above queer authors speaks for all translesbigay voices but is aware of wider concerns of other sexual minorities. Farajaje-Jones is the only open bisexual theologian to date who has committed his theology to writing. Bisexuality undermines the either/or categories of heterosexual and gay/lesbian, for it represents definitionally a both/and connection between heterosexuality and homosexuality. Victoria Kolakowski has pioneered transgendered theological reflection and raised the question of trans oppression.[24] Transgendered theology promises to destabilize our rigid notions of gender and proposes more than two genders. As bisexual and transgendered voices break silence, the complexion of queer theologies will evolve with new particularities and shades of differences. They will flesh out bi/transphobia, forcing earlier queer theologians to engage expanded definitions of sexualities and genders. They will assist us in seeing sexual and gender oppression from novel perspectives.

Queer theologies proceed from critical analysis of the social context that forms our sexual/gender experience in the web of interlocking oppressions and from our innovative and transgressive practices. Queer theology is an organic or community-based project that includes queer sexual contextuality and our particular social experiences of homo/bi/transphobic oppression and other forms of oppression, and our self-affirmations of sexual/gendered differences will impact upon the future developments of liberation theologies.

Queer theologies have inclusive potential that ghettoized gay theology previously lacked. It offends some Christians holding to earlier gay theology because it moves beyond binary divisions of straight/gay and blurs the constructions. Queer theologies comprehend gender, race, homophobia, class, ethnicity, and disability as shaping our sexuality in addition to our sexual desires. All these factors contribute to our constructions and experience of human sexuality, and no single location is capable of speaking for all other social locations. Queer theologies have the potential to unite people over a range of genders, sexual orientations, races, classes, physical abilities, and ethnic barriers. One danger of queer theology is gay theological hegemony and false inclusion of the voices of translesbigays with various shades of contextuality.[25] In the American Academy of Religion, queers of colour are emerging along with lesbian and gay voices. A new generation is already beginning to speak, write and develop queer theologies from womanist, Hispanic, and Asian perspectives.[26] These shades, variants, and tonalities in queer theologies will develop in imaginative configurations that will stretch earlier queer theologies and draw them into new sexual contextualities.

The implications of queer theory in the reformulation of a Christian theology of sexuality are profound and exciting. Queer theologies no longer attempt the dead-end route of various Christian theologies of sexuality but reconstruct theology within a sexual paradigm. Queer liberation theologies leave behind the bankrupt theologies of sexuality of the churches and challenge the churches to recognize their betrayal of God's gift of human sexuality in all its diversity. They have betrayed God's gift of sexuality and gender by refusing to bless queer relationships, recognize our families, or accept our calls to ordained ministry. Most churches have an impoverished theology of sexuality that has lent itself to gender and sexual oppression.

Sexualities and new gender constructions become a paradigm for reconstructing Christian practice and traditional theology. They represent a millennial paradigm shift in theological discourse, or what Michel Foucault has described as the 'insurrection of subjugated knowledges'.[27] Sexual and gender diversity provide a new paradigm for reinvesting the dead doctrines and practices of an erotophobic, gender-rigid Christianity. Queer sexual theologies have begun to concentrate on several questions: how sexuality and spirituality are connected; the fluidity of sexual identity and gender constructions; sexual relationships; rereading the biblical texts and the Christian tradition from a queer perspective; how spirituality and sexuality affect our attitudes and practices, towards God, self, and neighbour; how the Church relates to sexuality/gender in its mission, worship, sacraments, and rites.

Nancy Wilson, Elizabeth Stuart, Carter Heyward, Michael Kelly, and myself have made initial contributions to a sexual theology, connecting eros to justice.[28] The challenge for queer theologies is whether they can integrate sexuality and spirituality. Can our sexual theologies raise questions of justice? Dan Spencer has developed the feminist reclamation of the erotic into a gay ecological framework of justice.[29] Can such liberation theologies transform queers into erotic contemplatives and freedom fighters? Can they continue to expand our vision of justice?

Sex, relationships, and families are reconstructed into new categories of queer experience. Queers will reclaim family values through new patterns of community and new families of choice.[30] Elizabeth Stuart embeds our sexual relationships with a retrieved Christian tradition of friendship, while I queer the procreative privilege of heterosexist theology, arguing for a reconstructed procreativity inclusive of the reality of our sexual relationships and our families.[31] Nancy Wilson develops a Sabbath sexual theology, paraphrasing the Sabbath saying of Jesus: 'Humans were not made for sexuality, but sexuality was made for humans.' Wilson's sexual theology weaves pleasure and bodily hospitality into a promising framework for further ethical refinement.[32]

Sex can open us to a spiritual dimension. Michael Kelly reclaims the Christian heritage of Scriptures and medieval spiritual writings as resources to re-envision our sexuality and spirituality, and he does it very well in a series of video talks titled *The Erotic Contemplative*.[33] In *Revisioning Sexuality* (vol. 2), Kelly proposes that deep spiritual experience draws us to sexuality and that deep sexual experience draws us into spirituality. Kelly's proposal is not really revolutionary, for Christian mystics have been drawn to use erotic metaphors found in the Song of Songs to describe their union with Christ. It is God who draws us from spirituality to sexuality and from sexuality to spirituality, for God is the source of the longing for physical and spiritual union. For most of its history, Christianity barely tolerated sexuality, or tolerated it only within heterosexual marriage. Awaking to God in our sexual love-making is a transformative journey that includes a journey into the desert where we taste exile, rejection, and stigma. In *Liberation* (vol. 5), Michael Kelly notes that there is a turning point on our spiritual journey towards liberation where we are asked to make love to God. For Kelly, it is in making love with the crucified Christ that we learn to be sexually receptive to God as divine lover and learn solidarity with all suffering peoples. Thus, we who have been forbidden love by our churches are asked by God to become the Lover. From this love-making with the crucified Christ, we embark on building God's reign.

Outing, visibility, and transgressive reinscription of traditional symbols are the tools of queering. Nancy Wilson, Mona West, Thomas Hanks, and Victoria Kolakowski have used outing as a hermeneutical strategy for surfacing the voices of sexual minorities and gender benders in the Bible.[34] Heterosexist hegemony in the biblical academy has prevented imaginative interrogation of the biblical traditions. Much of gay scholarship has expended too much energy in deconstructing the biblical texts of terror that have been used to justify violence against us. New queer hermeneutics may reclaim those texts as part of our erotic history. Many gay theologians (including myself) have typically related Leviticus 18: 22 (and 20: 13) to cultic prostitution and idolatry. Perhaps we need to shift our hermeneutical gaze from reacting to homophobic biblical interpretations to claiming these texts of terror as part of our history. Our ancestors with homoerotic desires found social space and location in the Israelite and surrounding cultures as sacred intimates in temples.[35] They lived a connection between sexuality and the divine which biblical patriarchs had rejected. The Levitical proscription underscores patriarchal violence perpetrated against men who defied the gender codes because of their homoerotic desires. Queers are becoming sacred intimates once again through our love lives, uniting spirituality and sexuality.

Towards a sexual reformation of the churches

The seeds of queer theologies planted at the end of this millennium will blossom in the next. The challenges before queer theologies are to determine the implications of God's revelation through a community primarily consisting of queer Christians and what this means for life and ministry to the mainline churches and the world. Queer theologies espouse an ecumenical vision of community, doctrine, human sexuality, prophetic ministry, and human liberation. Queer theologies aim for the sexual reformation of the mainline, evangelical and fundamentalist churches.

The greatest task for queer theologies will be to develop a comprehensive social analysis to delineate interlocking networks of oppressions. Can they provide liberated sexual theologies that will free the mainline churches of their erotophobia? Will they remain queer, or will queer theologies ultimately transgressively reinscribe themselves into something new? During the next century, queer theologies will undergo profound changes as contextual translesbigay theologies emerge from Eastern Europe, Asia, South America, and Africa. The development of bisexual and transgendered theologies will offend some by their inclusiveness, moving beyond binary thinking of hetero/homo and deconstructing rigid gender boundaries. Bisexual and transgendered theologies will be far more threatening to those who want to assimilate into society. There are many ways to be queer, and future queer theologians will connect those ways with the networks of power relationships which shape race, gender, sexuality, ethnicity, class, physical conditions, age, and our relationship to the earth. Rather than assimilate, future queer theologies will mainstream and celebrate diversities.

The theologians of the post-denominational churches will embark upon a community-based project of theological reflection on the experience of sexuality and oppression. Already the post-denominational UFMCC requires a course in sexual theology for all future and transfer clergy. Such a course promotes the diverse voices of translesbigay, their views on sexuality and gender. New generations of erotic contemplatives, theologians, and freedom fighters in the post-denominational churches will have the tools to widen their theological discourse and practice as they encounter the emergent theologies of translesbigay Christians in other cultural contexts.

Such sexual theologies will prepare queer Christians for the next millennium and their mission to become theological troublemakers or prophets that will shake the theological roots of other Christian communities and challenge them to undertake a more inclusive theology of sexuality and justice-based sexual theology. Queer sexual theologies will remain troublesome and even provocative for churches with their impoverished theologies of sexuality. Can our churches become 'open and affirming' of heterosexuals without the tokenism many queers now experience in open and affirming congregations? Can we envision the full inclusion of heterosexuals at our table? Can we assist the churches in overcoming their erotophobia? Our vision and mission of justice involves healing the split between sexuality and spirituality within the Christian churches and assisting those churches in rediscovering God's gift of diverse sexualities/genders. Our mission is the sexual and gender reformation of the churches.

Is it so queer to dream of liberation in its entirety? Or perhaps is it queerer to accomplish the full liberation of oppressed and oppressor alike in future generations?

Notes

1 D. S. Bailey (1975) *Homosexuality and the Western Christian Tradition.* (Hamden: Anchor Books).
2 Robert Wood (1959) *Christ and the Homosexual.* Tom Horner (1978) *Jonathan Loved David: Homosexuality in Biblical Times* (Philadelphia: Westminster Press). John McNeill (1976) *The Church and the Homosexual* (Kansas City: Sheed Andrews and McMeel). Virginia Ramey Mollenkott and Letha Scanzoni (1978) *Is the Homosexual My Neighbor?* (San Francisco: Harper & Row).
3 John Boswell (1980) *Christianity, Social Tolerance and Homosexuality* (Chicago: University of Chicago Press).
4 Robin Scroggs (1983) *The New Testament and Homosexuality* (Philadelphia: Fortress Press). George Edward (1984) *Gay/Lesbian Liberation: A Biblical Perspective* (New York: Pilgrim Press). L. William Countryman (1988) *Dirt, Greed and Sex: Sexual Ethics in the New Testament and Their Implications for Today* (Philadelphia: Fortress Press).

5 Robert L. Brawley (ed.) (1996) *Biblical Ethics and Homosexuality* (Louisville: Westminster/John Knox Press). Sally B. Geis and Donald Messer (eds) (1994) *Caught in the Crossfire* (Nashville: Abingdon Press). Jeffrey Siker (ed.) (1994) *Homosexuality in the Church* (Louisville: Westminster/John Knox Press). Marion Soards (1995) *Scripture and Homosexuality* (Louisville: Westminster/John Knox Press). Thomas Schmidt (1995) *Straight and Narrow* (Downers Grove: Intervarsity Press). Daniel Helminiak (1995) *What Does the Bible Really Say about Homosexuality?* (San Francisco: Alamo Square Press).

6 Chris Glazer (1990) *Come Home* (San Francisco: Harper & Row). John Fortunato (1982) *Embracing the Exile* (San Francisco: Harper & Row). Maury Johnston (1983) *Gays Under Grace* (Nashville: Winston-Derek Publishers). John McNeill (1988) *Taking a Chance on God* (Boston: Beacon Press).

7 Jeannine Grammick and Pat Furey (eds) (1988) *The Vatican and Homosexuality* (New York: Crossroad). Robert Nugent (ed.) (1983) *A Challenge to Love: Gay and Lesbian Catholics in the Church* (New York: Crossroad).

8 Bernadette Brooten (1996) *Love Between Women: Female Homoeroticism in Early Christianity* (Chicago: University of Chicago Press).

9 Dan Spencer (1994) 'Church at the margins', in James B. Nelson and Sandra P. Longfellow (eds) *Sexuality and the Sacred* (Louisville: Westminster/John Knox Press), pp. 397–402.

10 Robert Goss (1993) *Jesus ACTED UP: A Gay and Lesbian Manifesto* (San Francisco: HarperSanFrancisco), pp. 123–5.

11 Troy Perry (1990) *Don't Be Afraid Anymore* (New York: St Martin's Press).

12 Wilson uses the wonderful metaphor of a loose thread on a coat to explain the threat posed to the NCC by UFMCC. When you pull the thread, it begins to unravel. In the same fashion, the NCC's inability to deal with homosexuality indicates the impoverishment of its theology of sexuality. When confronted with homosexuality, its whole homophobic/heterosexist theologies of sexuality come unravelled. Nancy Wilson (1995) *Our Tribe: Queer Folks, God, Jesus, and the Bible* (San Francisco: HarperSanFrancisco).

13 Marilyn Bennett Alexander and James Preston (1996) *We Were Baptized Too: Claiming God's Grace for Lesbians and Gays* (Louisville: Westminster/John Knox Press), pp. 98–100.

14 See Joseph Colombo's review of *Jesus ACTED UP*, in the *Journal of Men's Studies*, **4**, 3 (1996), pp. 318–20.

15 See Robert E. Goss (1996) 'Erotic contemplatives and queer freedom fighters'. *Journal of Men's Studies*, **4**, 3, pp. 243–61.

16 Ron Long (1995) 'Toward a phenomenology of gay sex: groundwork for a contemporary sexual ethic', in *Embodying Diversity: Identity, (Bio) Diversity, and Sexuality, Gay Men's Issues in Religious Studies*, vol. 6 (Las Colinas: Monument Press).

17 J. Michael Clark (1993) *Beyond Our Ghettos* (Cleveland: Pilgrim Press).

18 Gary Comstock (1993) *Gay Theology Without Apology* (Cleveland: Pilgrim Press). Richard Cleaver (1995) *Know My Name: A Gay Liberation Theology* (Louisville: Westminster/John Knox Press).

19 Mark Thompson (1995) *Gay Soul: Finding the Heart of Gay Spirit and Nature*
    (San Francisco: HarperSanFrancisco). Robert Barzan (1995) *Sex and Spirit:*
    Exploring Gay Men's Spirituality (San Francisco: White Crane). Randy P.
    Conner (1993) *Blossom of Bone* (San Francisco: HarperSanFrancisco).
20 Bruce Bower (1993) *A Place at the Table* (New York: Poseidon Press).
    Andrew Sullivan (1995) *Virtually Normal* (New York: Alfred A. Knopf).
21 *Webster's Third New International Dictionary of the English Language* (1986)
    (Springfield: Merriam-Webster).
22 Jonathan Dollimore uses the notion of 'transgressive reinscription' to
    describe the process of reclaiming queer meanings. Jonathan Dollimore
    (1991) *Sexual Dissidence* (Oxford: Clarendon Press), pp. 323–4. See also
    Robert Goss (1996) 'Erotic contemplatives and queer freedom fighters',
    Journal of Men's Studies, **4**, 3, pp. 243–61.
23 Robert Williams (1992) *Just As I Am* (New York: Crown Publishers). Elias
    Farajaje-Jones (1993) 'Breaking silence: towards an in-the-life theology', in
    James H. Cone and Gayraud S. Wilmore (eds) (1993) *Black Theology*
    (Maryknoll: Orbis), Vol. II, pp. 139–59.
24 Victoria S. Kolakowski, 'The concubine and the eunuch: queering the
    breeder's bible', in Robert E. Goss and Amy Squires (eds) *Our Families, Our*
    Values (forthcoming).
25 Mary Hunt (1993) 'Catching up to queer theology', *Frontiers*,
    10 September, pp. 59–60. Robert Goss (1996) 'The insurrection of the
    polymorphous perverse: queer hermeneutics', in J. Michael Clark and
    Robert E. Goss (eds) (1996) *A Rainbow of Religious Studies* (Dallas:
    Monument Press).
26 Renee L. Hill (1993) 'Who are we for each other? Sexism, sexuality, and
    womanist theology', in James H. Cone and Gayraud S. Wilmore (eds)
    (1993) *Black Theology* (Maryknoll: Orbis), Vol. II, pp. 345–54. Juan Oliver
    (1996) 'Why gay marriage?' *Journal of Men's Studies*, **4**, 3, pp. 209–24. Irene
    Monroe (1993) 'The Ache sisters: discovering the power of erotic in ritual',
    in Marjories Proctor Smith and Janet R. Walton (eds) (1993) *Women at*
    Worship: Interpretations of North American Diversity (Louisville:
    Westminster/John Knox Press).
27 Michel Foucault (1980) *Power/Knowledge* (New York: Pantheon Books),
    p. 82.
28 Carter Heyward (1989) *Touching Our Strength: The Erotic as Power and the*
    Love of God (San Francisco: Harper & Row). Elizabeth Stuart (1995) *Just*
    Good Friends: Towards a Lesbian and Gay Theology of Relationships (London:
    Mowbray). Robert E. Goss (1996) 'Erotic contemplatives and queer
    freedom fighters', *Journal of Men's Studies*, **4**, 3, pp. 243–61.
29 Daniel Spencer (1996) *Gay and Gaia: Ethics, Ecology, and the Erotic*
    (Cleveland: Pilgrim Press).
30 Mark Kowalewski and Elisabeth Say (1994) 'Lesbian and gay family:
    iconoclasm and reconstruction', in *Spirituality and Community: Diversity in*
    Gay and Lesbian Experience, Gay Men's Issues in Religious Studies, vol. 5 (Las
    Colinas: Monument Press). For more radical reconstructions, see Kathy
    Rudy (1996) 'Where two or more are gathered: using gay communities as a
    model for Christian ethics', *Theology and Sexuality*, **4**, pp. 81–9.

31 Robert E. Goss (1997) 'Challenging procreative privilege: equal rites', *Theology and Sexuality*, **6** (Spring), pp. 33–55.
32 Wilson (1995), pp. 231–80.
33 Michael B. Kelly, *The Erotic Contemplative*. Produced by EroSpirit Research Institute, Oakland, California.
34 Wilson (1995), pp. 110–64. Several essays in the forthcoming anthology *Our Families, Our Values* pioneer a hermeneutical shift: Mona West, 'The Book of Ruth: An Example of Procreative Strategies for Queers'; Thomas Hanks, 'Paul's Letter to the Romans as a Source of Affirmation for Queers and Their Families'; Kolakowski, 'The Concubine and The Eunuch'.
35 See Conner (1993).

LGCM chronology

1976

April 3   Inaugural General Meeting of the Gay Christian Movement at Sir John Cass School, City of London. Constitution, Statement of Conviction and Aims agreed; first elections. Peter Elers, Vicar of Thaxted, Essex elected first President. Over 100 attended.

May   First issue of the *Bulletin*, forerunner of the *Journal* printed. Editor, Michael Johnson from Bangor.

Sept 18   GCM's first conference, 'Sexual Expression and Moral Chaos' with Sara Coggin and Jim Cotter in Birmingham. Leads to publication of the first two GCM pamphlets.

1977

Feb 24   Death in motorcycle accident of Michael Harding, a founder member of GCM and priest, aged 25, working in the diocese of St Albans.

March 26   First AGM at Hinde Street Methodist Church, London. Speakers Malcolm Macourt and Alison Hennegan. National membership stands at 365. Denis Lemon (editor *Gay News*) and Richard Creed (Director) address meeting on *Gay News* prosecution for 'blasphemous libel' by Mary Whitehouse. Collection for *Gay News* Defence Fund taken.

April 17   Showing on BBC1 of *The Lord is My Shepherd and He Knows I'm Gay*. First TV coverage of the movement.

May 21   Extraordinary General Meeting in Manchester after the furore over the BBC TV programme, in which according to the majority of members GCM was portrayed as 'too Anglican, too male and too clerical'. Positions of President and Vice President abolished.

Oct 1   'The Bible and Homosexuality' GCM Conference at Bloomsbury Central Baptist Church, London. The *Baptist Times* refuses to print advertisement for the event. A GCM pamphlet of the same name follows.

Nov   Memorandum submitted by GCM to the Home Secretary's Committee on Obscenity and Film Censorship, prepared by our Think Tank under the direction of Dr Timothy Potts, Department of Philosophy, University of Leeds.
   Towards a Theology of Gay Liberation, ed. Malcolm Macourt (SCM Press) published. The book claims that 'for the first time it presents the debate about same-sex relationships from those who recognise that such relationships exist, are often loving, and are often between Christians'. It serves as a manifesto and focal point for those taking up the challenge from GCM.

1978

Jan 7   Conference on 'Blasphemy',
Speakers Richard Creed, David Craig
and Neil Richardson.

March 18   Annual National
Conference at St Botolph's Church,
Aldgate, London. Kennedy Thom
delivers the First Michael Harding
Memorial Address (publication made
possible by a memorial fund in his
name) 'Liberation through Love'.

April 21   GCM picket of Nationwide
Festival of Light rally on homosexuality
at All Souls' Church, Langham Place,
London, extensive media coverage of
the protest.

Sept 30   Malcolm Johnson, Rector of St
Botolph's, leads GCM conference in
Bristol on 'Exploring Lifestyles:
Blessings of Gay Unions'. Pamphlet
follows. Believed to be the first attempt
to provide suitable liturgies for what
were then novel occurrences. In the
intervening years LGCM has arranged
for thousands of same-sex couples to
receive a Blessing on their relationship.

1979

Jan 1   Appointment of Richard Kirker
as, initially, part-time Administrative
Secretary. Post becomes full-time later
that year as funds are secured from a
special appeal supported by the
membership.

Jan 8   Conference in Leeds 'What the
Church should be Saying to
Homosexuals', speaker Dr Una Kroll.
The Evangelical Fellowship within
LGCM is formed.

March 31   Annual National
Conference and Second Michael
Harding Memorial Address 'The Gay
Christian Movement and the Education
of Public Opinion' by Fr Harry
Williams, CR. Lecture published.
Twenty-four Local Groups in existence.
The Conference venue had to be altered
at short notice (to Notting Hill
Methodist Church) due to a
cancellation, and breach of contract, by

Canon Kelly of Westminster Cathedral
Conference Centre.

May   Three specially commissioned
GCM Working Papers published, *Some
Notes on an Ethic for Homosexuals*
(Norman Pittenger), *Christian Love and
the Concept of 'Maturity'* (Michael
Keeling), and *What the Church Should be
Saying to Homosexuals* (Una Kroll).
   Submission from GCM to the
Criminal Law Revision Committee and
the Policy Advisory Committee on
Sexual Offences.

Sept   *Statement of Conscience in Regard
to the Ordination of Homosexual Persons*
signed by 23 bishops of the Episcopal
Church, USA, meeting in Colorado,
dissenting from colleagues who had
reaffirmed the 'traditional' view. GCM
distributes this historic *Statement*
widely.

Sep 22   Conference in Southampton
on the three reports which had been
issued that year by the Church of
England, Methodist, and Roman
Catholic Churches with Rupert Davies
(past President of the Methodist
Conference) and Clifford Longley of
The Times.

1980

Jan 5   Conference at Hemel
Hempstead 'Our Resources for the
Future'.

March 22   Annual National
Conference and Third Michael Harding
Memorial Address, at the University of
London Union, 'Our Common
Humanity' by Jack Burton, Methodist
minister and bus driver in Norwich,
latterly Sheriff of the City. Address
published.

April 18–20   'Pastoral Approaches to
Homosexuality', Conference, Pitlochry,
Scotland. *The Pitlochry Papers*, edited by
James Anthony SSF and Ian Dunn later
published, by the Scottish Homosexual
Rights Group. Forerunner of the
'Changing Church Attitudes?'
Conference, a decade later.

Sept 20   Conference in Manchester 'Gay and Catholic' with speakers Maggie Reading (Catholic Lesbian Sisterhood) and Martin Stephens (Chairman of Quest).

Nov   British Council of Churches publish *God's Yes to Sexuality* edited by Rachel Moss.

1981

Feb   General Synod of the Church of England makes a desultory attempt to debate its Report *Homosexual Relationships: A Contribution to Discussion*. The Report is henceforth, effectively, ignored. Edition 20 of *Gay Christian* (edited by Diarmaid MacCulloch) comments on the Fifth Anniversary 'we've an immense amount to thank God for, and a stimulating and exciting task ahead. We've made enough mark to have the mickey taken out of us by *Not the Nine O'Clock News*'.

April 4   Annual National Conference and Fourth Michael Harding Memorial Address 'Godly and Gay' by Rabbi Lionel Blue.

June 20   Fifth Anniversary Celebrations and Service held at St Botolph's. Sermon 'Gay Christian Maturity' by Canon Douglas Rhymes.

Oct   Conference in Cambridge 'Worship: An Expression of Ourselves' led by Brian Frost.
   Submission by GCM to the Law Commission on Offences Against Religion and Public Worship.

1982

Jan 9   Conference in London 'Can Gay Christians Afford to Tolerate The Churches?'

Jan 17   Young Gay Christian Group launched.

March 27   Annual National Conference and Fifth Michael Harding Memorial Address, in Birmingham, 'Rediscovering Gay History' by Professor John Boswell, author of the widely

acclaimed *Christianity, Social Tolerance, and Homosexuality*. His address was published and became our most popular pamphlet. GCM organized a tour for John Boswell which was launched at the RAC Club in Pall Mall, and included a packed meeting chaired by Kenneth Woollcombe, formerly Bishop of Oxford at Friends Meeting House, London.

June 27   Gay Pride Week Service at St Botolph's, sermon by Elaine Willis.

1983

Jan   Conference in Cardiff 'Healing Wounds'.

March 19   Annual National Conference at St George's Church, Hanover Square, London 'Creating The Future Together'. Management consultant works with the conference to try to identify and resolve the Movement's problems of growth and its priorities.
   LGCM establishes Discrimination Commission with Professor Tony Coxon as Chair, in an attempt to monitor and challenge cases of unfair treatment.

May   Final Report of the GCM Working Party on worship completed by Brian Stone, Chairperson.

June 11   Conference in Glasgow on the Church of Scotland's recently published *Report on Homosexuality*. Wide media coverage including a debate on Scottish TV with Frank Gibson, the Church of Scotland Director of Social Work.

Oct 15   Extraordinary General Meeting in Birmingham resolves to alter Constitution and establish gender parity on National Committee, and implement a fairer voting system to ensure greater participation by women.

1984

Jan 14   Conference in Bristol 'Towards a Gay Ethic'.

June 2–3   First GCM delegation to
Forum for Gay Christian Groups in
Europe, Amsterdam.

June 23   Annual National Conference
and Sixth Michael Harding Memorial
Address, at Conway Hall, Red Lion
Square, London, by Sheila Briggs
'Gayness as God's Choice'.

Oct 20   Conference in Manchester
'Spirituality' with Alan Gaunt.

Oct 31   HM Customs and Excise seize
copies of *The Joy of Gay Sex* en route to
GCM.

Nov   Decision to contest Seizure
Notice taken: Defend GCM Fund
launched. All copies were eventually
returned in a momentous climb-down,
but not before we joined Gay's the
Word in defending a similar (but larger)
action against them.

Dec   The Evangelical Fellowship
publish *Challenge of Freedom*.

1985

Jan 12   Conference in Southampton
'The Gay Community Under Threat'
with Chris Smith, MP, Martin
Pendergast and Terry Munyard (NCCL).

April 23   Annual National Conference
and Seventh Michael Harding Memorial
Address, in Sheffield, 'The Other
Country' by Jim Cotter. Address
published.

June 1   Extraordinary General Meeting
in Birmingham, called by Save GCM
Campaign, decides to maintain post of
General Secretary as first priority.
National Committee resign, and
completely new Committee elected.

Oct   GCM submits its response to
Goals for our Future Society, a
Consultative Document, eventually a
Report, published by the Board for
Social Responsibility.

Oct 19   Conference 'The Bible: Friend
or Foe for Gay Christians?'

Dec   GCM publishes submission to the
Archbishop of Canterbury's

Commission on Urban Priority Areas
(ACUPA) jointly with Christians Against
Racism and Fascism.

Formation of AIDS Faith Alliance
(AFA) a joint venture with Quest and
MCC to foster a truly religious response
to AIDS.

1986

Jan 4   Publication of AFA leaflet *Is
AIDS God's Wrath?* with support from
the Terrence Higgins Trust.

Jan 11   Conference in Leeds, 'The
Family – the Gay Dimension'.

March 12   Death after long illness of
Canon Peter Elers, former President of
GCM. Survived by Gill his wife, staunch
GCM friend, and member.

April 4–6   Tenth Anniversary
Celebrations and Residential Conference
at Goldsmith College, London. Eighth
Michael Harding Memorial Address
'Masculinity, War and God – A Case to
Answer' by Brian Wren.

June 22   Peter Elers Memorial Concert,
and Memorial Fund established to raise
£5000 for the London Lighthouse AIDS
centre.

Sept 3   Customs and Excise return
seized books. The protests and
campaigning succeeded.

1987

Jan 10   Conference in Cardiff 'The Joy
of Lesbian and Gay Faith'.

Feb   Paper on Equal Opportunities
submitted by LGCM to Board for Social
Responsibility.

News slowly emerges of an initiative
by the Archbishop of Canterbury for
the appointment of a Working Party on
Homosexuality. Much secrecy
surrounds its membership, terms of
reference, and timetable.

April 24   Annual National Conference
in Birmingham votes to alter name to
Lesbian and Gay Christian Movement
(LGCM).

June LGCM Submission to the Department of Education review of sex education titled *Positive Images*.

June 21 Ninth Michael Harding Memorial Address by Jean White, Pastor of MCC South London.

Aug 28–31 Young Lesbian and Gay Christian Group summer camp.

Oct 17 Conference in Liverpool, 'AIDS – How Should We Be Speaking to the Churches?'.

Nov 9–13 Church of England General Synod 'debate' a Private Members' Motion on Sexual Morality, chiefly an attack on homosexuality, and with minor amendments condemn the practice. LGCM lobbies vigorously, produces four special Briefings and has a higher media profile than ever before. In fact from now the issue is clearly 'discovered' by all branches of the press and this has the effect of legitimizing our campaigns. Alongside the ordination of women debate ours assumes almost equal prominence.

Nov 15 Diocese of London, through Archdeacon George Cassidy, opens its campaign to have LGCM's Offices removed from the tower at St Botolph's Church where it has been located, at the invitation of the Parochial Church Council, since 1978.

1988

Jan Defence Fund launched to pay for costs of defending our right to remain at St Botolph's. Counselling helpline inaugurated, a response to the hundreds of pleas for in-depth advice received each year.

April Legal proceedings, in the Consistory Court, result in its refusal to grant a Faculty, which would have enabled us to remain *in situ*.

April 15–17 Annual National Conference endorses decision taken by National Committee to oppose the Diocese of London by all legal means.

May LGCM's Theological Commission (Chair, Canon Douglas Rhymes)

publishes its submission to the Archbishop of Canterbury's Working Party.

May 12–15 Forum for Gay Christian Groups in Europe holds annual Conference at Brunel University, co-hosted by LGCM. Speakers include John Yates, Bishop of Gloucester (and Chairman of the 1979 BSR Report *Homosexual Relationships*) and Dr Una Kroll.

May 14 Extraordinary General Meeting confers authority on National Committee to constitute the Movement as a legal body in its own right so as to enable itself to be a party properly recognizable by the Court in the continuing wrangles. St Botolph's withdraws from case three days before the final hearing.

May 16 A full day's hearing in open court takes place. QCs and legal teams from both sides appear in the Guildhall, City of London. We win and lose. The Judge (Chancellor) says we should never have been involved in the proceedings in the first place. We would still have to leave the premises, although costs were not awarded against us as the Diocese had been urging, which we had most feared. Our costs were £8000 and the Diocese over £30,000. Considerable media interest and sympathy for LGCM.

Sept 10 Spectacular, joyful Service of Passover and Exodus with preacher Ken Leech, to mark LGCM's formal eviction, on 14 September 'giving thanks for all we have received through the hospitality of God's people at St Botolph's Church in the last twelve years; in painful rejoicing at being found worthy of persecution and in eager anticipation of God's love in leading us to new freedom in light and love'. *Speaking Love's Name*, edited by Ashley Beck and Ros Hunt (Jubilee Group) published to coincide with the eviction. Office moved temporarily for one year to Camberwell, South East London, courtesy of helpful intervention by London Churches Resettlement Agency!

Archives deposited at the London School of Economics and Political Science (LSE).

Nov   Relaunch of enlarged and redesigned members' *Journal*.

1989

Feb   General Synod member, Muriel Curtis, proposes Motion to ban LGCM entry in 'semi-official' Church of England yearbook directory. Attempt fails resoundingly.

March   Peter Elers Memorial Fund hands over £5300 to London Lighthouse to equip a private room, for people with AIDS, named after him.

April 8–10   AGM in London, with theme 'Pastoral and Campaigning Priorities'.

June   Move to newly refurbished office in Oxford House, Bethnal Green, adjacent to the City of London.

July 2   Tenth Michael Harding Memorial Address 'The Body's Grace' given by Professor Rowan Williams, Lady Margaret Professor of Divinity at Oxford University.
Lecture to LGCM Meeting by Bishop Jack Spong to launch *Living in Sin? A Bishop Rethinks Human Sexuality*.

Sept 23   The Institute for the Study of Christianity and Sexuality (ISCS) Launch Conference at Christ Church, Oxford, with speakers Monica Furlong and Jim Cotter.

Dec   Rumours that the Archbishop's Working Party Report is to be held back from publication indefinitely.

1990

Feb   The *Report on Homosexuality to the House of Bishops* (given the name Osborne, after its Chairperson) is leaked on Granada TV documentary. Widespread media interest ensues – all curious to know why the Report seems destined to be suppressed. At General Synod the Archbishop says the Report is to be revised by another group of unnamed people, believed to be

bishops, widely expected to weaken the recommendations of the Osborne Report itself. LGCM located at centre of the ensuing controversy, as we call for its immediate publication.

April 21   Annual National Conference with Keynote Speaker Dr Bill Countryman, author of the esteemed *Dirt, Greed and Sex: Sexual Ethics in the New Testament and Their Implications for Today* (SCM Press).

April 27–29   'Changing Church Attitudes?' Conference at Dunblane. Over 100 in attendance, with speakers Mary Hunt, Norman Shanks, Clare Sealy, and Harvey Gillman. Successor event to the Pitlochry Conference of 1980. Conference decides to reconvene in 2000, in Scotland.

May 24–27   European Forum for Lesbian and Gay Christian Groups meets in Strasbourg. Speakers include John McNeil, author of *The Church and the Homosexual*. Paul Scroxton elected President.

July 3   Bishop Jack Spong, of Newark, New Jersey, meets LGCM members at a Reception for him and his wife Christine in Oxford House.
Report of the Commission on Human Sexuality presented to the Methodist Conference, Cardiff.

Sept 10   Roman Catholic Caucus Study Day with Fr Bernard Lynch at Oxford House.
Channel 4 documentary *Out on Sunday*, covering the ever more evident confusions within the Church of England.

Nov 6   *Call to Action*, edited by Elaine Willis published jointly by LGCM and Stonewall Group for use as a resource to help initiate change in the churches. Distributed to all members of the newly elected General Synod, who are all invited to its Launch at the Palace of Westminster, hosted by Keith Vaz, MP.

Dec   *Roman Catholics and Homosexuality* by Dr Elizabeth Stuart, Convenor of the RC Caucus published by Channel 4 for its two profiles on

Fr Bernard Lynch, broadcast on the same evening just before Christmas.

1991

Jan World Council of Churches Assembly in Canberra sees formation of Lesbian and Gay Caucus for the first time ever, with key input from Alison Webster.

April 13 Annual National Conference with Keynote Speaker Sara Maitland, author and broadcaster whose lecture 'Divine Imagination' delivered on the 15th Anniversary.

Nov Publication of the URC report *Homosexuality: A Christian View* which refuses to endorse traditional condemnations of same-sex relationships.

Dec Publication by Anglican bishops of *Issues in Human Sexuality* which forbids same-sex relationships amongst the clergy but not the laity.

1992

March The Archbishop of Canterbury, George Carey, steps in to prevent SPCK from publishing Elizabeth Stuart's book of gay and lesbian prayers and liturgies, *Daring to Speak Love's Name*.

April 24–25 Annual National Conference in London and keynote address by the Rev David Norgard, Director of The Oasis, Diocese of Newark, USA.

July LGCM sets up a commission of enquiry under Tony Green to investigate the aims and working practices of the ex-gay movement.

July 21 Publication of the Congregation for the Faith's notorious attack on anti-discrimination legislation in America. LGCM's Roman Catholic Caucus organizes an open letter of protest which gathers widespread support.

Oct 27 Service of celebration at Methodist Central Hall to mark the publication by Hamish Hamilton of Elizabeth Stuart's book *Daring to Speak Love's Name*.

1993

April 16–18 Annual National Conference in Liverpool. Keynote address 'Daring to Speak Love's Name' given by Dr Elizabeth Stuart.

April 23 LGCM Catholic Caucus Study Day on 'Homosexuality and the Roman Catholic Priesthood'.

June 29 Meeting of the Methodist Conference in Derby at which all members receive information packs from LGCM's Methodist Caucus. It adopts contradictory resolutions which reaffirm the Church's support for chastity outside of marriage, but refuses to change its candidating procedures, and celebrates the ministry of gays and lesbians in the Church.

1994

April 15–17 Annual National Conference and keynote address by Professor William Countryman 'The Priesthood of Being Gay/Lesbian'.

September Revelation that the Bishop-elect of Durham, Michael Turnbull, had once been cautioned for cottaging leads LGCM to accuse the Church of England of hypocrisy. In the same week the Anglican Children's Society announces that it will, contrary to government guidelines, no longer accept gay and lesbian foster parents.
Setting up of Lesbian Matters as the coordinating group for women within LGCM.

Nov 11–13 LGCM Retreat led by Helen Loder and Malcolm Johnson at the Royal Foundation of St Katherine.

1995

April Success for LGCM as the Methodist Conference refuses to change its candidating procedures as conservatives have demanded.

April 28–30 Annual National Conference in London with keynote address by Dr Grace Jantzen 'Off the Straight and Narrow: Toward a Lesbian Theology'.

May 25–28   Conference organized by the European Forum of Lesbian and Gay Groups at Dreibergen in the Netherlands takes as its theme 'Changing Church Attitudes?'

Aug 17   LGCM becomes a limited company and a registered charity.

Sept 29   Evangelical Fellowship Conference at Offchurch, 'To Be and To Do'.

Nov   Publication of *Reconsider: A Response to Issues in Human Sexuality* edited by Christina Sumner.

1996

Jan   At the start of the 20th anniversary year, public launch of LGCM's new status as a limited company and a registered charity. Generous sponsorship from the English Teddy Bear Company.

Lesbian Matters holds a national gathering at Charney Manor, Oxfordshire which discusses lesbian ethics.

May   Publication of the commission of enquiry into the ex-gay movement is critical of its aims and lack of professional standards.

May 15–23   LGCM 20th anniversary holiday pilgrimage to Brittany.

May 16–20   European Forum for Lesbian and Gay Groups meets in Oslo.

Oct 10   An attack on BBC 4's *Thought for the Day* by Anne Atkins on the LGCM service at Southwark is condemned by the Church of England's communications director as inaccurate and preposterous.

Oct 11   Richard Kirker debates with Anne Atkins on the *Today* programme.

She accepts his offer to attend the service but does not subsequently do so.

Nov 16   2000 people pack Southwark Cathedral for a joyful celebration of LGCM's first 20 years at which the Bishop of Guildford, John Gladwin, preaches.

1997

April 11–13   Annual National Conference in London. Keynote address by Dr Sean Gill 'Making Rivers in the Desert: Reflections Upon the Past and Future Agenda of LGCM'.

July 8   A lengthy campaign including the preparation of a video and a booklet *Voices from Within* by the URC Caucus, is successful when the Church's Assembly refuses to change its ministerial procedures and thereby exclude sexually active gay and lesbian candidates from the ministry.

July 14   The meeting of the Church of England's Synod accepts an LGCM sponsored motion calling upon the Church to reflect further upon the questions raised by the 1991 bishops' report.

July 19   After an 18-month investigation the Crown Prosecution Service finally admits that LGCM has no case to answer over the charge of putting the banned poem 'The Love that Dares To Speak Its Name' on the Internet.

Nov 8   A memorial service held in Cambridge to celebrate the life of LGCM founder member and author of *Time for Consent*, Norman Pittenger. LGCM sets up a Memorial Fund in his honour.

Index

Index

Index

Stacey, Rev David   40
Stephens, Martin   205
Stone, Brian   34, 205
Stonewall Group   85, 86, 208
Stonewall Riots (1969)   39, 171
Stuart, Dr Elizabeth   vii, 76, 80, 81–2, 84,
   87, 196; *Daring to Speak Love's Name*
   209; *Roman Catholics and
   Homosexuality* 208
Student Christian Movement (SCM)   39
Sumner, Christina, ed.: *Reconsider: A
   Response to Issues in Human Sexuality*
   210

Tatchell, Peter   63, 82
Terrence Higgins Trust   55, 57, 206
Thatcher, Baroness   51, 52, 53, 56, 59, 67
Thaxted, Essex   8, 9, 15, 28
Thistlethwaite, Susan   25
Thom, Kennedy   9, 12–13, 23, 28, 29, 32,
   132, 145–50, 204
Thompson, Geoffrey   63, 108
Thompson, Jim, Bishop of Bath and
   Wells   78
Thompson, Mark: *Gay Soul*   193–4
Thorne, Brian   132–6
Thought for the Day (radio programme)
   96, 210
Thurston-Smith, Trevor   108
Towards a Quaker View of Sex   5
Towards a Theology of Gay Liberation
   (SCM)   39
Treacy, Eric, Bishop of Wakefield   10
Trillo, John, Bishop of Chelmsford   8, 9,
   28
True Freedom Trust   27, 55–6, 93
Turnbull, Michael, Bishop-elect of
   Durham   88, 209
Turning Point   55–6

United Fellowship of Metropolitan
   Churches   3
United Reformed Church (URC)   11,
   92–4; caucus in LGCM   73, 75, 93, 94,
   210; General Assembly   94
Universal Fellowship of Metropolitan
   Community Churches (UFMCC)
   191–2, 199

Vasey, Michael   168
Vatican   4, 79, 80, 81, 82, 83, 179
Vaz, Keith, MP   208
Vik, Aasmund   76
Voices from Within (LGCM)   94, 210

Walker, Iain   68, 69
Walsh, Jerry   80, 121, 125–7
Walton, Lieutenant Colonel   43
Webber, Rev Janet   94
Webster, Alison   72, 76, 85, 171–2, 209
Webster-Gardiner, Graham   53, 54
Weeks, Judith   121, 127–9
West, Mona   197
Westminster Cathedral   82
Westminster Cathedral Conference
   Centre   38, 204
Westwood, Bill, Bishop of Peterborough
   61
Whistler, Humphrey   43
White, Jean   207
Whitehouse, Mary   36, 51, 52, 203
Whitelaw, Lord   55
Williams, Fr Harry, CR   204
Williams, Robert   194
Williams, Professor Rowan   68, 208
Willis, Elaine   33, 85, 205
Willis, Elaine, ed., *Call to Action* (LGCM
   and Stonewall Group)   85–6, 208
Willis, Lord   37
Wilson, Nancy   192, 194, 196, 197
Wolfenden Committee   5, 7
Women's Group (LGCM)   128–9
Wood, Robert: *Christ and the Homosexual*
   187
Woods, Canon Michael   78
Woollcombe, Kenneth, Bishop of Oxford
   205
Workman, Michael   57
World Council of Churches   76, 209
Wren, Brian   206

Yates, John, Bishop of Gloucester   41, 43,
   207
Young, David, Bishop of Ripon   61, 62, 64
Young Lesbian and Gay Christian Group
   (LGCM)   35, 73, 205, 207